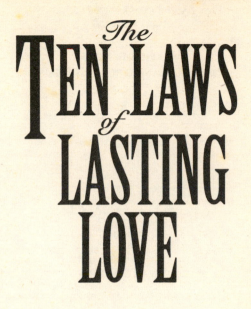

The TEN LAWS of LASTING LOVE

Other Avon Books by
Paul Pearsall

MAKING MIRACLES:
FINDING MEANING IN LIFE'S CHAOS

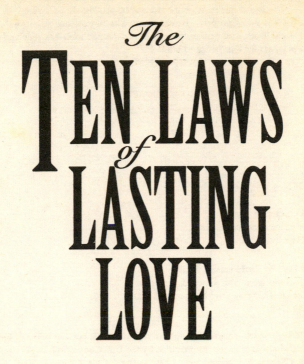

The TEN LAWS of LASTING LOVE

PAUL PEARSALL, PH.D

AVON BOOKS ◆ NEW YORK

AVON BOOKS
A division of
The Hearst Corporation
1350 Avenue of the Americas
New York, New York 10019

Copyright © 1993 by Paul Pearsall, Ph.D.
Published by arrangement with Simon & Schuster
Library of Congress Catalog Card Number: 92-42016
ISBN: 0-380-72307-7

The Simon & Schuster edition contains the following Library of Congress Cataloging in Publication Data:
Pearsall, Paul.
    Ten laws of lasting love/ Paul Pearsall.
    p.   cm.
Includes bibliographical references and index.
1. Marriage. 2. Love. I. Title.
HQ734.P325   1993   92-42016
646.7'8—dc20   CIP

First Avon Books Trade Printing: February 1995

AVON TRADEMARK REG. U.S. PAT. OFF. AND IN OTHER COUNTRIES, MARCA REGISTRADA, HECHO EN U.S.A.

Printed in the U.S.A.

OPM 10 9 8 7 6 5 4 3 2 1

For my wife, Celest, for the miracle of our love and for all the miracles our love has made

CONTENTS

We are all angels with but one wing. We fly only when we embrace.

—Leo Buscaglia

ACKNOWLEDGMENTS

This is the sixth book I have written and, as with the first five, my wife Celest and my two sons, Roger and Scott, made it—and me—possible. Without three remarkable miracles among the many made by my marriage, I would not be writing books, teaching, or swimming in the warm ocean in Maui. The two most cherished miracles, my sons Scott and Roger, give meaning to my life and motivation to my work. The third miracle was the loving energy from my marriage that helped save my life and cure me of cancer.

I'm sure my mother Carol would have written several books herself had she not given her life to caring for my brother Dennis and me. Her courage to carry on after my father's death is testimony to the immortality of their love and the true nature of High Monogamy. The memory of the gentleness of my father Frank and the love he had for my mother gives me the faith, hope, and joy to work. I know my parents, like my wife and me, will be together forever.

For the concepts shared in these pages, I depended on the great physicists and other scientists and researchers quoted throughout this book. I learned from them two facts their work has revealed. I know that all boundaries are illusions and that the startling lessons from new physics profoundly influence our personal lives and how we relate to one another. I learned from the psychologists whose work I have included in this book that, as Carl Rogers said, those things which are most personal are most general.

Like making a marriage, publishing a book can be a frustrating and wonderfully challenging chaos. I appreciate the efforts of my editor, George Hodgman, and the staff at Simon & Schuster to bring this book to print. I value the persistence of my good friend and former agent Susan Cohen—it kept this book alive. I thank all of my patients and their marriages for teaching me the lessons of love. I hope my readers will feel the energy and creativity of all the people I mention here to help them make the miracle of lasting love in their own lives.

An Invitation to a Wedding:

PETE AND LITA'S MIRACLE

Where Does the Love Go?

It's the most often asked question in the world. Everyone will ask it sometime during his or her life. Countless hours are spent worrying about and contemplating this question. This book provides the answer. My patients ask the question every day, and this woman's words typify the many ways the question is asked:

"Where does the love go?" she said, between sobs. Her tears fell rhythmically on her wrist as she twisted her wedding band in circles around her finger. She repeatedly dug the ring into her skin, but her pain seemed blocked by the deeper ache within her heart. "We seemed to love so much, but now it seems gone. How can I be married and feel so divorced? How can I seem to be in love yet feel so alone. How can I sleep every night with him, make love with him, raise children with him, go to funerals with him, and live with him every day and still feel so disconnected from him? How can we be so together and yet so apart? Why do I feel so lonely every night even when he is right there beside me? Why don't I really know him? Why doesn't he really know me? Why can't marriage be more than this? Is this all there is? Where does the love go?"

During my twenty-five years as a marital therapist, I have seen hundreds of wives and husbands just like this woman. Disappointed, confused, lonely, and angry, these forlorn people find themselves despairing over their inability to feel lastingly fulfilled in a loving relationship. They ask it in many different ways, but they always ask the same vital question: Where does the love go? By following the steps in this book, most of these people have found their answer, and you can too.

I have seen resignation, surrender, and numbness in response to the terrible havoc, cruelty, and pain caused by the failure of intimacy. I sensed an emotional anesthesia that seemed in one way or another to plague every patient I saw. I have spent my career trying to help families pick up the pieces of a shattered loving relationship, and I have seen passion turned to poison. I have grieved with my patients for the love they lost or never found, and I have wondered if there wasn't another way to love that brought more joy, tenderness, fulfillment, and persistent exhilaration to the daily life of the American marriage. I know now that there is. I know we can love much more deeply, lastingly, and tenderly. I have seen such love, and I have felt such love myself. My patients and I have discovered the miracle of lasting love.

I know there is such a thing as a miracle marriage. When my own marriage rescued me from almost certain death, I felt the miracle of love's power. Through my experiences with a remarkable group of patients who had discovered the magic of lasting love—twenty-five-year-old "silver survivor" marriages and fifty-year-old "golden oldie" marriages—I learned that love can grow, endure, and be exciting forever. My experience was sobering, and it was awesome. If you feel lonely tonight, remember that there is hope for a new feeling of mutual devotion beyond your wildest fantasies. There is not only an answer to the question "Where did the love go?" There are ways to go and get it.

I learned that it is possible to love so deeply, so spiritually, and so completely that marriage not only survives crises but thrives because of them. I have discovered startling new secrets of lasting love and how to put them to work in any relationship. I have seen how marriages can survive any crisis, and I have witnessed others that flourish through the most chaotic and terrible times. I am astonished at the power of couples to make miracles out of the worst messes. I know now that a miracle marriage is within the grasp of anyone willing to accept the challenge of making marriage the primary focus of his or her life rather than the secondary support system for self-fulfillment. I have learned that our wish for the miracle of lasting love can come true.

Would You Make Midas's Mistake?

If you could have one wish, what would it be? Would you wish for health, wealth, or happiness? King Midas's one wish was that everything he touched would be turned to gold. He thought that the guarantee of self-wealth and eternal self-sufficiency would make him happy. His wish was granted, but he nearly starved to death—alone. Surrounded by glittering riches, he too asked, "Where did the love go?" The persons who gave gold its meaning had been rendered lifeless by his touch—themselves turned to useless gold.

What would be your own one wish of a lifetime? Would you make the Midas Mistake and forget the one aspect of your living upon which all else depends—the love of another person? Would you wish for some*thing* or some*one*? Would you wish for lasting love?

If you wished for your own health, what would your health bring you if you had no one with whom to celebrate your well-being? If you wished, as Midas did, for personal riches and material goods, what could your wealth buy for you if there was no one with whom to enjoy your treasures? If you wished for happiness, what would your happiness mean without someone to share your joy? This book is an invitation to a wedding of human spirits in a love that can help you be free of wishing because you will have someone with whom to share all of life's gifts.

A Miracle-Marriage Portrait

I saw a miracle marriage today. I was invited to attend a wedding ceremony celebrating the sixtieth anniversary of two remarkable people. I want to describe the marriage I saw at this "rewedding" because it is the kind of marriage you can have by following the steps presented in this book. My invitation read, "The honor of your presence is requested at the celebration of the love of Pete and Lita. Please come and help us commemorate and enjoy the power of the union of our souls. We married for each other and for all of us, and we want you to join us in the solemnization and reconfirmation of our love." Allow me to introduce you to this miracle couple as an example of the type of loving you can have.

Both Pete and Lita are eighty-one years old. Almost all the time of their life is spent together. They walk together, talk together, sit together, and sleep together. They tell me that they make love almost every night, but they don't have sex very often. First and foremost, the time of their life is for the love in their life. Their love and their marriage is primary and above all else.

Pete said, "I can't seem to get a love handle on Lita. She's always been a mystery to me and she always will be." Lita says, "In some ways I know everything about him, but in other ways, I have to learn about him every day." Pete and Lita never take each other for granted, but they take it for granted that they will always love each other and give that love priority over all else.

Lita said, "All weddings are happy. It's staying happy when you're married that's difficult." Pete said, "Marriage isn't a state of 'mine.' It's a state of 'ours.' Whatever is worth having, we have together." Pete and Lita feel, look, and move as one, and all that happens to them seems to be experienced by them as an Us. When I spoke with them, I seemed to speak to one person rather than two.

Pete said, "When I look at Lita, I don't see how old she is. She's just my Lita." Lita said, "When people call him 'old Pete,' I don't see it. He's my Pete. By the time you're our age, I guess you get the face you deserve, but I still just see the same Pete I always saw." Pete and Lita see each other "their" way from their loving point of view.

Lita says, "He's always tinkering around with his tools. He talks about variable-speed drills and overdrive. Sometimes I wish he'd look at me like he looks at his tools. He's always puttering around. He breaks more things than our great-grandson. He drives me nuts. But that's what makes me love him." Pete said, "She's always watching those talk shows. She drives me crazy wasting her time on that junk and telling me about them. She always says I'm too involved with my tools. I joked with her and told her if she had variable speed and overdrive, I would look at her like I look at my tools. She's got Oprah and I've got the Handy Man." Pete and Lita are empowered as a couple by their tolerant, subtle, patient, and playful enjoyment of each other's uniqueness.

Pete said, "I can feel her with me anytime. When I was sick in that hospital, she was with me no matter where she was. I felt her with me." Lita said, "We can communicate without words anywhere. I'll always be with him, and he'll never leave me alone." Pete and Lita have their own power of communication beyond words.

Lita says, "We've had more problems than you can count. Maybe that's why we still love each other. We don't have time not to. We're too busy living and loving." Pete says, "Anybody can love a little when things are going good. The trick is to love a lot when things go really bad. That's how we are. The worse things are, the more we need and help each other. All of our problems made us love each other more." Pete and Lita accept the natural chaos of life and face it together.

Pete said, "Almost anybody can laugh together, but we can cry together. That's really harder to do, and it takes a lot of practice and a lot of love." Lita says, "Whenever I'm sad, he comforts me. Sometimes he tells me to stop crying and start fighting. One time, he brought me his new drill just to distract me. He knew I'd have a fit. He comforts me his way, but he's always there." Pete and Lita's love grew stronger through the sad times of their life.

Lita says, "We used to dress up for Halloween. We pretended we did it for our grandchildren, but we both knew we did it for ourselves. You have to get away from the real world, or the real world will get you." Pete says, "I think you have to face facts. I just think you have to pick which facts you face and which ones you choose to turn your back on. That's the advantage of being married for a long time. You can watch out in both directions. You can watch each other's back." Even as they coped with the "real" world, Pete and Lita constantly created their own private reality unique to them.

Pete said, "I know we don't have many years left. One of us is going to be alone here on earth sooner than we want. But we know we will never be too far from one another even when one of us is gone." Lita said, "We've made something together that time won't stop. We'll be married forever somewhere and somehow." Pete and Lita had discovered the miracle of infinite love beyond physical limits.

Within the words of this wonderful couple are the secrets and rewards of a miracle marriage. To laugh, to cry, to work, and to love together forever is the most remarkable accomplishment imaginable—a true miracle. There is nothing quite like the miracle of a marriage that defies the obligations of a pressuring and self-oriented modern world. There is something powerful about a marriage that is the center of our life.

After the wonderful rewedding of this miracle couple, I asked Pete and Lita if they ever felt lonely and wondered where their love had gone. Pete laughed and said, "If you wonder where your love went, you forgot that you are the one who makes it. It's not out there, it's in here between Lita and me." Lita nodded in agreement, leaned over and kissed her husband's cheek. She looked at him with tears in her eyes and added softly, "Nobody can find love if they go looking for it alone."

I invite you to experience the joy of a miracle marriage like Pete and Lita's. If you do, you will never feel lonely again.

PART I

Understanding the Laws of Lasting Love

The meeting of two personalities is like the contact of two chemical substances; if there is any reaction, both are transformed.

—*Carl Jung*

Total Marriage:

TWO WAYS TO WED

Human love is not a substitute for spiritual love. It is an extension of it.

—*Emmanuel*

A Cosmic Coincidence

A coincidence of cosmic proportions took place today. From my lanai at my home in Maui, my wife and I watched together as the moon raced at twice the speed of sound to thrust our Polynesian dawn into darkness. As the bright morning sun began to sparkle in the deep blue sky over the peak of Haleakala (a dormant volcano—its Hawaiian name means "house of the sun"), a total solar eclipse created a day like no other.

Legend has it that the demigod Maui snatched the sun and held it so his people could thrive, and this morning the sun seemed captured once again. It hung just over the highest ridges of Haleakala and, as if Maui's hands were closing around it, was blocked by the moon in what astronomers call a "totality"—a complete eclipse of the sun. The moon's deep-black silhouette slowly crossed the sun, and a dancing halo of fiery light exploded around the moon's shadow. As the entire landscape was transformed by an ethereal glow, a transcendental silence confirmed the moment's spiritual intensity. The air was filled with positive ions or particles charged with a power that seemed to slow the passage of time. The birds stopped their singing, and the night-blooming flowers opened their petals. Some people screamed, others sobbed, and still others fell to their knees in prayer. As many couples did, my wife and I held each other, cried, and gave thanks for a miracle of love that had given us more time to be together.

A Couple's Eclipse

I had nearly died of cancer two years earlier, and the power of our love had helped to save my life numerous times. Now the cosmic connection between sun and moon reminded us that love can be a totality or wholeness that follows the laws of the cosmic and quantum world.

The totality of our love as husband and wife had overwhelmed the selfish cancer cells in my body. Each cell had been unwilling to sacrifice its own singularity. Cancer cells seek their own re-production until they kill the very system that gave them life. Through the strength we drew from the combination of our two spirits, my wife and I seemed to make a new totality that eclipsed my disease and overwhelmed the selfish cells. Like the solar eclipse totality, my wife and I had made our miracle by making our own totality of loving and healing energy.

This special day seemed to provide cosmic clues for coupling. This book will describe how the same cosmic and quantum principles that underlie the totality of a solar eclipse (the spinning of electrons in orbits around the center of an atom, and the functioning of everything in the universe) also show us the way to High Monogamy and how to make the miracle of lasting love.

Low or High Monogamy? The Choice Is Ours

There are two general types of marriage—Low and High Mo-nogamy.[1] Each form meets different needs for different people. Most books about marriage have focused on the modern form of marriage—Low Monogamy—because it is the most common and is well suited to contemporary society's emphasis on personal success and self-fulfillment. Low Monogamy is ancillary to our selfish motives. It is supportive to our life, but secondary—not the primary, principal, or fundamental aspect of our living.

The principles of Low Monogamy are drawn from psychology, psychiatry, economics, sociology, and biology. They are supported and enforced by a complex legal system designed to see that "marriage serves us." This book, however, is about how to make the adventurous and difficult commitment to the rarer way to love—High Monogamy, based on the principles of the quasars rather than quarrels, the laws of the cosmos instead of rules of the courts. What follows is a description of the two ways to wed, and the two styles of being monogamous from which we have to choose:

Low Monogamy: A marriage of two confident selves *for* the purpose of enhancing the individual spouses. This marriage evolved from socioeconomic, cultural, religious, and legal systems as the expected modern way to marry, and its rules of maintenance come from the new social sciences. Low Monogamy is maintained inertia, the timidity of one or both partners to change, and its efficiency as a means for getting children raised, careers conducted, tasks accomplished, and taxes paid. The goal is finding a happier Me through a partner who is also looking for someone to make him or her more content.

High Monogamy: A marriage of two people who consider themselves incomplete for the challenge and adventure of making a new Whole that is more than the combination of their two Halves. This relationship transcends the socioeconomic, cultural, religious, and legal legacies of the modern marital institution. It is based on the higher cosmic laws and quantum physics. It is primary rather than secondary to the spouses' lives and provides a way for both people to create a growing and adapting microsystem through which they can positively influence the macrosystem of the world. This is a marriage designed to help the world and not just to survive within it.

High Monogamy is not for everyone. It is the marital road less traveled.[2] Many persons find Low Monogamy to be a happy, easier, more secure, predictable, and less demanding way of leading their lives. Just as a valley is not inferior to a mountain or a raindrop to a snowflake, Low Monogamy is not worse or inferior to High Monogamy. It is well suited to the modern lifestyle of personal growth and self-enhancement. It is a different degree of marrying based on different assumptions, promises, and goals. This book, however, is about total marriage, the demanding, perplexing, often turbulent journey toward the complete and absolute merging of two spirits with the ultimate purpose of making the world a better place.

The Us-Fulfillment Movement

Low Monogamy—based on ground rules and guidelines taken primarily from the courts, the psychotherapy couch, or the church—adapts to the world instead of trying to help the world adapt to love. Therapeutic, legalistic, and religious rules determine its rituals of begining and ending, the marital contract, and ways for mediating problems. While many men and women have found happiness in Low Monogamy, other couples are considering another way to wed.

Many individuals are beginning to look beyond the demands of modern society to be independent, to succeed, flourish, accomplish, and consume. They are looking beyond "doing" to "being," and they are considering a more ecological orientation to life, a global "save and give to the earth." Individual meditation, self-help books, personal visualization, self-improvement courses, getting one's fair share, self-assertiveness training, and trips to various gurus for self-enlightenment are being replaced with attention to the meaning of marriage. There is an Us-fulfillment movement underway: men and women are accepting the challenge of making their marriage their lives.

People who choose High Monogamy don't *have* a marriage, they *are* their marriage. Their relationship is primary over all else and dictates every decision, wish, and prayer. Having transcended the ability to think for themselves, people in High Monogamy learn to think, feel, fear, and grow together. Low Monogamy is modern, efficient, and convenient. High Monogamy is a miracle of spiritual union that is timeless, challenging, and dynamic.

Two Ways to Find Your Bliss

I hope you will read this book as a means of considering your own choice between Low and High Monogamy. There will always be both types of marriage, and your own relationship may pass through its own phases. One way to wed or join is not "better" than the other, any more than a solar eclipse is "better" than a lunar eclipse.

Both a modern and a miracle marriage are ways to find your bliss or your own chosen goals and dreams.[3] Nothing is ever quite as glorious as it sounds and things are seldom as bad as they seem, and both the modern Me marriage and the miracle Us marriage have their strengths and weaknesses and positives and negatives. The Me marriage is efficient, simple, fast, adaptive, and less demanding of personal time and effort. It is a good way to fulfill oneself and "make it" through life. High Monogamy—a marriage for the making of miracles together—is the more difficult choice. It requires effort, time, patience, tolerance, forgiveness, and a willingness to learn what Us-fulfillment means. This book is intended to help you consider that choice and show you how to succeed should you elect the hard way to wed. If you choose that way, this book will help you learn to make a miracle marriage through the application of ten new laws of lasting love.

A Preview of the Ten Laws of Lasting Love

The ten laws of lasting love revealed themselves in the totality of the solar eclipse that cast its glow on our Hawaiian home. Within this cosmic coincidence were metaphors that served as hints about the lessons of loving forever that I will describe throughout this book. The totality seemed to raise important questions for my wife and me and several other couples who witnessed this magnificent event. What follows are the questions we asked and some answers to these questions as suggested by the laws of science. I hope you and someone you love will ask yourselves these questions, too.

QUESTIONS ABOUT LOVE

1. Are we making enough time for the two of us to love? The Two-Time Law

As the sun and moon made a totality that would not happen again in Maui until 2106, we realized that none of us now watching this event would be here again for the next cosmic coincidence. We sensed the preciousness of our time together and its *relativity* to the priorities we assign to the limited moment of our life. Albert Einstein's theory of relativity revealed that our time is not absolute and static. Einstein showed that how we think, where we are, and how fast we are traveling alter our perception of time and give it its meaning. My wife and I wondered if we were making enough "Two-Time" for love in our life.

People in Low Monogamy work hard to find some quality time to put into their marriage. High Monogamists work hard to invest the major quantity of their time into making a quality marriage.

2. Should we be so certain of each other? The Confident Uncertainty Law

A part of the power of the eclipse was the complete darkening of a segment of the earth. The brief and sudden night shortly after dawn—followed by a second dawn in one day—fooled the roosters into crowing in confusion and the birds into flying, roosting, and flying again. For a few moments, everything seemed *uncertain*. We sensed that—although it often seems that we have tamed, controlled, and learned to manage our world—nothing about life is really certain.

Physicist Werner Heisenberg's uncertainty principle teaches that the more we know of one thing, the less we automatically know of another. The more we know about light's wave quality, the less we know about its particle quality. We make a serious error when we think we know for sure. As my wife and I shared the totality, we felt a deeply reverent and renewed uncertainty about our love that seemed to make it more alive, mysterious, and invigorated.

Low Monogamy spouses feel that the more confident they are of one another and themselves, the more stable their marriage will be. High Monogamists work hard to be more certain of their marriage, but they are never certain of themselves or each other. A chief objective of a miracle-making marriage is to develop confidence constantly in the strength and power of its loving. A main goal of Low Monogamy is for husband and wife to become more "self"-confident and assured.

3. Are we too selfish? The One-Love Law

As the sun and the moon became one in a pitch-black sphere, the power of life's *oneness* overwhelmed us much as it had when we had faced my near-death together. When I felt the cold shadow of death and suffered the fire of the pain of my cancer, my wife suffered with me. During the totality of the eclipse, we felt that same sense of marrying or merging as one. Quantum theory suggests the law of oneness by showing that everything in the universe is both "particle and wave"—lump of stuff and jump of energy. Science has shown that matter and energy exist as one.

Secondary Monogamy is a union of one plus one equals two. High Monogamy is a union of one-half plus one-half equals one.

4. Do we really see each other? The Love-Look Law

As we joined the thousands of persons who came out at dawn to worship and be awed by the heavens, my wife and I wondered why we so seldom study the beauty and majesty all around us. In some parts of Hawaii, a thick cloud cover blocked clear viewing of the eclipse. The actual merging itself could not be seen, but people kept looking up with their solar shades in place to protect their eyes from a light they could not see. One old Hawaiian man said, "They said we couldn't see it, but we believed we saw it. We didn't have to see it to believe it. We believed it so we could see it. They said we couldn't see Maui's hands around the sun, but we did." This person's statement revealed the science principle called the *participant observer,* and my wife and I wondered if we were looking with love at each other often enough. The science principle called observer participancy teaches that what is seen depends upon the nature of the person doing the seeing. When we look lovingly, we are more likely to see love. As another observer of the eclipse pointed out, "You have to look while and when you can. You may not get another chance."

Some people looked up and said they saw the face of God in the shadow of the moon and prayed to the totality Others looked down and wondered at the night flowers fooled into blooming at dawn. These people looked for biological reflex and saw the effects of light. Others, like my wife and me, looked into each other's eyes and saw their totality there.

People in Low Monogamy look "for" love. A High Mongamist looks "with" love.

5. Do we remember how incomplete we are without each other? The Complementary-Love Law

Science speaks of physicist Niels Bohr's principle of complementarity, which states that there are always two sides or parts to all the wholes in the cosmic and quantum world. A piece of sand is both matter and energy, and light is both wave and particle. The sun's hot, powerful explosiveness and the moon's cool, calm mellowness complement each other in the totality of their mutual making of the miracle of their eclipse. The totality reminded us that a miracle marriage is made when a person is willing to see himself or herself as a "half-self," searches vigorously for the missing half, and gives fully of his or her own half to make a new whole.

A person in Low Monogamy tries to be as complete as he or she can be and looks for a "complete" person to help him or her be even more complete as an individual. A High Monogamist accepts and forgives his own and his spouse's natural halfness and looks for the complementarity to make a new whole marriage. As one husband put it, "We have a marriage of wills because we were really willing to marry."

6. Are we aware enough of each other often enough and everywhere? The Transcendent-Love Law

When scientists speak of the concept of nonlocality, they are describing their discovery that space or time does not restrict the interaction of the particles and waves of the universe. When the moon and sun pass within millions of miles of each other, the power of their energy and their respective forces of gravity transcend this distance instantaneously. Both celestial bodies in this cosmic couple are influenced *now* and their mutual effect on each other impacts all over the earth at exactly the same time. The positively charged ions we could feel surging through the warm Maui air at the moment of totality were transformed in outer space, but we felt their effect immediately, faster than the speed of light, and as if there were no distance at all between us and the cosmic coincidence.

As we felt the strange sensations of the charged air, my wife and I remembered how I could always feel her love even when she was isolated from me physically at the time of my bone marrow transplant to cure my cancer. Through the plastic walls of my isolated world, I could feel my wife's love heal me no matter where she was.

Spouses in Low Monogamy pine for each other when they are separated and feel isolated and vulnerable when apart. High Monogamists feel close no matter how far away each lover may be, and their loving energy extends anywhere, anytime.

7. Do we appreciate the opportunity to have each other to go through crises with? The Creative-Chaos Law

Every night, when my wife and I look up at the deep, dark Hawaiian sky, we see a dazzling chaos of white dots over the West Maui Mountains spilling out over the Pacific Ocean. The totality we observed on eclipse day was a sudden pairing that occurred from within this cosmic clutter—an order within the evolving disorder and an encounter with a regularity between nature's regimes of chaos. We were reminded how fortunate we were, after my near-death, to have each other as companions through life's constant turmoil.

Scientists developing the new chaos theory have learned that the eerie order beneath the natural disorder of life is caused by "strange attractors"—a mathematical term that explains why smoke from a cigarette finds a patterned swirl as it curls up from the first puff and flooding water finds its point of ebb and flow. Our loving is made from two personal strange attractors drawn to each other to make windows through the chaos of living.

People in Low Monogamy view life's chaos as an obstacle, hindrance, or encumbrance in their quest for self-fulfillment. For them, the necessary turmoil of life is a distraction or barrier to "getting their own way." High Monogamy marriages see chaos as a necessary and natural life process. Pandemonium and tumult are the challenges that contain the lessons that help their marriage make their miracles.

8. Do we love as if we remember that our time here on earth together will end? The Law of Shared Sadness

Scientists have developed a principle they call the Second Law of Thermodynamics, which predicts that, since the Big Bang 20 million years ago, everything is slowly but surely burning itself out through a process called "entropy," or increasing disarray. New science teaches that it is more accurate to refer to living things as experiencing *negentropy,* or the process of burning up or out as a reordering dance of evolution toward a higher, newer, more mysterious order.

As my wife and I witnessed the eclipse, we were strengthened in our faith that—whether or not the physical stuff of the universe is heading for a Big Burn or a Big Crunch—there seems a higher purpose for all our suffering. The inescapable reality of the totality's passing seemed to tell us to enjoy our togetherness now. Lasting love is based on the faith that the burning up may become the fire of an evolving loving spirit that can transcend the physical end.

Spouses in a Low Monogamy marriage thrive on sharing joy and accommodate, cope, and survive together during the ending and sad times. Spouses in a miracle marriage capture energy from the natural endings and times of sadness and thrive through the crises of life. They use sadness to become stronger and more compassionate for each other and for everything and everyone in the world.

9. Are we imaginative and creative enough to see many possibilities and many "realities" rather than consumed by the need to discover and comply with the "one" reality? The Law of Loving Realities

Seventeenth-century science seemed to prove that there was one way of explaining everything—scientific reality. The scientific revolution of the twentieth century shows that there are many ways to view the world and many *realities.* The natural inquisitiveness and curiosity of science can also be applied to the reality we have come to accept in our day-to-day life so that we can learn to imagine and discover many realities together.

During the totality of the eclipse, people shouted out their respective feelings of what was real for them. Some even questioned whether or not what they were seeing with their own eyes was real. One husband looked through his solar shade and said, "I never saw the sun's shape and outline so clearly." His wife said, "I never saw the mountains and valleys on the moon before." As each spouse saw the other's reality, they shouted out in unison, "Oh! I see how you're seeing!"

The total eclipse suggested to us that lasting love also involves the acceptance and mutual enjoyment of many realities and different points of view. Miracle marriages require spouses to expand their minds to be free of the limits of one way to see, know, and explain their world. High Monogamy capitalizes on the fact that one collective, inventive, and open mind is better than two individual, prosaic, and closed brains.

People in Low Monogamy work hard to help each other see and understand what each of them experience as their respective and valid reality. They apply a "protective couple cynicism" against anything that is not "factual" or based on reality. High Monogamists apply a "creative couple cynicism" to any certainties, "facts," or demands to face "the" true reality. They discover new realities together by assuming that each spouse can bring many realities to the marriage.

10. Are we open enough to feel the energy of our love? The Energizing-Love Law

I have described the positively charged ions resulting from the unique atmosphere created by the dark dawn of totality. We could feel them surging around and through us. In 585 B.C., the fighting Middle East armies of Medes and Lydians stopped in midbattle because of their sense of this strange energy from a total solar eclipse. The Polynesians, ever the romantics, saw the sun and moon as merging together in sexual embrace. They experienced romantic energy coming from the totality and began several days of their own erotic eclipsing spurred on by the astro-aphrodisiac of the sun's and moon's combined sensuous glow.

For my wife and me, the totality reminded us of the power of an *energy* beyond the mechanical and here-and-now that provides love's "forever force field." We had felt that energy as I faced my death, and it healed us both.

Low Monogamists put energy "into" their marriage. High Monogamists are energized by their marriage, and the whole world basks in the love emitted by their union.

All of the above laws of love hinted at by the metaphorical movement of the heavens and the symbolism of the totality will be described in detail in the Miracle Marriage Manual in Part II of this book. From each of these remarkable laws, new lessons for accomplishing High Monogamy—a miracle marriage—may be learned and applied. If you feel your marriage is in distress and that there is urgency in finding a different way to be married, Part II is also a marital guide through couple chaos. You may want to read that section first and then return to Part I.

The first part of this book explores the theories, problems, challenges, and a new psychology for making a miracle marriage. This material is based on what I learned from my own experiences when my miracle marriage saved my life and from what I call the Twenty-five Silver Survivors—twenty-five couples I studied for more than twenty years in my Problems of Daily Living Clinic at Sinai Hospital of Detroit. What follows is a preview of ten of the lessons you will learn in Part I. If they seem different or contradict marital advice you may have read and heard before, it is because these are not lessons to help you survive in a modern marriage. These are the lessons of thriving in a miracle marriage. One Silver Survivor said, "Modern marriages sometimes work well for two people, but miracle marriages are made by two people working well at their marriage." The more common Low Monogamy lessons precede each lasting-love lesson.

TEN LASTING-LOVE LESSONS

Low Monogamy Lesson: You can't love anyone unless you love yourself first.

High Monogamy Lesson 1: Deciding where we are going in life and whom we will take with us is the same question. Learning to love yourself takes place at the same time you learn to love and be loved by someone else.

If you don't feel you are lovable, you cannot give or receive love. You find your "self" by joining with someone else in a shared search for the meaning of life.

Low Monogamy Lesson: A good marriage is based on compromise.

High Monogamy Lesson 2: Compromise compromises a marriage.

Meeting someone "halfway" guarantees that your relationship will never find "its way." Partners in a miracle marriage don't give in or give up, they try out, try on, and sample from the half their partner brings to the relationship. High Monogamists persistently pursue their own point of view, and with vigor and convincing energy, they model the behavior they hope to observe in their partner. By encouraging one's spouse to do the same, a person can make his or her miracle marriage stronger, because each partner will then try new ways to think and behave instead of giving in or giving up.

Low Monogamy Lesson: The more communication in a marriage, the better.

High Monogamy Lesson 3: Communication can bore a marriage to death.

Many couples talk themselves out of love. Less talk and more development of other means of communication is the way of a miracle marriage.

Low Monogamy Lesson: Good and frequent sex makes a happier marriage.

High Monogamy Lesson 4: Sex can be a risk to intimacy.

Too much sex can diminish sexual mystery. Sex can become a shortcut means of expressing intimacy or trying to elicit intimate feelings—a type of marital work-saving device that ultimately wears out and becomes ineffective. Persons in Low Monogamy try to have sex often in order to feel love. High Monogamists feel love always, which sometimes results in having sex. Partners in miracle marriages don't necessarily "do it often," but when they do, they experience a deep and profound intimacy. Sexual frequency and variety are not predictors of the quality of a High Monogamy marriage.

Low Monogamy Lesson: Love is an irresistible and profound feeling that overcomes and involuntarily overwhelms you.

High Monogamy Lesson 5: Loving is a way of thinking, not a way of feeling.

Love is a choice of a point of view regarding another person and a decision about how to relate with someone you elect to invest your life in. It is volitional, not emotional. Low Monogamists believe that you'll know you're in love when you feel it. High Monogamists believe that when you truly think about and know love, you'll begin to feel it. The biological imperative to bond and procreate results in powerful biological urges, but spiritual merging requires choice, commitment, effort, and behaving and thinking lovingly to feel love and be loved. Miracle monogamists don't "fall" in love—they think themselves through it.

Low Monogamy Lesson: Be sure to find the perfect partner for you.

High Monogamy Lesson 6. Good marriages are made by being the right partner, not by finding the right partner.

In a miracle marriage, what I "am" is what I "get." More people want to be loved than are willing to put the mental, physical, and spiritual effort into loving.

Low Monogamy Lesson: Be sure that marriage is for you and know when it is the right time for you to marry.

High Monogamy Lesson 7. The question is not "Should I marry?" or "Is it time to marry?" High Monogamists reflect on the question "Would I want to be married to me as I am now?" and "Am I ready now and forever to make the time to be totally married as the prime focus of my life?"

Low Monogamy Lesson: Don't marry unless you're a complete person and be sure to marry someone who himself or herself is totally together.

High Monogamy Lesson 8. The template of lasting love is composed of two half persons. We marry so we and our partner can become whole together, two halves.

Low Monogamy Lesson: Be assertive and represent yourself. Know what you need and want and let your spouse know it.

High Monogamy Lesson 9. No one gets his or her own way in a miracle marriage.

High Monogamists struggle together to make a new way to live and to create a marital way to experience all that life offers. Miracle marriages are more tolerant than confrontive, more forgiving than argumentative, and more compliant and docile than demanding and assertive. By looking together for "a" way to live and love, the spouses avoid the trap of battling to get their own way.

Low Monogamy Lesson: Try to apply the principles of psychology to your marriage.

High Monogamy Lesson 10. The principles of psychology work well for modern marriages. The principles of physics—the laws of the cosmic and quantum world—are the way to a miracle marriage.

A miracle marriage is not made by giving ourselves away. It is not a product of one lonely star dominating another. If you choose High Monogamy, you choose to try for a complete merging of spirits forever with someone else. Miracle marriages revel in the joy and power of all the love there ever was, is, and will be in the world and reflect that love back throughout the world. Like the totality of a solar and lunar eclipse, we move back and forth together forever through the shadows and the light. Sometimes, one of us shines more brightly and the other's shadow temporarily darkens us, but the energy of our love keeps us moving and changing. No matter where we are, the gravity of our love influences us and draws us back together again. We are a totality even when we are separated. When we learn to eclipse the self, we make our own miracle total marriage.

Marriage or Me?

THE CHALLENGE
OF BECOMING ONE

*The goal of our life should not be to find joy in
marriage, but to bring more love and truth into the
world. We marry to assist each other in this task.*

—Leo Tolstoy

The Choices of a Lifetime

This book is about the two most important questions of life.
"Where am I going and who will go with me?" All of us must
answer these questions sometime during our lives, and the order
in which we answer them is as important as the answers
themselves.

If we go through life with a Me focus, we tend to answer the
two questions above by first trying to find out *who* we are as
individuals and where we want to go with our lives. After we
feel that we have resolved these issues, we turn our attention to
a search for someone to take along with us. First we settle on
our destination and then we consider a traveling companion.

If we go through life with a passion focus and are enthralled
by romantic lust, our first issue is finding the companion to make
life's journey worthwhile. We think that once we have found the

perfect traveling companion, our personal voyage will be made clear and easier.

Love the Hard Way

This book is about more challenging ways to answer life's two key questions. The first two ways mentioned above—finding Me first or finding someone who will help Me find Me—are ways of the modern marriage of Low Monogamy. Many people have found these ways satisfactory for them, but the way of High Monogamy requires that we ask "Where am I going and with whom?" at exactly the same time.

This is a book about how the two love and life questions can be explored along with someone else. Psychologist Nathaniel Branden warns that we should "never marry a person who is not a friend of our excitement." He is referring to accepting the challenge of trying to learn life and learn love together with someone else. Like me, he sees a miracle marriage as an infinite work in progress.

One of the Silver Survivors described the problem this way: "You can learn to love life first or you can try to find the love of your life first. Loving the hard way requires that you and your spouse learn to love by discovering life together."

Is Self-Love a Prerequisite for True Love?

The old cliché is "If we do not love ourselves, we cannot love anyone else." This is the orientation of Low Monogamy, learning to love me and then trying to find someone who can love me as much as I love myself. Low Monogamy marriages are built from two people who have learned to love themselves and then try to find a life and love together.

It is equally true, however, that we cannot love ourselves if we cannot make it possible for someone else to be able to love us. No matter how hard our lover tries to show caring, he or she feels frustrated if we cannot accept, receive, and reflect love because we don't feel lovable. The constant struggle in Low Monogamy is either figuring out to whom or to what we want to be devoted, or accepting the devotion of someone else as a means of finding out what is worth devoting ourselves to.

If we choose High Monogamy, we struggle with these same issues. The difference is, however, that we struggle right along *with* someone else who is grappling with them too. In High Monogamy, we join with a coexplorer in our search to discover who we are, who they are, and where we both might like to go, and to tune in to the lessons of those who have loved before us. Modern marriage employs Low Monogamy as a means of loving in today's world. Miracle marriage employs High Monogamy guided by the laws of loving that transcend time.

It is much more difficult to deal with "where and with whom" at the same time, particularly when both people are engaged in the same tussle. The choice to make a miracle marriage, however, means that we choose the more difficult way as a means to enlightenment. Miracles are never easy.

As an introduction to the challenges and choices facing marriage today, consider the story below, in which both husband and wife chose to answer the two questions described above by selecting the way of "self first" and—maybe—loving later.

Who Has Custody of the Marriage?

"There is just no question about it. He would be the best parent." The psychologist's words echoed through the large courtroom, and she spoke with authority and confidence. She glanced toward the seven-year-old twin sisters sitting frightened and confused just behind their father, then turned back toward the judge. The little girls seemed afraid to look up as they continued to color in their coloring books. They looked like uninvolved miniature court artists rather than innocent children watching the course of their lives being changed by adults who became stuck on the question of "Where am *I* going?"

"It is clear to me that the girls would be much better off with their father. Their mother is going through an important phase in her own development right now. She needs to search for her identity and pay attention to her own needs. She has to find her own fulfillment and to discover who she is. In a word, she needs space." The psychologist flicked her hair to one side, glared angrily at the father, leaned forward, and shouted, "She has a right to be who she wants to be and not a slave to his sexist macho ego."

Before the father's attorney could object, the judge swept his hand in apparent disgust and boredom. "That's enough, doctor, you may be seated," he said. It was my turn to testify next. The court clerk called my name as if announcing a fighter in the opponent's corner of the boxing ring.

As a clinical psychologist in charge of a large family clinic, I am often the "expert" in divorce battles over the custody of the spoils of marriage wars—children and chattel. That day, I was expected to advise the court about the status of this marriage and to indicate which of the parents of these two vulnerable little children would do the best job in protecting, nurturing, and helping them have a safe and healthy childhood. I had testified in such proceedings dozens of times, but this time when my name was called I could not move. This battle was between two parents who were each trying to force the other to *take* custody of the children! The *loser* would have to raise the little girls.

Mutual Mariticide: The Killing of Marriage

The psychologist who had just testified brushed past me with tears in her eyes, ignoring the father and the girls. She slammed into her seat as her briefcase slapped loudly to the floor. Try as she did to detach herself from her ordeal by speaking as if she were a therapist presenting a diagnosis, this sad woman was in fact the mother of these children and had been testifying not in her role as a psychologist but on her own behalf in the custody battle over which parent would be stuck by the state with a mandate to be a parent. The husband had testified earlier, saying that he felt his career was at a "vulnerable period" and that while he loved his daughters very much, he really could not be their father until he too "found himself," completed his own psychotherapy, and knew where he was going. He felt that his psychologist wife should take the twins because "she had the training" and because the two girls had been "her idea in the first place as a way of having the experience of motherhood."

Listening to their selfish diatribes was too much for me. I already knew that within any marriage that took place in 1980, the year prior to this trial, 80 percent of the resulting white children and 94 percent of the black children would no longer be living with both natural parents by age seventeen.[1] Most marriages were not even working well as day care centers! As marriages sank, children were jettisoned and left to single-parent homes or relatives, if they were lucky, or to an institution or to the street if they were not.

I asked to meet with the judge in his chambers. As the parents, attorneys, and I followed him in to his office, the judge walked over to the window, lowered his head, and began to sob. Without turning around, the judge unleashed in tears his years of frustration. He had witnessed and assisted at the death sentence of hundreds of marriages, and his black robe seemed appropriate for the job. Shoulders quivering, he said, "Is this what marriage has come to? A battle over who *must* have custody of the children? In God's name, what does marriage mean? What are we doing to it? We're killing it. What is it for? What is it all about? What good is it? Is there any hope for marriage at all? It's going to take a miracle to save marriage as an institution and to save the innocent victims of this ridiculous selfish slaughter of what should be one of the happiest parts of our life. Marriage deserves so much better than the people who are using it and offers so much more than we are getting from it. If there were a law against marriage abuse, the jails would be full of offenders. Who in the hell has custody of marriage?"

Monogamy and Monotony

The judge's words struck a chord I heard resounding beneath the drone of the marital discord I had struggled with through my years of clinical practice. What is marriage for anyway? What does it mean? More than 2,000 couples had come to my clinic for help, and I had learned that marriages are not failing—we are failing our marriages. We use marriage rather than respond to its challenge of making two into One. A key lesson beneath this course in making a miracle marriage is that lasting love depends much more on being the right partner than on finding the right partner—on being loved by the one you love by loving the way you want to be loved.

It is not marriage that is monotonous—we are! We are blaming our marriages for our boredom and unhappiness because too many of us fail to see the real challenge in being married—to share in the process of growth from lust to love to a loving life. One Silver Survivor said, "We've grown from being monogamous monotonists to marital miracle marriages. It's easy to be bored with yourself, but it's impossible to be bored when you are trying to live as two."

Three Challenges of a Miracle Marriage

In working with the couples in my clinic who had chosen to try for a miracle marriage, I asked them to remember the following:

Challenge 1: Never Marry to Change or Expecting Change in Someone Else

We are all married to failures, and so are our spouses. The challenge is to learn as an imperfect person to live and love with another imperfect person, understanding and accepting our differences, expecting no more than we give, and changing and improving oneself in the direction of changes hoped for in our spouse. As flawed as we all are, a major challenge of being and staying married is to try to love as and how we would be loved.

Challenge 2: Lust Always Lapses

Marriage is designed so that we fall out of romantic love and into loving reality. The challenge is to expect and be ready for the inevitable change from unrealistically passionate and exciting loving to a different loving of predictability, comfort, safety, and joy in learning about and with each other. The natural decline from romantic high and passionate longing is a sign of maturing love, not a failing marriage.

Challenge 3: Couples Conflict Kills or Creates Love

Conflict in marriage is natural, necessary, and a part of the process of evolving real love. Conflict is the necessary chaos that makes change and growth possible. If you marry to settle down, that's exactly where you will find yourself. Marital conflict is the forge of the shared development of human spirits. The challenge is not only to stand *with* your spouse but to stand constructively *against* him or her when adjustments are called for. The difference between the heat from the friction of two egos and the warmth of the forging of two spirits is the guarantee that the two of you always stand *behind* the marriage itself. High Monogamists are willing to take the risk of coming into conflict with their lovers as a means of making a better marriage for both. Low Monogamists come into conflict when their ego is threatened.

There can be little monotony if we respond to the challenge of trying daily to support our spouse when he or she is threatened, trying to change ourselves instead of expecting changes in our partner, and confronting our lover when he or she seems unwise or unreasonable or when poor judgment threatens someone's welfare. Miracle marriages are safe places for two lovers to take growth risks and to learn more about loving. When we fight in our marriage, our loving suffers. When we fight for our marriage, our loving grows.

Popping the Right Question

When people "pop the question," they are often thinking that they have finally found the right partner. It may be assumed that the challenge is over, because the discovery of the perfect lover has been achieved and the two lovers can now "settle down." As I said above, the miracle marriage described in this book is based on the challenge that getting married is a way of stirring things up in our lives. It is taking on the most important life challenge—to silence the search for the self and try instead to make a whole new searching and growing loving unit.

If we are really ready to pop the question or to answer it, the real question to be popped is not "Will you marry me?" The miracle marriage question is "Am I marriable?" If we want the miracle of a lasting and growing marriage for life, the question to be asked is not "Do I want to marry him or her?" We should ask, "Would I want to be married to me?"

As obvious and simple as it may seem, we sometimes forget that marriage is for two. The challenge of a lasting marriage is not to find someone to go through life with but to find within ourselves the willingness and strength to try to make an entirely new way to live. A lasting marriage is not the "two of us trying as two individuals to survive side by side." It is "the total union of Us creating together in order to thrive together," and therein lies the prevention of any possible monogamy monotony.

You will learn in Part II of this book that marriages designed or covertly directed primarily by the need for selfish gain, growth, and fulfillment seldom survive. They tend to lack purpose other than the parallel pursuit of the separate individual goals and wishes of the respective spouses. Low Monogamy provides an avenue for self-fulfillment, but "self"-fulfillment is not what High Monogamy promises. Miracle marriage is for all of us everywhere.

The Great Marriage Myth

The best way of two becoming and staying One is for each of the two to love according to what mythologist Joseph Campbell calls that Great Marriage Myth.[2] Myth in this sense means universal lesson or the meaning a culture gives to its most basic institutions. Rather than a fictional story or false belief, great myths are the moral guideposts of our personal spiritual development. Great cultural myths reverberate with the energy of past loving. They teach us timeless lessons about what makes life meaningful. They help a society survive and evolve. Great myths are life lessons that have been learned by and passed on from our ancestors.

In Hawaii, passing on the great myths is called "talking story," or the word-of-mouth teaching of morality that makes up the core of culture. The Hawaiian word *mana* means "energy," and the native Hawaiian is taught that the love of our ancestors is all around us, influencing all that we do. The Polynesian miracle marriage of hundreds of years ago was a union of two lovers to discover the aloha and mana, the love energy of ancestors vibrating through time and to channel that energy to those around them. Miracle marriages are mana marriages.

There are many great myths, including the myths of spiritual beliefs, the value and meaning of work, and enduring symbols, ceremonies, and rituals for giving meaning, significance, and dignity to the cultural aspects of our birth, life, and death. The last chapter of this book presents a "miracle marriage ritual" to help you discover the mana or mythic love energy of our human past. Modern marriage seeks answers from the present about what might be needed to survive in the future.

The miracle marriage of the Great Marriage Myth tries to discover the spiritual energy from all the loving that ever was. The Great Marriage Myth teaches that we are not human beings capable of a loving experience but loving spirits experiencing the human side of loving.

The Great Marriage Myth also teaches that one of our most important life choices is whether to approach life as a self or as a unit. We can agree to suffer and celebrate together in a total union or high marriage as One spirit. Or we can choose to go it alone and, if we legally marry, seek personal fulfillment beside but not with our partner. The challenge of living by the Great Marriage Myth is to choose to help someone be happy and healthy and to make that goal unqualifiably and unconditionally fundamental to our own individual bliss.

By being creatively and lastingly married—the state of High Monogamy—we share in a give-and-take of the world's loving. Our unqualified caring for one another and for all the products and processes of our union, including birth, parenting, working, playing, suffering, healing, growing old, and dying, helps makes us better and helps make the world a better place. Our world needs High Monogamy because the task of the evolving human spirit is too difficult for millions of single selves who are seeking to solve life's many mysteries.

The Great Me Myth

The decision concerning which great myths we will follow in our search for bliss and happiness fundamentally determines the nature of our life and the life of those around us. The last decades have seen the emergence of the Great Me Myth of Low Monogamy, and it continues to be a guide for many relationships. In contrast to the Great Marriage Myth, the modern Me Myth asserts that our gratification will best be found by self-protection and self-assertion as we seek our own path to our own individual goals, healing our own "inner child," and essentially "doing our own thing."

The Great Marriage Myth tells us to try to "do the Us thing."

While the Me Myth urges us to find our space, know "where our head is at," and be a strong, independent, and self-sufficient person, the Great Marriage Myth teaches that we should make space for another person in our life, learn to think as one, and be vulnerable, interdependent, and mutually supportive.

What We Are *for* Strengthens Us

In the Great Marriage Myth, needing someone is good and necessary, but the Me Myth teaches that needing someone else is a sign of immaturity. Giving in, going along, and putting up with are good things to do according to the Great Marriage Myth, but self-representation, asserting our own intentions, making our point, and not putting up with anything from anyone are good things to do according to the Me Myth.

The Me Myth is primarily oriented toward "standing against" invasions on our own psychological turf. The Marriage Myth is oriented toward "standing for" the marriage rather than the protection of individual egos. What we stand for strengthens us, and what we stand against saps our energy, so the Marriage Myth allows for an energizing rather than energy-draining daily life.

One Silver Survivor who is president of his own company described the contrast between living by High Monogamy, or the Us Myth, and Low Monogamy, or the Me Myth, when he said awkwardly, "There is always some crap up with which I will not put from anybody—except my wife, that is. In my business, I'm assertive, but in my marriage I'm accommodating. I'm an authoritarian administrator, but I just try to be agreeable in my marriage. I'm a demanding boss, but I'm a docile husband."

In the tradition of the Great Marriage Myth, we marry not "to" but "with" one another to be happy together, to struggle and change together. The objective is to stir things up and to agitate our life instead of each other. Miracle marriages are made by two people disturbing the status quo instead of each other, in order to find creative and challenging ways to change and improve themselves and the world. Another Silver Survivor supported the orientation of the Great Marriage Myth by saying, "If you marry for yourself and 'to' someone, you want a marriage that smooths things over, gets things done easily, and is as free as possible of hassles so you can go about the business of being

happy. If you marry 'with' someone, you choose to struggle together and mess things up so you can discover a whole new way
to put them back together again. My husband and I accommodate to one another, but we don't expect or accept life to be easy
and predictable."

The Great Marriage Myth says that making our world a better
place is not a job that can be accomplished one person at a time.
A world of peace and loving is built by units composed of these
same qualities and not selfish, assertive, and defensive egos. Millions of "ones" living by the Me Myth only add up to millions of
single strivers doing their own thing and hoping that getting
their way is a good way for the world. Millions of lasting and
strong marriages add up to much more than two plus two plus
two. Miracle marriages add up to unions of one-half plus one-
half combining in totalities that can change the world. These are
lofty goals indeed, and that is why I have chosen the phrase
"miracle marriage" and not "mediocre marriage" for the goal of
the love lessons to be described in this book.

Questions of Lasting Love

We have seen that the choice of living by the Great Marriage
Myth carries with it an entirely different set of questions from
the choice of living by the Me Myth.

• People of the Great Marriage Myth ask themselves, "Would
I want to be married to me?" instead of "Do I want to marry
him or her?"
• People of the Great Marriage Myth ask, "Am I loving just as
I want to be loved?" instead of "Why isn't he or she loving me
enough or in the way I want to be loved?"
• When things go wrong in the marriage, people of the Great
Marriage Myth ask, "How have I changed?" instead of "Why has
my partner changed?"
• When things go right in the marriage, people of the Great
Marriage Myth ask, "How have we done it and what have we
learned?" instead of "How did I do it and does he or she ap-
preciate it?"
• Finally and ultimately, people of the Great Marriage Myth

constantly ask, "What are we giving to the world?" rather than "Are we each getting all we can out of life?"

The End of the Affair

Joseph Campbell writes, "Marriage is not a simple love affair, it's an ordeal, and the ordeal is the sacrifice of ego to a relationship in which two halves become One."[3] This union is much more than the sum of its two members. It is an ongoing ordeal of merger that, if we stay the battle, results in a strong bond beyond the combined strengths of its components. Lasting marriage is as much agony as ecstasy because two becoming One is always a trial of wills, ways, and wishes. The lasting and growing marital relationship is a miracle deserving of our awe and reverence because it symbolizes just what the world needs now, the victory of unity over separatism. It shows the world that the struggle for love is worth it and that we can be victorious together without vanquishing each other or the world in the process.

The Momentum for Merging

None of us is complete or perfect. All of us need something more to be whole and to move closer to our bliss. Nature imparts the momentum for merging and the template for totality. Marriage is the process through which a loving wholeness is possible here on earth. When, as the parents did in the example at the beginning of this chapter, we seek *only* "self"-fulfillment through marriage, our marriage can end up burdening instead of helping society.

As you will read later in this book, the greatest principles of new science teach the same lesson as the Great Marriage Myth. There is no such thing as a lonely electron—they always spin in pairs. The energy of the universe is in every particle and wave. From quarks to quasars, the universe is built two by two by the merging of opposite complementary pairs to combine and share their energy. When we choose Low Monogamy, we defend or apologize for our halfness and regret the incompleteness of our partner. When we choose High Monogamy, we forgive our own and our lover's halfness, and we willingly take on the challenge of trying to make a stronger One. While marriages of the Me Myth struggle against incompleteness, miracle marriages are energized by it.

A Gentler Science

Paradoxically, as the hard sciences have become more metaphorical and interested in the miracles and magic of the cosmic and quantum worlds, psychology has grown to seem more cynical and mechanical in its view of the world. Physics speaks of the fact that, once connected, nothing can ever be completely separated, and scientists have extended this principle to understanding the entire world system. Quantum physics speaks of "instantaneous" communication and faster-than-light speeds that allow for communicating beyond words, and we have extended these concepts to explain the power of prayer in miraculous healings. Popular psychology and its "reality" scoffs at such thinking and has become more focused on the tangible, measurable, mechanical, desacralized dimensions of life. For the mental health field, self-help and health, verbal-communication gimmicks, and sexual posture and timing adjustments seem more in vogue than loving across time and being together forever.

Einstein warned that "God may be subtle but he is not malicious." The modern world, however, seems to assume that being clever, fast, powerful, and fully "self"-developed and autonomous is protection against the ravages of a malicious and senseless chaos that will ultimately consume us all. As you will discover in later chapters, however, many great scientists—Einstein, Planck, Heisenberg, to name only three—have discovered that the way to wellness of the spirit is through the principles of lasting union they see in their cloud chambers and telescopes and not through the independent striving they see in the daily world around them.

We can only find the meaning and purpose of quarks, electrons, atoms, stars, and planets by focusing on the laws of their lasting unions. The secrets of the universe are revealed when we understand how its components merge their opposite halves and by seeking the nature of the infinite energy that bonds them as one. The traditional approach of mechanically oriented science is to take things apart to understand how they work. Modern science is learning to look at how they exist forever together in ebbs and flows of waves of energy.

The Me Myth is based on old science. It follows the laws of separate and colliding particles and isolated energy systems burning themselves out as they are dragged to their end by limited one-way time. The Great Marriage Myth asks us to try to follow the way of waves and particles merging into One.

A Brief History of the Great Marriage Myth

Great myths and the influence they ultimately have on our lives take centuries to evolve. The Great Marital Myth of true spiritual merging beyond selfish needs and sexual drives goes back far into history. The Countess of Champagne, the "Miss Manners" of the year 1174, wrote, "We declare and we hold as firmly established that love [romantic love and lust sought for self-fulfillment] cannot exert its power between two people who are married to each other. Married people are duty-bound to give in to each other's desires and deny themselves to each other in nothing."[4] The countess's point was that marriage was intended as a system for learning to be a unit rather than a place to guarantee self-gratification.

Records from Mesopotamia, an ancient country in Asia between the Tigris and Euphrates rivers (in the area now referred to as the country of Iraq), contain few references to selfish or romantic love motives for marriage. Marriage was intended to serve the higher purpose of making a new union of two individuals and to quiet selfishness and egoistic pursuits damaging to the welfare of the state. The Great Marriage Myth evolved as a means to transcend each person's individual personality. By so doing, it was thought, we would make society stronger, unified, and more whole. No society survives that fails to learn the lesson of unity.

Early Romans arranged marriages on the basis of the durability of the community's political and economic alliances. Individual happiness was never considered. The chief objective was to make as many building-unit blocks for the society as possible. Boys were rushed to marriage at age fourteen and earlier, the girls at age twelve and often younger.[5] As impractical, exploitive, and damaging as this early-marriage practice may have been for these children, the rationale is clear. Marriage was not seen as "for" the spouses. Marriage was for the good of the society.

In India, marriage was intended for a purpose beyond romance and self-fulfillment. Marriage for financial gain and enhancement of social status by the parents of the spouses is still often found in India, and the early roots of marriage for purposes beyond the individual spouse's needs was evident in early Indian culture.

The ancient Romans' contribution to the evolution of the Great Marriage Myth is found in their strong sanctions that marriage not only should but almost *must* endure and survive for the good of society. To foster a viable union between men and women, the Romans devised three types of marriage. They considered the highest-level marriage to be the *confarreatio,* which was highly ceremonious and almost impossible to end by any legal or socially approved means. The welfare of the Roman society and cultural system came first over all else, and High Monogamy was supposed to be strong enough to survive for the general welfare of everyone else. As the Roman citizen was expected to put the state above all else, spouses in the *confarreatio* marriage were expected to place their own needs below the welfare of the marital union. The Romans saw marital survival and not individual assertiveness as the sign of personal maturity and responsibility.

The next level of marriage was the *coemptio* union, in which the Romans had little faith. After a brief legal ceremony, the bride was given to the groom to "use" as he wished for cooking, cleaning, and sex. In trade, the wife received financial support and security. This form of "very low monogamy" was tolerated but never admired or advocated by the Romans. Some of our modern-day marriages have a *coemptio* quality, but they typically fail because they do not effectively meet either the needs of the Me Myth spouse, the aspirations of those in search of High Monogamy, or the requirements of society.

Finally, the Roman system of marriage included the *usus,* or "trial marriage" for one year. If the couple qualified after that year, they could decide to try for the High Monogamy of the *confarreatio* marriage. The *usus* marriage was one of the earliest institutionalized arrangements for cohabitation. Just as evidence clearly shows that cohabitation seldom results in a marriage of High Monogamy, the *usus* marriage failed the Romans because only a small percentage of these marriages survived the one-year trial period.

High Monogamy requires a promise of commitment to join forever. The idea of "trying it for a while first" negates the very basis of the Great Marriage Myth. Rather than asking, "Am I ready to be a good spouse?," cohabitation or trial marriage asks, "Is marriage ready to be used by me at this time in my life?"

The church has always been a source and purveyor of our greatest cultural teaching myths. Most church doctrines have historically been direct and explicit in their attempt to make marriage a place of lasting union not threatened by selfish romanticized loving. During the 1800s, marriage was seen as an antidote to selfishness and the pursuit of romance. Church leaders often suggested marriage as a means of curbing lust and egocentrism. Some church leaders went so far as to recommend "spiritual diets" designed to prevent a spouse from becoming self-indulgent and thus vulnerable to lust. (The Graham cracker was invented by preacher Sylvester Graham as a nonstimulating and tasteless food capable of preventing any gastric-to-genital lust-arousal cycle.)[6] Some churches recommended marriage at as early as eleven years of age to prevent the emergence of selfishness and immature lustful strivings.[7] The philosophy seemed to be to "get married before you get too selfish."

Of course, marriage by a child to another child or to an adult is the worst example of exploitation and abuse, but evolution of any great myth, including the Great Marriage Myth, contains within its gestation many abuses and much human suffering. The brief history of the Great Marriage Myth I have outlined here evolved the idea of "wedding for the world" instead of the self. It reflects the fact that marrying for Me is a relatively new and modern wrinkle in the development of the meaning and purpose of marriage.

The early cultural and religious influences discussed above provided the early impetus for one part of the Great Marriage Myth—wedding for the good of more than the individual. Unfortunately for our ancestors, the parts of the myth that concern a tolerant, egalitarian loving of mutual respect, caring, and the facing of life's chaos together failed to emerge as rapidly and powerfully as the greed, abuse, sexism, and pandering to the lowest form of economic gain that came with the social priority for marriage. In deemphasizing the self, these cultures also often neglected mutual love in the process.

Unfortunately as the development of the Great Marriage Myth continued, our more recent contribution to the ever-evolving Marriage Myth has been an overemphasis on getting as much love as possible for the self. This manual for making a miracle marriage is an attempt to promote the further development and refinement of the Great Marriage Myth. It is a reminder of our ancestors' lessons that High Monogamy, or "rightful marriage," serves a higher purpose than the self. It is a challenge to make marriage a great and safe place for two selves to grow together not only for the good of all of us but also for the well-being of the spouses.

Silencing the Self

The Great Marriage Myth is enhanced by the new discoveries of science that stress nature's submergence of individuality as necessary for the evolution and enhancement of the universal system. Miracle marriages are based on the silencing of the self. You will learn in the pages to follow how we can live up to the miracle potential that marriage holds and how we can discover the universal laws of love that can result in a new impetus for the maturing and enhancement of the Great Marriage Myth. To find the *One*, we must first silence the *one*.

Silencing the one, or the selfish self, means giving in, letting things go by, being docile or teachable, and seeking happiness by making a better life for Us instead of looking for a better life for Me. Silencing the self is not giving up the self and allowing oneself to be abused, used, and hurt. I speak here of an ego silencing and the quantumlike paradox of giving up our "particlehood" or individuality to merge with the energy of someone else to become a stronger unit. The silenced ego is freed from asserting, demanding, urging, and telling. With this freedom comes the opportunity to learn, understand, ask, hope, and discover mutually *with* someone else.

When the self is silenced, it does not become forever mute. When it speaks again, the self is ready to stand with or against the spouse in the service of the enduring relationship rather than to reclaim perceived lost territory. Silencing the self means replacing "my way" by allowing time to learn an "our way." The silenced self learns, accepts, and searches for its other half. It is us-assertive rather than self-assertive.

"When I asked myself why I got married in the first place, I was hard-pressed to find an answer that wasn't selfish," said one of my patients. "I guess I just thought that school, college, your job, and marriage were ways for me to make a life for myself. When you asked me what I thought my marriage was for, all my answers seemed to point to Me. I think I'm gradually learning that my marriage should be for Us and that is a real challenge. It means a marriage not only for my wife and me but for everyone everywhere. I think it's a lot easier to try to find your own happiness in marriage than it is to make a happy marriage that makes everyone happier."

This husband's response to my question as to the purpose of his marriage reflects his new attempt to silence his self. A miracle marriage becomes something that doesn't burden society, desert children, or fill the courtrooms with endless squabbling over "things," ownership, and personal rights. Miracle marriages provide a source of mature and stable loving that—like the energy of the electrons spinning around us—can be felt by others anywhere. There can be no greater cultural story or myth than that.

We do not have to suffer as the parents in the courtroom at the beginning of this chapter who became so consumed by the Me Myth that they came to see their marriage as a self-help program. We do not have to fall into the trap of blaming and abandoning marriage because "it" didn't work. *We* are it! We can choose to marry to enjoy a quieter Me and the birth of an enduring Us. If our marriage seems empty, it is because the ego has drained it of its energy and purpose.

Looking to the Cosmos Instead of to the Counselors

As I pointed out in Chapter 1, traditional psychology, marriage counseling, psychiatry, and most psychotherapies are the sciences of Low Monogamy. They offer little to help in making a miracle marriage. The mental health movement has evolved largely alongside the Me Myth, so it does not acknowledge or understand marriage other than as a vehicle for self-actualization or source of guaranteed availability of romantic love, unequivocal support, or convenient sex. To be "happily married" has become similar to becoming "fulfilled in our career" and "self-actualized." It has become a secondary objective to larger life goals and a place we live while we are busy "doing our own thing." Marriage often becomes something we use to help us get what we want for ourselves instead of something we are making with someone else.

As psychologist Lawrence LeShan points out, "Psychology has so lost contact with real human experience that there would be no point in asking it to solve major human problems."[8] This is why we must look not to the counselors but to the quantum scientists to understand the ways of a miracle marriage. These are the men and women who have learned from studying systems rather than individuals, from studying mergings rather than separations. These are the voyagers into the worlds of the untouchable, unseeable, and mysteriously paradoxical happenings far beyond mechanical cause-and-effect. New physicists are the archaeologists who have discovered the ancestral foundations of the Great Marriage Myth.

Philosopher Meister Eckhart once said that if you are searching for God, you should look in the place you lost Him. If we have lost the Great Myth of Marriage, we might consider looking where we ourselves lost it—within our loving relationships where we have failed to silence the self and transcend the ego. The science that best understands and studies the process and impact of merging and transcendence is the same science that studies the workings of the cosmos and the quantum particles and waves.

Lonely Atoms and Selfish Stars

What is lacking in the mental health movement is the realization that *individual fulfillment is impossible*. The perfectly happy person who is totally alone has no one with whom to verify and give meaning to the joy. Adjustment rather than transcendence has been psychology's goal, but we have failed to ask, "Adjusted to what?" Psychology offers ways to be healthy but offers little in the way of answers to such questions as "What is the purpose of health?" or "How can we make the whole world happier?" It has offered ways to be happier in marriage but not much help in ultimately answering the questions "So what?" and "What for?"

Modern science, aside from psychology and psychiatry, has

emphasized the idea that individuality and independence are impossible. Scientists know that everything and everyone is connected. The Einsteins, Plancks, Bohrs, Heisenbergs, and other great minds of new physics have shown that the principle of oneness and unity is incontrovertible.

The well-known expert on the behavior of apes Wolfgang Kohler said, "A solitary chimpanzee is not a chimpanzee." If it were possible to have just one star in the sky, that star would have no reference group and therefore the concept of a star would have little meaning. We lose who we are when we leave our own constellation of the people around us. When lovers say, "I am nothing without you," they are not exaggerating. Our identity is formed more by who we are with than who we try to be alone. If we choose High Monogamy, our marriage becomes our constellation, and a Me without an Us no longer has meaning. Kohler was stressing the fact that all of us lose our meaning and identity if we are unable to merge with, compare ourselves with, and reflect off someone else and to be "with" the whole of the universe.

The single atom cannot be a "chair atom." Atoms are "just atoms," and the lonely atom from a star or a chair is really nothing at all until it gains meaning by joining with other atoms to form a mass. Atoms alone are just quanta, or cosmic stuff, sitting there doing nothing, being nothing, and going nowhere. Only in a large group of atoms does the singular atom find its identity so that it becomes something we can sit on, fly in, or fly to, or someone we can fly with.

To illustrate the importance of unity rather than individuality, one of the Silver Survivors who taught physics at her local university said, "What a waste of matter we are when we try to be our 'selfs.' Matter is really only resting energy waiting to merge and become—to do, fly, buzz, explode, and evolve. We're just stuff when we're 'self,' but we're up there with the stars when we really marry."

One of the greatest thinkers of all time, Albert Einstein, "saw the light of unity." One of his greatest discoveries surprised even him. He showed that light is not just a wave of energy. Light is also made up of individual light quanta. Until a light quantum joins with millions of other light photon particles to form a "wave of light," it never really shines. Einstein reflected on the profound implications of this amazing discovery until his dying day.

A piece of star is only static stellar stuff, but when it begins to join piece by piece with other star stuff, it glitters through the cosmos for millions of years. When a star shines with millions of other stars, constellations are made. When constellations join, galaxies are made. Billions of galaxies spread out through our ever-expanding universe. Like stars merging, a miracle marriage is the process of soul merging in which two "people particles" become something much more than two individual pieces. Couple by couple, each partner joining with a complementary partner, we become a loving universe.

Marriage is our process of loving fusion, our primary method of two becoming one and finding our complementary "ego silencing" partner. There will probably not be lasting peace and joy in our families or the world until we find peace and joy by learning how to merge permanently in a miracle marriage. We will not find our bliss by, as Andy Warhol put it, each of us being stars for fifteen minutes. The real challenge is in working two by two toward being a part of a loving constellation forever.

Toward a New Science of Lasting Love

The central premise of this book is that if we choose to make miracle marriages, we need a new science upon which to build our love. In Chapter 1, I introduced ten laws of lasting love based on findings from new physics. What follows is a brief restatement of each of these laws. In each case, I have contrasted the modern psychology, or Low Monogamy, view.

Love Law 1: Two-Time

TIME MANAGEMENT VERSUS RELATIVITY THEORY

Psychology helps us seek an "absolute truth," emphasizing assertive representation of one's confident personal point of view. It teaches us to defend and manage our "own time" and find time for ourselves. The new science of love teaches that all events, including time and loving, are relative, dynamic, and boundless. Lasting love doesn't require "time management"—it requires "time merging." There is no-lasting love unless we make time relative to our love and make plenty of time for two. We make "two time" by choosing to make loving time our first priority and not allowing "real" time to take our loving time away.

Love Law 2: Confident Uncertainty

SELF-CONFIDENCE VERSUS THE UNCERTAINTY PRINCIPLE

Psychology is helpful in establishing self-confidence and self-esteem and in helping us to be sure of ourselves. The new science of love replaces self-confidence with Us certainty and the fact that the more we think we know of our lover, the less we really know. Knowledge, like time, is eternal and infinite, and lasting love is an eternally unfolding mystery.

Love Law 3: One Love

BREAKING THINGS DOWN VERSUS THE HOLISM PRINCIPLE

Psychology's effectiveness depends on solving problems by isolating their component parts and determining who or what caused a problem. But the cosmic world can only be viewed as a whole. It cannot be understood in terms of individual particles of matter or quanta of light. The new science of love teaches that problems can only be understood by studying wholes instead of parts. The challenge for the miracle marriage is to find what is wrong and right with Us and our loving system.

Love Law 4: Love Looks

SEEING THINGS CLEARLY VERSUS THE OBSERVER PARTICIPANCY PRINCIPLE

Psychology concerns itself with "seeing things objectively," but the new science of love asserts that complete objectivity is impossible because we are always an inseparable part of whatever and whomever we are observing. As author Leo Rosten states, "We see things not as they are but as we are." That we observe, how we observe, and who and how we are as observers determine what is observed. Nothing "is" until there is an Us. Our marriage is defined by how we choose to see it and be it; it is not a thing we can stand back from, look at, or try to stay in or get out of.

Love Law 5: Complementary Love

THE COMPLETE PERSON VERSUS THE PRINCIPLE OF COMPLEMENTARITY

Psychology teaches us how to be a complete person. The new science principle of complementarity shows that there is always an opposite partner to everything and every event in the universe. We are all half people seeking our other complementary half. Partners in miracle marriages know that the viewpoint of one partner is never complete without the other partner's view and that when one partner is center stage, the other is stepping back to wait for his or her turn in the spotlight.

Love Law 6: Transcendent Love

EFFECTIVE COMMUNICATION VERSUS THE PRINCIPLE OF NONLOCALITY

As I have pointed out, psychology emphasizes "effective verbal communication" and teaches effective speaking and listening skills. We are taught to "tell" him or her how we feel. But the new science of love has discovered nonlocality, or the universal presence of the energy of the spirit everywhere in all time. We call this an energy-wave approach to loving. A miracle marriage doesn't "take time," it transcends time because we work to be aware of, sensitive to, and receptive to our connection with our lover beyond words.

Love Law 7: Creative Chaos

GETTING YOUR LIFE IN ORDER VERSUS THE DETERMINIST CHAOS THEORY

Marriage counselors often see conflict and chaos in marriage as a symptom of marital weakness and work to reestablish order, structure, and simple cause-and-effect predictablity in a relationship. The new science of love has discovered that dynamic and deterministic (not random and external) chaos and patterned disorder are the natural state of the universe. Conflict in marriage is the natural process of love's constant evolution. Couple chaos is not a symptom but rather a constantly rhythmic and alternating process of standing with and against the partner so both spouses can learn to stand more strongly together behind their marriage.

Love Law 8: Shared Sadness

CURING DEPRESSION VERSUS THE SECOND LAW OF THERMODYNAMICS

Psychology has borrowed from mechanical science and the science of steam engines to use the Second Law of Thermodynamics as proof that all love—like everything else in the universe—is burning itself out. New science has discovered, however, that the increasing entropy or disarray of living contains within it wonderfully mysterious patterns, so that lovers can relish their journey even as they struggle together to understand their ultimate destination. The fact that there is a physical end to our loving makes the fact that we can love in the Now more urgently vital and poignant and not a source of desperation.

Love Law 9: Loving Realities

FACING REALITY VERSUS THE PRINCIPLE OF MULTIPLE REALITIES

While therapists struggle with their patients to help them find "true reality," the new science of loving shows that there are *many realities*. The reality of the cosmic world is different from the reality of the quantum world, but neither reality is more real than the other. Miracle marriages are based on the premise that arguing over what is real is a waste of time. If we begin with the premise that there are many realities to which each partner may have different access and awareness, we open our marriage to endless ways of finding the mysterious order beneath the chaos and crises of living.

Love Law 10: Energizing Love

SAVING YOUR ENERGY VERSUS THE PRINCIPLE OF FIFTH ENERGY

Psychologists speak disrespectfully of what they see as the New Age fads of "bad and good vibes." Energy is seen as something physical or biological. New science has shown that there is a "fifth energy" stronger and more pervasive and potent than gravity, electricity, and strong and weak nuclear energy. We know that this is the true bonding energy of life and loving and that it can be mobilized for miraculous healing, serve as the energizer of loving at times of crises, sadness, and loss, and bond us together through time and physical separation.

To begin your course in making a miracle marriage, however, your first step is to make a choice between Low Monogamy's psychology principles and High Monogamy's new physics principles as your way to wed. To begin making your own miracle marriage, you must acknowledge that there is no "self" without "other," no I without Thou, and no Us without a choice to follow the lessons of the Great Marriage Myth instead of the Me Myth. By making this choice and trying to determine where we are going and who we will take with us at one and the same time, we can reawaken our sense of the universal laws of an enduring, loving union. The Great Marriage Myth is well within our grasp if we learn to search together where we lost it—somewhere between us.

3

Falling Apart at the Dreams:

HOW WE FAIL OUR MARRIAGE

I'm a wonderful house keeper. Every time I divorce a man, I keep his house.

—*Zsa Zsa Gabor*

A Comic Tragedy

"Marriage is a great idea. Somebody should try it someday," said the young comedienne with more wisdom than she seemed aware of. The audience laughed in agreement as she fired off a series of antimarriage one-liners. "You don't know what real happiness is until you get married . . . but then it's too late," added the entertainer as she pointed to a man in the front row. "Look at this bald old guy in the front here with this young fox. What did you do when your first wife turned forty . . . turn her in for two twenties? You probably cheat on her. Eighty percent of married men cheat in America . . . the rest cheat in Europe. As for me, my life was incomplete until I got married . . . then it was finished!"

Since there has been a 700 percent spurt in the divorce rate since the beginning of this century, and 64 percent of marriages still end in separation or divorce, the comedienne was playing to an experienced and knowledgeable audience.[1] Almost one-fifth of marriages will end within eighteen months of the birth of the couple's first child.[2] As Shakespeare suggested, perhaps we laugh for fear of crying and deny through our mockery the misery of our failing marriages.

The state of matrimony is not in a very good state. Perhaps we make jokes about marriage and its problems because something within us tells us that there is a better way to wed. Perhaps something within tells us that something magnificent can happen when we merge forever with someone else. The tragic comedy of couple distress is a sign of grieving for a lost opportunity to love forever and a soul signal that all of us can make the miracle of a lasting love.

Sleeping Together or Dreaming Together

I suggest that the grief that is felt when divorce takes place or a relationship ends or turns combative is a good grief—a signal from our soul that we are missing out on something miraculous and that we should be trying more vigorously for a lasting love. The turmoil of divorce stems from the pain of a dream turned nightmare, and we are startled and awakened to a sense of profound reality of emptiness and despair. Our grief is a teacher. The lesson is the availability of a higher love.

When one partner dreams of Us loving together forever and the other dreams of Me finding happiness somewhere, this "dream difference" will almost certainly result in legal or emotional divorce. When both spouses dream only in images of the Me Myth, total spiritual union is impossible. The goal of the miracle marriage is to find a mutual marital dream. One Silver Survivor said, "Marriage is more than sleeping together. It's dreaming together."

When I have asked my patients to describe their dreams to me, I have noticed one factor common to the theme of every dream. No matter what the scene or the dream drama, the dreamer is wishing for or struggling with relationships. We dream of other people or their absence. We dream of people we loved and lost, of our relationship to others in our life or of those we wish were in our life, and of pursuing or being pursued by an "other." Beneath the more obvious content of our dreams rests the message of our longing for merging and terror at its ending.

When a relationship ends and we feel the anger, disruption, loneliness, self-doubt, and even the rage of a lost loving that I will describe later in this chapter, it should signal to us that marriage is much more than we have yet been able to discover—a dream yet to be fulfilled. When we feel that our lover has failed us and we become furious and forlorn, we should consider these feelings as divine defenses against the challenges and demands of a higher monogamy. When the self gets defensive, depressed, or demanding, it should tell us that the soul is crying out for some real loving.

Is Divorce Possible?

Divorce may be a legal term, but it has deep spiritual significance. In the most human sense, true divorce or an ending of a bond is impossible. We may think we can divorce ourselves from things and people and that a divorce can be won or declared, but the end of a loving relationship is only a victory if it teaches us more about how to love and bond more strongly. Marriage is not just a legal agreement through which two individuals made paper promises to stay together. Whether we are aware of it or not and even when we think we have voluntarily chosen Low Monogamy, marriage is much more a merging of souls than we may realize. Ultimately, our love defenses will weaken and fail us. The anger will numb us, depression will cripple us, and we will fall into a state of divorce shock.

Perhaps the courts are crowded with couples fighting over "stuff" or even fighting over who has to be forced to take responsibility for their own children because we have developed a divorce-court social-denial system to match our personal denial systems. This immense, complex, overwhelmed institutionalized, and ceremonial marital-ending system is intended to protect our delusion that a merging can be declared ended forever. One husband said, "You can end a marriage formally and institutionally, but you can't end its feelings and intimacy. Something of the two of you together always remains. The courts may award you a legal divorce, but you never really get spiritually divorced. Something of the two of you together always remains."

Good Grief and Soul Signals

Our legal system provides ritualistic ceremonies that allow us to avoid and distance ourselves from a confrontation of the true emotional and spiritual impact of failed relationships. It cannot show us how to find a higher monogamy than the Great Marriage Myth and teach us the skills necessary for enduring, rewarding, growing love. Our marriages may be declared null and void, and the Me may think that it has been freed to look again for someone "right" who will make it happy, but our spirit does not understand what happened to its loving connection. Our soul grieves, and it feels suddenly empty, deceived, and confused rather than independent and free.

When we try to end loving, our soul feels that something has died. To annul means "to bring to nothing." To annul a marriage means to declare by legal or religious code that a relationship was in fact "nothing" and never really existed. But our soul is too powerful to be nullified. It knows something of profound significance was attempted, and it is not bound by the creations of our social and legal systems. While we are busy joking about, ignoring, or even celebrating a relationship's end, the soul is busy searching for answers to where the love went. While we go through the motions of our endings, the soul is grieving for love.

The "good" grief of ending a relationship can give birth to a new freedom of hope and commitment to see what the Great Marriage Myth promises—a love that will never end. A divorce and its accompanying emotions can help us develop not toward a new Me but toward a more loving Us.

Divorce Dependency

We have become a divorce-dependent culture, and marital failure is the base for an entire growth industry. If all divorce stopped tomorrow, our economic system would undergo a radical change. Between 1970 and 1979, the divorce rate doubled in the United States, and more than one of every three marriages this year will end in divorce.[3] An entire legal, therapeutic, and socioeconomic system has evolved that depends on this marital distress inflation rate for its continued growth. Our court systems, lawyers, drug companies, doctors, hospitals, marriage mediators, psychotherapists, child-care centers, school counselors, financial advisers, banks, popular-song writers, movie makers, and even our comedians, depend to varying degrees on the psychological and economic ebb and flow that accompanies the divorce cycle and its related divorce diseases.

As common as divorce has become and as strong as the divorce-denial systems may be, the entire process is one of the most severe emotional and physical shocks a person can suffer. No one gets used to it. When a human bond is wrenched apart, no matter how much both spouses may think that "divorce is better for everyone concerned," the ending of a marriage results in a trauma on every human level that extends to everyone touched by that union. The emotional and physical trauma of divorce has become one of our most common socially transmissible diseases.

Dropping Out or Diving In?

Living in a nonloving, unhappy, even abusive relationship is devastating. Sometimes legally ending a marriage is the only option and a necessary step to stopping abuse and toward learning how to love more maturely. This book, however, is dedicated to seeking a new way out of loving dilemmas that are so hurtful for everyone involved by learning how to make a miracle marriage out of a messy marriage. This book focuses on learning how to reinvest in rather than pull out of a troubled marriage. One Silver Survivor said, "We had a choice. It seemed like dropping out of the marriage was the only way out. As we started to end it, we suffered more, and we seemed to be suffering only for an end. We thought it might be wiser—if we were going to suffer anyway—to suffer for a new beginning. We didn't drop out, we dove back in, and I think we are learning to swim. Before, we were like swimmers with one arm and each of us kept going around and around in circles. Now we're joined together to swim as one, and we're finally getting someplace."

Even if divorce is necessary, the expected relief from anxiety, depression, anger, loneliness, and more serious emotional disorders does not always occur. In fact, research indicates that each of these conditions may worsen.[4] Divorce never works as a *solution* to love problems, only as a step toward learning how to love. Given the devastation of divorce that you will read about in this chapter, it is often better to stick it out and suffer through the difficulties of learning how to love on a higher and more difficult level.

During several decades of treating couples going through separation and divorce, I have rarely seen both spouses made much happier by the process. Only when they learn to love again does joy return to their life, and even then the separation scars are deep. Thousands of professional intervention hours are spent treating what I call the "divorce shock syndrome," and as you consider making a miracle marriage, I hope you or someone you know will learn to recognize the serious symptoms of divorce disease.

The Risk of Collective Heart Attack

The "divorce shock syndrome," or DSS, is one of the most common afflictions of our society. It results not only from legal divorce but from divorce in the broader sense—an attempt to terminate or distance oneself from a relationship even if a legal divorce is not sought. Sometimes divorce is sought because the partners failed to merge by the guidelines of the Great Marriage Myth, and now one or the other seeks to move from Low to High Monogamy. Other times, couples tried but failed to make a miracle marriage because they were too consumed by the Me Myth. In yet other instances, a couple may tire of the effort necessary for a miracle marriage and seek the easier road of Low Monogamy. No matter the reason, emotional shock is inevitable.

Divorce shock syndrome, or DSS, is contagious. It affects not only the marital partners but the entire family system and society as a whole. Much as a heart attack can result from poor health habits, self-indulgence, and a hyperaggressive pursuit of self-success, DSS can result from malnourished loving and unhealthy love habits. Just as our arteries become clogged when we eat selfishly and ignore our system, our self-indulgent Me Myth loving can block our loving system. As a result, we can suffer a mutual emotional heart attack—DSS—that can kill our love and our ability to love and impair the health of those around us in the process. If we survive the emotional heart attack, learn what caused it, and begin a "we wellness program," we can learn to love better in the future and lower our risk of DSS.

The Divorce Shock Syndrome

Based on my interviews and the research of others, what follows are the twelve major symptoms of divorce shock syndrome, or DSS.[5] The staff in my clinic saw these symptoms so often that they began to call them the divorce dirty dozen. I have included sample statements from my interviews of divorced people that illustrate each symptom and the shock of failed marriage and hint at the importance of learning how to make miracle marriages.

THE DIVORCE DIRTY DOZEN: TWELVE SYMPTOMS OF DIVORCE SHOCK SYNDROME

1. The Sleep of the Separated

• Many divorced or divorcing people experience disruption of sleeping patterns, usually in the form of difficulty sleeping accompanied by a feeling of constant fatigue. Less frequently, some patients reported what they called "the divorce coma," in which they would sleep deeply for long periods and have difficulty waking in the morning.

"The only time I could get away from the pain was when I was asleep," said a forty-seven-year-old divorced physician. "I got into what I called my 'divorce coma,' which was my place of escape. I curled up under the blanket like a fetus in the uterus. I had many intense dreams which I have forgotten, but I must have been getting a lot of stress-caused REMS." (REMS are rapid eye movements associated with dreaming and indicative of deep sleep.)

2. DIDS: Divorce Immune Deficiency Syndrome

• Separated or divorced people are among the most frequently admitted patients to hospitals. They also suffer serious illness and disability at a higher rate than any other group.[6] Another major symptom is increased frequency of colds, allergies, flu, infection, and sometimes life-threatening illness. Separation and divorce are a shock to the immune system, almost as if the immunity cells are no longer sure who or what is a part of the person and what is not. When we reject someone else, our immune system often tries to reject us or becomes uncertain as to what or who is an invader to our system. Divorce confuses our immunity, since cells of defense are no longer clear on who or what is to be protected or attacked.[7]

"I felt like I was cut off from life," reported a thirty-year-old teacher. "Just like an uprooted plant, I felt separate from living. I never had colds before, but then I started to have cold after cold. It was like my immune system had shut down, tired out, become confused, or been disconnected. I was always teared up and snorting as if my body were crying for me."

3. Lost-Marriage Migraines

• People facing divorce report more headaches and bodily aches and pains, increased use of over-the-counter pain relievers, and in many instances growing dependence on prescription medications. One contributing cause of divorce may be substance abuse, but divorce is also a contributing factor in the development *of* substance abuse.

"I thought my life was a headache, but when we separated, I began having real lost-marriage migraines," said a thirty-six-year-old mechanic. "Aspirin didn't work, and my head throbbed just like the time I was hit in the head by a wrench at work. It just shows you what a blow my divorce was when I thought it was going to be a new and better life."

4. Divorce Depression

• Divorce depression is pervasive in the form of lack of energy, long periods of pensive rumination, tears for no apparent reason or in reaction to episodes on television shows and songs on the radio, and mental flashbacks to the good and bad times of the marriage. I suggest that marriage is a miracle union on a physical and psychochemical level—truly a becoming "of one flesh"—and merging results in intense neurohormonal and body chemistry changes. When a marriage falls apart, there are actual physical withdrawal symptoms when the flesh is torn asunder. We become neurohormonally linked and cross-dependent on one another when we bond, and when our bond ends, we lose our psychochemical companion.

My interviews revealed that the more depressed divorced people become, the more likely it is that they actually have an *accurate* and realistic view of how much their spouses and others really liked or disliked them. As you will learn later when you read about the new science love law of multiple realities, one sign of a decrease in divorce depression is that the person's sense of what is real expands to include many realities. The person sees many new possibilities, broadens his or her imagination and fantasy, develops what I call "enlightened denial," and is not trapped by one here-and-now version in a single and inevitable cause-and-effect reality.

Research indicates that life is much less depressing when we move beyond one way of determining what our "real world" is or has to be—however accurate that way may be.[8] In effect, data indicate that depressed people are often right in their assessment of the state of their world, at least on one level of reality. One of the newest approaches to treating depression is based on helping the sad person find what new science proves exists—many other "options for optimism."

The real problem is not that depressed people are "too realistic." The difficulty rests with the fact that they have too few reality options and explanatory modes. When scientists could not explain how electrons did not seem to exist in space or time according to the then current laws of cosmic reality, they made a new and equally workable quantum reality in which time and space were relative. We rise from the depression of lost love when we learn to make new, more optimistic realities for our love to live in.

"I used to go into these separation spasms," said a forty-three-year-old waitress. "I would be waiting for an order at the counter and just space out. I wouldn't be thinking or anything, I would just be gone for a while until somebody practically shook me back to this reality. I would daydream of someone loving me as much as I love him and loving with someone forever and ever. When I dreamed like this, it was a better reality, and I want to take part of that reality into my everyday reality because I really need some new reality. In this real world, I'm getting a painful divorce. In a new reality, I may be able to find love again."

5. Coupling Incompetence

• Divorcing people have a tendency to feel ineffective, incompetent, and inferior. They perceive themselves as failures at loving. They report feeling "unmatchable" or "unpairable" or not knowing how to "make a marriage work."

"I know they say that divorce is very common, but I still think that divorced people feel like they screwed up," said a fifty-two-year-old accountant. "We can joke all we want, but when you're divorced, no matter how bad your husband was, you feel at least a little like it was you who did something wrong or who was unable to love enough. You feel that even if they don't say it, everyone else knows it, too."

6. Partner Paranoia

• Divorcing people can become distrusting of potential partners and suspicious of friends, family, and colleagues who attempt to help them by introducing new possible mates.

"I couldn't get over the feeling that everyone was talking about my divorce and why it happened," said a thirty-three-year-old dentist. "I would meet a patient and wonder if she knew about my divorce, and if she was busy putting me down to somebody about it. I worried that my patients would think that someone who couldn't do marriage right couldn't do dental work right. I began to feel that even my family and friends weren't on my side. When anyone tried to set me up for a date, I began with the assumption that the person would be a jerk. When I saw some of the people my friends thought were a good match for me, I began to wonder what my friends really thought of me."

7. Affective Assertiveness

• Because psychology emphasizes the value of the direct and immediate expression of all our feelings, some divorcing people become overassertive and overexpressive of negative or angry emotions. They become short-tempered and assume the posture of "I'm not going to take it anymore." They erroneously assume that failing at making an Us resulted from the failure to be a more powerful self.

"Once burned, one hundred times warned—that was my new marriage motto," said a forty-four-year-old travel agent. "Nobody was going to walk over me again. I began driving more assertively, demanding faster service in stores, and hanging up on customers who got me mad. I probably scared a lot of people off, but I couldn't help it. I was making up for lost chances to tell someone off. No one was going to take advantage of me again."

8. Negative Self-Image

• Divorcing people begin to doubt their own intellectual capacity and their physical and sexual attractiveness. This insecurity is sometimes accompanied by compensatory drastic changes in hairstyle and fashions. Some of my separated or divorced patients seemed to be turning into the person their spouse had wrongly accused them of being. Others tried to become the image that their partner had wanted them to project. This behavior is a form of self-fulfilling prophecy derived from unconscious acceptance of the partner's accusations, criticisms, or unrealistic expectations.

"I noticed that I began looking in the mirror more often," said a thirty-five-year-old secretary. "I knew on one level that I was attractive, but how could my husband leave me if I was such a beauty? I changed my hairstyle and even thought about breast augmentation. I started looking at myself almost to validate my husband's criticisms of me. I seemed to want to become the person he thought I had failed to be. I know it sounds crazy to focus on my looks, but as stupid as men may be, they are seldom blind."

9. Increased Sexual Activity

• Many divorced people begin to act out sexually. In spite of the threat of AIDS and other sexually transmissible diseases, sexual experimentation may begin. Fewer than one of every five divorced persons in my data and the data of other researchers reported abstinence during the first twelve months following their divorce or separation.[9]

"I think you sort of get horny after a divorce," said a twenty-seven-year-old artist. "I went on three or four dates a week with several different men and had sex with some of them. Usually, it wasn't even good sex, probably because I wasn't really making *out*. Instead, I was probably trying to make *up* for missed sex or to dispel any self-doubt about my sexual desirability. I guess it was a distraction or some type of sexual reaffirmation. I thought my ex-husband must be doing it, so why should I be deprived? It scares me now to think what a risk I was taking, but it was kind of aggressive, as if I were screwing *him*."

10. Marriage-Wrecker Projection

• Some divorcing people focus to the point of distraction on a projection target or someone other than the divorcing spouse—another family member, a therapist, a doctor, a minister, an attorney, or a friend or lover of the former spouse. They begin to blame this target for "wrecking" their marriage. But it is the marriage partners, not an outside person, who have destroyed their marriage; DSS only causes them to look for an easier and more available hate target outside the primary relationship.

I typically warned my patients, "Do not divorce someone you don't know, including yourself." I meant that learning about both spouses and their respective strengths and vulnerabilities was a prerequisite to understanding the real problems in a failed marriage and preparing to try to love more knowledgeably in the future.

The following statement reflects the divorcing person's tendency to project rather than be introspective. Unfortunately, the comment also reveals something about the ethics of some marriage counselors in the divorce industry and their tendency to take advantage of one of the most vulnerable times in a person's life.

"Can you believe that our marital therapist was the one my former husband finally married?" said a thirty-seven-year-old dance instructor. "Here we had gone to her for help with our marriage, and she helped herself to my husband. The bitch. I could kill her."

11. Pop Philosophizing

• Some divorcing people begin searching for a new philosophy of life. They may return to a long-neglected childhood religious belief system or embrace a new "psychology of life" or "philosophy of love," often in the form of a self-help pop psychology, religious cultism, or so-called New Age spiritualism.

"I thought I was dead and then I almost died," said a thirty-two-year-old computer operator. "I mean, I've learned in my LAD—life as death—encounter group that we all need to die symbolically many times in our life. I got a divorce as one of what my group therapist calls my transitional learning deaths necessary for my growth as a person. No matter how dead you think you are, you can always die again. You can't be born again unless you die again, and my divorce was one of my chosen learning deaths."

12. Sexist Cynicism

• Divorcing people often develop a cynical view of intimacy, lasting love, the nature of their opposite gender, and any potential for real caring between the genders. Both divorced men and divorced women often become at least temporary man- or woman-haters.

"I've heard it said that most men owe their success to their first wife and their second wife to their success," said a thirty-seven-year-old English teacher. "That's how I feel. I helped my husband be what he is, and he used what he is to find someone else. I was his coach, and he made a new team. As far as I'm concerned, men are all broken and use women to get fixed. Then they go out and get a fix by finding a new woman. I'm out of the male-reclamation business. I've sworn off men forever."

Divorce shock syndrome is so severe that most of my divorced patients require more than three years to return to the consistently adaptive equilibrium and clearer thinking that overcomes the symptoms of DSS. Children and other family members affected by divorce also experience varying degrees of these symptoms. Unless we learn to make miracle marriages, more than half of our adults and more than three-quarters of our children can be expected to experience some or all of the DSS symptoms sometime during their lifetime. A review of the literature on divorce reveals that, as the symptoms above indicate, the end of a marriage is the single most widespread threat to the health and welfare of the American family![10]

Till Parting Do Us Die

The crisis in lasting loving leaves thousands of men and women without a place to love, with their mental and physical health at serious risk, and with the overwhelming sense that something within them has died. Something within *has* in fact been seriously assaulted in many marriages because the ego and the screaming self have ravaged the marital system. What is attacked is the sense of Us, but this book will teach you that a miracle can be made to resurrect our sense of sharing love.

My own interviews and the work of other researchers indicate that divorce can cause early death and is capable of eliciting the same sense of bereavement and grief usually associated with a loved one's death.[11] Divorce has about the same effect on health and poses the same risk of early death as smoking one pack of cigarettes a day.[12] As I pointed out at the beginning of this chapter, if we learn how to make a miracle marriage and follow the ten laws of lasting love of new science and the lessons of the Great Marriage Myth, our grief can guide us to a rebirth of loving. A divorce can be a beginning, but only if we are willing to assume self-responsibility—not blame self or others—for the ending of a love. A divorce can be a beginning if we acknowledge that no matter how bad the relationship seemed to be, something important happened that should not be denied and dismissed.

The Phases of Failing in Love

Sadness may be a sudden reaction to a transitional life event, but depression festers and endures. It lingers, feeds on itself, and usually has its beginnings in sadness we failed to pay sufficient attention to. Except in the case of death, the loss of love is never sudden. The problem festers malignantly until we feel helpless to do anything about it. Many of my patients who suffer divorce shock syndrome say things such as "How could I have missed it?" or "I think I knew something was wrong but just didn't let myself face it."

There are four stages in the divorce process. Remember that I am using "divorce" beyond its legal definition and to refer to the failure of a merging love and not just a legal act:

• The distress stage: This is the "little things" stage. During this phase of failing love, small signs of selfishness that never seemed present before reveal themselves. This period of gradual falling out of a lasting love can last for months or years while one or both partners fail to acknowledge their sense of trouble and impending disaster. Their dreams of what love means become more and more different. One Silver Survivor called this "falling out of lustful love and into a rotten reality."
• The decision stage: During this phase, one or both partners consciously resolve that they will leave the relationship. There is often a brief and sudden announcement that, despite years of marital distress, may surprise one of the partners. Emotional suffering is extensive during both of these first two stages, but denial and anger often mask the depth of such despair. One husband said, "I was just stunned. I was numb. She just took a drink of her wine, looked up, and said she wanted a divorce. We sat for a while and then we discussed the quality of the meal. Can you imagine that? A few days later, I was devastated."
• The separation stage: During this third stage of the end of a marriage, the separation or death stage, grief and bereavement occur. Bereavement is the ending of an intimate personal bond, and grief is the necessary physical and emotional reflexive reaction to bereavement. Grief is a universal characteristic. Animals, including us, go through it as a physical and mental means

of purging, cleansing, and adjusting to the recognition of the obligatory endings we all must endure. Whether the partners of a divorce report leaving a relatively good or a relatively bad marriage, they almost all report the grieving I have described.[13] This is a key phase in the ending of love, because as I pointed out earlier in this chapter, grief can be as much a call to loving as it is a purging of the pain of love's ending. A Silver Survivor wife said, "I went into a long period of grief. I don't think I smiled for months after we decided to divorce. I felt I could never love again. Then it hit me. Why was I so devastated if I wasn't as capable of a lot of love as I was a lot of grief? If I could feel this bad about love problems, I must be able to feel pretty good about the joy of love, too."

• The postparting-depression stage: The fourth and final stage of divorcing—the postparting period—lasts for several years. A marriage never truly ends—it only changes in terms of type and extent of emotion, expression of emotion, and physical proximity. One of the Silver Survivors said, "When you enter into postparting depression, you are really suffering through a remarriage to something or someone. You just are getting a new type of marriage that is long-distance, even more awkward, but at least you are usually no longer sleeping with the enemy."

As I stated above, legalities notwithstanding, no marriage can be declared null and void. All marriage—Low and High Monogamy—is forever. As my patient above states, "postdivorce" is really a form of "new approximate marriage." No matter how many marriages a person may enter into, some bond on some level always remains with each spouse. To deny this is to deny the natural bereavement and grief of all human endings. Our soul will not let us separate from someone without letting us know how it feels. Some type of relationship with the divorced husband or wife, if only on an emotional-imagery-and-memory or a trace-of-turmoil level, always remains. One of my patients called this lasting bond the "us imprint that never gets erased, only blurred." If children are involved in a divorce, there are contacts with and necessary discussions about the children, visitation and planning issues to be resolved, forced contacts with the former spouse and in-laws over practical problems, and financial concerns.[14] Somehow, some way—a bond is forever.

Who Suffers Most?

While women are stereotypically portrayed as more dependent on marriage than are men and are viewed as more devastated by divorce, my data indicate quite the opposite. The men I interviewed were more likely than the women to experience severe depression, psychopathology, and physical illnesses requiring hospitalization, and other researchers have borne this out.[15]

Women's reactions to divorce tended to be less severe than the male's reaction but more generalized to all areas of their life. The impact of divorce seems to be more common among women, and it is longer-lasting.[16] Part of this difference may be due to the fact that, after divorce, a woman's standard of living drops 75 percent, whereas a man's jumps 42 percent. This difference results in life-adjustment stress from more protracted and sometimes delayed socioeconomic impact.[17] Over one-third of all households headed by women are below the poverty level.

Who really suffers most from divorce? We all do. Society is shaken to its roots by families shattered by love deprivation and the failure of the central loving bond. Both men and women become physically and emotionally sick, although men are more likely to experience their distress as actual and immediate physical symptoms. Women struggle over a longer period of time trying to pick up the pieces of a disrupted household in a sexist society. The real answer to who suffers most is that, in the battle over who may have loved the most or lost the most, nobody ever wins.

The Six Cs of Coupling

When our marriages fall apart "at their dreams" or lose their hope, shared goals, and joyful anticipation of a lasting and growing love, they typically do so because of six major marital mistakes caused by overemphasis of the great Me Myth. Hundreds of test items were administered to hundreds of couples who came to my Problems of Daily Living Clinic at Sinai Hospital of Detroit. I have selected some of the most predictive items—those items that correlate most with lasting love—to illustrate where our dreams of love turn to nightmares.

What follow are the six Cs of coupling—completion, caring, communication, coitus, children, and compromise. When each of these Cs was practiced by the guidelines of the Great Marriage Myth, loving flourished. When these Cs were corrupted by over-dominance of the Me Myth in a marriage, they turned to demons, and our marital dreams turned to nightmares.

1. The Quest for *Completion*: Marriage as a Stumbling Stone

Very few people enter marriage with realistic expectations about what it is really like.[18] The underlying common mistake is that people usually marry to "develop" themselves or move toward the completion of their own individual life dreams rather than to find a partner to develop with and to share in helping to develop and enhance the world. The pitfalls of marrying to enhance one's own individual *life* are illustrated by the following statement by one of the Silver Survivors:

"I got married the first time at age sixteen," said a woman who later was able to make a miracle marriage. "It was the only way I could think of to grow up and get out. Since I thought that kids didn't get married, I thought that if I got married, then I wouldn't be a kid. It was a young girl's way—from high school to the marriage altar and out. I had four sisters, and I think we all got married to grow up and get out, and we all ended up divorced. Ironically, by trying to get out of being a daughter, we seemed to skip being our own woman and ended up being the mother to an immature man. I think most women end up being daughters, then mothers, but seldom themselves."

As I pointed out in Chapter 1 and as related to the Complementarity Principle of new science, a primary motivating energy behind the lasting love of a miracle marriage is to become "whole" together by joining as half people into a new One. Complementarity means for each of us to seek through our marriage the other half of us left intentionally lacking by nature's hard-wired design. Nature's built-in incomplete love map makes us want to merge to find our spiritual completeness with someone who has the missing half.

Because we are half-people, our life goals are half and never high enough. Marrying to gain an advantage in life or for mere support for individual life objectives always renders us half-ful-filled, even if we find ourselves at our individual destination.[19]

High Monogamy is not finding a guide or assistant as an adaptive step through what psychologists call the "personal passages of life,"[20] but rather, in the words of another Silver Survivor, "Marriage is a stepping-stone toward two people finding happiness or a stumbling stone that gets in our selfish way. You should enter into it as something to help and to be helped and *not* to help you. Marriage is a decision to work for years to make an 'us' with somebody and not a way to be more of yourself over the years."

My data and that of other marriage researchers reveal that women tend to marry "instrumentally" or as a step toward independence or the enhancement of their perceived lot in life.[21] Men, on the other hand, seem to seek their "completion" through what I call the "acceptable-bystander principle." Men tend to take on a companion for help with what one wife described as "the five Cs of why a man marries." She said, "They 'take' a wife to help them with their career, do their cooking and cleaning, take care of their children, and provide them with easily available coitus."

One Silver Survivor husband supported this wife's view: "You sort of knew you were going to get married, so you married the one you were with when it seemed to be time. She was the nearest acceptable bystander who had the necessary skills and fit your spouse's job description. It's just too big of a coincidence that so many guys seem to meet just the right girl at just the exact time that they have finished school or it seems to be time for them to settle down and start their career. If you're a man and you feel like it's the time to love, I guess you love the one you're with."

2. Caring for Me or Caring for Us?

If men and women vary in the way they seek self-completion through marriage, they also differ on the issue of caring in marriage. If women are "instrumental marriers" and men are "bystander marriers," then the caring each seeks and receives in marriage is also destined to be insufficient in terms of their Me expectations.

Married men live longer, report more happiness and less depression, and have fewer mental and physical illnesses than single, divorced, or widowed men.[22] On the other hand, marriage can be a serious risk to a woman's health. Married women report more depression, lower self-esteem, and poorer health than single women.[23] Divorced and widowed men tend to remarry very quickly, while women remarry much less often. The irony may be that the "instrumentally marrying woman" invests much more to get the caring she seeks but she does not often get the independence she bargained for; she herself becomes an instrument of caring for and attending to the male.

In contrast, the "bystander marrying man" initially seems to invest much less but gets much more out of marriage. He often finds support and a form of marital health insurance on which he becomes dependent. When the man ends up in the "intensive caring unit" of a marriage to a woman willing to exchange her caring and support for socioeconomic security, however, he discovers that he becomes much more invested in and dependent upon his wife than he ever anticipated. If the relationship ends, he may be more devastated than he would have imagined.

The caring of a miracle marriage is not a caring for self or each other. Caring in a miracle marriage has a much higher purpose—to join together to take care of the development and enhancement of two spirits as One. By contributing a strong One to the world system, families are stabilized, children are nurtured with less disruption, and the marriage fulfills the objective of the Great Marriage Myth of bringing "more truth and love into the world."

3. Too Much *Communication:* Talking Yourself Out of a Marriage

"I've been married to this man for fifteen years and he hasn't said one word to me," said the frustrated wife. "Not a single word in our whole marriage."

"Why don't you talk to your wife?" the stunned therapist asked the husband.

"I would," said the husband, "but I don't want to interrupt her."

Just as good marriages are wrongly assumed to depend on completing the development of the self or caring for the self of someone else, folklore about communication in marriage abounds. They are based on the third C of marital crisis: the Me Myth concept that the best relationships are based on being sure that our self is heard. Our partner works just as hard to make himself or herself heard in return. One wife in my clinic shouted at her husband, "I can't hear you when you holler at me!" Marital therapists teach that more communication can save or enhance a marriage, but my work with the Silver Survivors indicates that the *less* dependence there is upon verbal communication in a marriage, the more likely that marriage is to survive and grow.

A consistent finding among the Silver Survivors was that the more comfortable a man becomes in a relationship, the less he tends to talk. Conversely, the more comfortable a woman becomes in a relationship, the more she tends to talk. Miracle marriages are made by the establishment of a level of communication far beyond these verbal factors and the "power" words and simple verbal techniques often practiced in marriage encounter groups.

"One thing you have to deal with in a marriage is the ramble-rest ratio factor," said one Silver Survivor. "When men settle down, they rest, but when women settle down, they begin to ramble. Both genders have to learn to set up an entirely different communication system based on sensing one another, feeling one another, and using EMP, or extramarital perception."

I will be describing the EMP mentioned by the woman above later in this book. The point here is that the *more* a couple relies on talking, the *less* likely the marriage is to stay together. The problem is not how much communication there is but *what type* of communication develops. The challenge of High Monogamy is not to talk to each other but to learn to speak as One in a language beyond words.

4. *Coitus as a Marital Risk: Screwing Up the Marriage*

"I think a good marriage is based on three things: congeniality, coitus, and children," said one husband. "And the first leads to the second which leads to the third."

"Well . . . if God had wanted sex to be fun, he sure wouldn't have created children as punishment," responded his wife.

As discussed earlier, it is a common misconception about successful marriages that "the better and more frequent the sex, the better and stronger the marriage." Over the last fifty years, all the research on sex in marriage indicates that most couples, no matter what the state of their marriage, have sex less than two times per week.[24] Compared with everything else that is happening in a marriage, just by time investment alone, sex is not the big deal that marital therapists and "sexperts" say it is.

In the famous studies done by Alfred Kinsey and his associates, more than one-third of the wives reported having good sex with their husbands but at the same time reported being unhappy in their marriages. One-third of the sample of wives who reported having bad sex with their husbands reported very happy marriages—and most of these same wives said that they stopped having orgasm once they were married. "One thing marriage did for me," said one wife, "was clear up my complexion and my orgasms. I haven't had a pimple or an orgasm since my wedding day." Subsequent studies by other researchers have shown that good or frequent sex really has little to do with a good marriage.[25]

My data from the Silver Survivors and interviews with couples in counseling indicates the opposite of the good-sex-equals-better-marriage hypothesis. My interviews revealed that the more sex there is in a marriage, the less intimacy there seemed to be and the more likely that marriage is to fail! Marriages in which one of the partners sought sex outside the marriage were characterized by frequent sexual activity and mutual reports of satisfying sex. Sex was often a "quick fix"—a compartmentalized act of pseudointimacy—for many couples, so frequency of coitus did not necessarily reflect an intensity of loving.

As sexuality has evolved through the sexual revolution begun in the 1960s, it has become yet another avenue of "self"-fulfillment and the physical manifestation of the Me Myth. Diagnostic categories of sexual problems are based exclusively on individual and not couple dissatisfaction. The tyranny of the orgasm and coming fast enough or lasting long enough has been imposed on modern marriage. Sex surrogates offer "treatment" to improve the sexual prowess of the husband (seldom the wife), as if sex were a transferable skill brought *to* a marriage rather than an act of intimacy *from* the marriage.

The modern sexperts tell men to slow down, women to hurry up, and everyone to do it more and try hard to "come together." If a man "comes" too soon, the wife is shown how to choke the penis (called the "squeeze technique") to delay the ejaculation. If a woman takes too long to "come," she is told to vibrate herself up to speed with an electronic device. Mechanical sex manuals abound to such a degree that one of my patients said, "I think

I'm going to write my own sex manual and title it 'Ouch! Get Off My Hair.' "

The miracle marriages of the Silver Survivors, on the other hand, varied greatly over time in their marriage's amount of sexual interaction, sexual satisfaction, and interest in sex. Their strength seemed to rest less in satisfaction with sex or frequency of sexual encounters than with both partners' faith in the continuing and changing nature of their development of intimacy, and in the emergence of multiple ways of expressing that intimacy.[26]

5. Children as Marriage Wreckers: When the Kids Take Custody of the Marriage

"I take my children everywhere," said the mother. "But they always seem to find their way home."

Low Monogamy is dependent on children. Marriages based on the Me Myth see children as a means of drawing spouses together, making the marriage stronger, or as a way for the self to have a "parenting experience" or pass on its genetic code. My evidence indicates that children are *always* a problem for *every* marriage. Few of the husbands and wives I studied were ready for the constant turmoil, fatigue, demands, financial stress, and general pressures of parenting. "Your kids think that your life is completely for them and that your marriage is theirs and not yours," said one mother. "If you're not careful, they'll take custody of your marriage and your home. If you really value your marriage and the welfare of your children's future marriage, you'll learn to say the magic words 'Go away and leave us alone.' We have a sign we hang on our bedroom door that says, 'Do not disturb—marriage in progress.' Our sex life depends on a lot of Vaseline. We've had to put Vaseline on the outside bedroom doorknob so the little monsters' hands slide off, and they don't break in on us during sex."

The miracle marriages of the Silver Survivors were characterized by the acknowledgment that the children were not beautiful, innocent gifts to marriage or vessels for genetic passage. The Silver Survivors put their marital union first above all else, expected the children to help parent the marriage as much as the parents parented the children, and were relatively free of the parental guilt that causes so many marriages to fall into the custody of their children.

"Children always make any marital problem worse, not better," warned one Silver Survivor mother. "If marital discord is a damaging thing for kids, so are kids a potentially overwhelming pressure on a marriage. Just being aware of the kid pressure and acknowledging it can help, and if the marriage is really a union, there is a lot more parenthood for everyone than there is motherhood and fatherhood."

In a miracle marriage—a union dedicated to joint caring *beyond the egos of its members*—the spouses are "familying *with*" instead of trying to be the "parents *to* their children." They are busy raising a family and not just children and are modeling love for one another as well as giving love to their children. When children learn to share a responsibility for the marriage just as parents are responsible for the welfare of their children, the stress of being a parent becomes less of a risk to the marriage itself.[27]

6. The Danger of Compromise: The Importance of Getting One's Way

"We went to what they call a marriage mediator," said the woman. "They are supposed to be the last stop before divorce court and a last-ditch effort at saving the marriage. Her buzz phrase was 'the power of compromise.' Well, we compromised all over the place. I didn't get what I wanted, and he didn't get what he wanted, and both of us think that the other got more. Nobody got their way so nobody is really happy at all now. I would have sooner lost out. If my husband wins, I can at least be a martyr for a while and set myself up for a later battle where I figure I have a win coming to me."

The Silver Survivors made sure that one or the other spouse got his or her way in a conflict. While at first glance this may sound like a selfish orientation, it is actually in keeping with the Great Marriage Myth that the marriage can be much more—not less or an approximation of—the sum of its parts.

By working it out until one partner convinces, persuades, tantalizes, influences, sways, demonstrates, coaxes, or educates the other to his or her point of view, the two partners manage to make the marriage grow by incorporating different points of view and behaviors that are not mere compromised approximations and amalgams of the individual partners. The union becomes much more than the sum of its parts not by combining modified approximations of each partner but through the ordeal of hard-won negotiation and experimentation. By trying out sometimes diametrically opposed individual ways of living, the two people in a miracle marriage find completely new ways to live.

Through the ordeal of establishing a clear "winner" and the ability of the miracle marriage to tolerate and even thrive on prolonged conflict and endure the absence of closure, the "surrendering" partner engages in and experiments with behaviors and orientations to life that he or she may never have tried had a compromise been reached. Instead of two slightly happy and slightly unhappy people, the marriage has one happy partner guiding and teaching the reluctant but willing other through a new experiment in living and loving. As a result, the marriage grows rather than accommodates and takes on its own identity and life instead of being the status sum of two compromised parts. One partner momentarily "wins" but *the marriage is ultimately victorious,* because both partners have faith in the Great Marriage Myth of the endurance of their union and the opportunity of the other partner to have his or her turn to drive. They know that the marriage will live to fight and love another day.

How this noncompromising orientation is accomplished will be explored in detail later, but the tribulation and ordeal of making a miracle marriage depends on avoiding the clichés of all of these six Cs of marriage. The Great Marriage Myth is discovered when both partners work toward a transcendent rather than self-adaptive "approximation" approach to loving.

Miracle marriages are not only compromised and destroyed by shattered dreams and sustained by their shared dreams. They are also created by shared and rational thinking. The final chapter of this introduction to the miracle marriage manual deals with the logic of love.

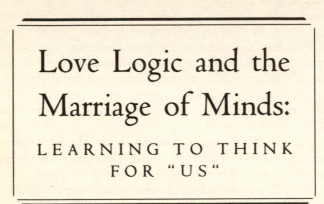

4

Love Logic and the Marriage of Minds:
LEARNING TO THINK FOR "US"

We only know what is on our mind, rarely what is in our mind.

—*Robert Ornstein*

Thoughts of Love

Lasting love is logical. It is a way we elect to talk to ourselves about others. It is how and what we think about commitment, what we consider to be caring and considerate behavior. The achievement of High Monogamy and the way of the Great Marriage Myth is based on learning how to put "mind over Me" to achieve a type of collective cognition or Us-type thinking about our lover and our daily life.

The brain is made for staying alive but not for staying in love. Our mind must make our brains stop thinking about Me and begin thinking about Us.

"Self"-Consciousness or Us-Consciousness?

Low Monogamy and the Me Myth are based on the brain's addiction to passion. The word "passion" literally means "suffering," and is based on thoughts about what we ourselves are experiencing, feeling, and contemplating. Compassion is "co-passion" or cosuffering. Compassion is thinking about the challenges and pain of life not as a self but as an Us. We can learn to control what psychologist Robert Ornstein calls our SOB, or "same old brain,"[1] and what I call the "selfish old brain" and all of its prewired dedication to the preservation and enhancement of the self. The miracle marriage is a melding of minds—we think "with" someone else rather than "about" them.

We can, as authors Anne Moir and David Jessel point out in their book *Brain Sex: The Real Difference Between Men and Women*, come to think rationally about our innate and neurobiological differences as men and women. We can learn to call out across the chasm rather than bellow insults at each other. By getting our minds on our loving, we can learn to respect and build from our natural differences by thinking as an Us rather than exaggerating them by magnifying the Me.[2]

Our brains have minimal standards. They are satisfied with merely staying alive. Our brain's first mission is *not* to think or to love but to keep its life-support system—the body—functioning. It is stimulated and alerted by the four Fs—"fighting, fleeing, feeding, and sex." But the mind is much more than just the physical brain. It is the self, and it uses the brain but is not limited by its physical capacities. The mind wants much more out of the spirit's brief journey through humanhood than living. It is dedicated to the four Fs of "feeling, forgiving, flourishing, and forever," and it is in search of another mind to think about love with.

While our brain thinks in the logic of subsistence, the challenge of making a miracle marriage is to think in the logic of love. The brain's "Me love" is ultimately immoral because it disregards the Us by seeking only the goals of the self. The brain does the thinking for the body, but the mind does the thinking of our soul. The brain's logic of life is "if it keeps me alive, it has meaning." The mind's logic of love is "if someone else can love with me, that is all that really means anything." The mind is where morality happens, because morality depends first and foremost on learning how to think responsibly about Us instead of protectively about Me.

At the end of this chapter, I will present a brief course in learning to think lovingly and illustrate how learning to be moral and learning to be less Me and more Us are the same cognitive challenge. Before we can learn to think lovingly, however, it is necessary to identify and overcome our brain's addiction to "self"-consciousness so our minds are freed for a collective consciousness.

The Brain's Passion for a Pretty Partner

The fourth F of the brain—sex—means that the brain is predetermined to react quickly to who it thinks is the best sexual partner. The brain does not ponder "being" the right loving spouse. It's the brain's evolutionary destiny to seek the continuation of its self. We all have prewired into us several factors that get mixed up with loving.

First, the brain is dominated by the "baby-face fixation," or its automatic response to what it sees as cuteness. As a result, the brain drives us to seek what our cortex interprets as a pretty partner, even though our minds know that cuteness in another person or ourselves has nothing to do with lasting love. If another person's brain finds you cute, his or her brain will take its body anywhere and get it to do almost anything to try to get some of your cuteness genes.

The brain is a follower by nature. For example, something quite remarkable takes place when a duckling hatches. When it turns eighteen hours old, the duckling will follow anything that moves because its brain is in a movement mode. The duckling becomes "imprinted" on the first passing object—be it a mother duck or a bowling ball.[3] Fortunately, the first moving object the duckling usually encounters is its mother, so imprinting leads to a greater chance of survival.

Such imprinting also takes place in children. During the first few weeks of the life of the child, he or she imprints on the nearest caretaker. This is usually the mother and, to a lesser extent, the father. Although it is much less rigid and biologically determined than imprinting in other animals, there are critical periods in humans when certain behaviors on the part of the child become linked with an adult nearby.

The parent is also imprinted or brain-linked to the child. A certain type of cry elicits an innate reaction in the mother, such as cleaning, holding, or feeding. These instinctive reactions, born of the brain's attachment mechanisms, work very well for seeing that our young are protected and cared for, but these same processes wreak havoc in our attempt to form a mature, lasting bond with another adult.

Our evolution dictates that our attraction and attachment be stimulated by "cuteness." All animals and human babies have much larger and more sloped and high foreheads, wider eyes, and higher cheeks than their adult counterparts.[4] This is called the "neotenic," or "baby," face, and few people can resist its appeal. The more a face approximates this "cutest little baby face," the more we ooh and ahh, goo and gaa, and hold and hug. Unfortunately for a more rational and logical loving, the brain remains blindly committed to these evolutional patterns through most of our life if we don't learn to use our minds to transcend them.

Things from little puppies and kittens to Mickey Mouse are seen as cute throughout the world. Adult men and women who approximate the neotenic face make the covers of our magazines and star in our films. They are awarded the coveted distinction of being the pretty people who "turn our heads" as if we have no choice. It is difficult to resist wanting to cuddle, hold, and love someone or something that is cute by evolutional brain standards. Imprinting of the neotenic face is so strong that some people avoid visiting pet stores for fear they will want to buy every puppy or kitten they see.

"I don't go out looking for somebody cute," said the woman. "I value brains, sensitivity, caring, and someone who will treat me with respect. Of course, it wouldn't hurt if he was cute, too!" Deny it as we may, our partner selection is to a large degree influenced by our brain's evolutionally fixed preference for someone the lower levels of our brain find to be a "real cutie."

Attracted to an Attractive Nuisance

While we may think that different people are attracted to different faces and that what one person finds appealing another would find appalling, the brain's subtle influence attracting us toward cuteness is powerful. We transcend it only when our mind takes over and we think about who, how, and why a person is with us rather than how someone may look to our brain. Our brain sees and reacts only to patterns, but our mind is drawn by people.

"I've noticed that a majority of the people in my courtroom are pretty good-looking," said the divorce judge I mentioned in Chapter 2. "I'm sure ugly people get divorced, too, but they must go to someone else's courtroom. Sometimes I think divorce court is a recycling center for couples consumed with their own or someone else's physical attractiveness." Although he was joking, it appears true that being unable to overcome our imprinting and strong attraction to the brain's preference for a pretty little baby face can cause us to end up with a very attractive nuisance for a marital partner.

As you will learn later in this chapter, romantic and passionate brain love is a danger and not a help to making a lasting marriage. Romantic love is fueled by a strong physical longing elicited by physical appearance. Persons succumbing to the cuteness reflex reflect it in their lover's language—such infantile terms as "baby, cutie, honeybunch, doll face, and sweetie." Even the tone of voice of someone responding to a cuteness fixation gives evidence of the infantilization of their lover.

However unconscious and powerful the cuteness response may be, it never lasts. If our children stayed as cute as they were when they were very young, and if we stayed as attracted to cuteness as we were when we were new parents, how could we ever hope that these cuties would get out of our house and leave us alone someday?

PCR Syndrome: Post-Cuteness Remorse

High Monogamy is not based on a parental type of caring or thinking about our spouse. Low Monogamy is often an extension of puppy love and represents an attempt to bring a marital partner home as a cute pet. It always ends in disaster. Miracle marriages require two maturing adults overriding their irrational predisposition toward cuteness in order to merge into a miracle marriage of two people who do not spend their time babying each other. Cuteness never lasts, and the brain's reflexive response to prettiness always ebbs away.

It appears that the cuteness response wears out much quicker in men than in women. Consider what we call male "postcoital remorse."[5] Shakespeare called this the "expense of spirit in a waste of shame." A strong biologically based sex drive focused exclusively on physical attractiveness can lead to this postcoital remorse in both men and women. Men particularly have this problem because of their highly testosteronized brains and highly genitalized response to what the brain perceives as erotic. Men have a strong predisposition to respond more intensely and quickly to objects and patterns than to persons and personalities.

Male sea lions will fight to the death in order to mount an extremely vague plastic replica of a female sea lion dragged across the beach. Thousands of even more vague rubber doll replicas of the human female are produced every year. An unknown number of men inflate and mount these sex dolls. The male brain's propensity for sex objects has a long evolutionary history. If you go home at night, however, with a well-patterned body and face that your brain fell for, you may be powerfully deflated and "re-minded" the next morning that there is more to loving than a pretty face.

The delusional power of the cuteness response and subsequent postcoital remorse is reflected in this statement by one of my students. "Late that night, she looked like she was well endowed with erotic capital. After we had sex and I saw her in the bright light, she looked like she was beauty-bankrupt. Now I know what morning sickness means." The woman to whom he was referring no doubt experienced her own rude awakening when looking at her new lover with logic rather than lust.

The Brain's Ultimate Aphrodisiac: Power and the Danger Delusion

Former Secretary of State Henry Kissinger once said that "power is the ultimate aphrodisiac." In addition to its temptation toward cuteness, the brain is also a power addict. Since it evolved in a constantly threatening world, the brain values power and control and is aroused by danger. When we are "out of our mind in love," the brain is on one of its power trips in its consumption with the need to "have" our lover, control him or her. It goes on the alert to protect its owner.

The brain was formed at a time that no longer exists and helped make a world for which it is no longer well suited. We don't have to pounce on a prospective lover and drag him or her away from competitors. (Contrary to cartoons, it was our female primitive ancestors who did the clubbing and dragging more often than the men.) Power and arousal to danger were necessary responses when every minute was a struggle to avoid being eaten by a wild animal or killed by an enemy. Our selfish old brain helped us survive millions of years ago by quickly selecting the cutest partner, and helping us to mate powerfully and rapidly and then move on. There was little time or need for the mind's pondering about the personality and mutuality of interests with a prospective partner when a growling predator lurked at the cave entrance.

The brain's obsession with self-power is another obstacle to logical loving, because when the brain focuses on hard fighting, fast fleeing, and quick eating, it generalizes this alert status to the fourth F—sex. Our brain still prefers hard, fast, and quick sex.

If our heart is beating fast, our palms are sweating, and our mouth is becoming dry, the brain reacts by "thinking" that we must be sexually excited. As a result, we come to feel as our bodies behave instead of trying to make our bodies behave as our minds tell us we feel. Most feelings *follow* the body's reflexes rather than lead it into its reactions, and the psychochemicals of danger are very similar to those that course through the body during sexual arousal. It is for this reason that we often mistake our aroused state for sexual and romantic feelings.

If our date is not arousing enough, the brain will seek more arousing input by telling us to try to do something dangerous to *make* it more arousing. Young people in particular drive fast on their dates, attend loud and wild parties, go to horror or violent movies, and ride on roller coasters. Dating practices in our society almost always involve some form of induced excitement and at least some element of danger, if only from an observer or audience point of view. If we are aroused by the danger and the activity is arousing to us, we wrongly assume that the *person* we are dating is causing our body to react as it is.

Pavlov's dogs were conditioned to salivate whenever they heard a bell. In similar fashion, our date becomes a conditioned stimulus for our aroused state. There are not too many sixty-year-olds who have been married for forty years who are roaring down the street in their cars or waiting in long lines to see two hours of murder and mayhem. With maturity comes the ability, in most cases, to differentiate between excitement and what or who is doing the exciting.

A classic study illustrates my point about the relationship between power and danger, on the one hand, and sex on the other.[6] A woman was asked to interview a sample of men after they had crossed one of two bridges. One of the bridges was strong and safe. The other was the Capilano Suspension Bridge, which is 450 feet long and 5 feet wide, and wobbles precariously over a 230-foot drop. The woman waiting for the men asked them to look at a picture and write a brief story about that picture. She then gave her phone number to all the men crossing either bridge and instructed them to call her if they had any questions about the experiment, which she said was related to how scenic attraction affects creative expression.

Only 12 percent of the men who had crossed the safe bridge called, but more than 50 percent of the men who had crossed the dangerous bridge called the woman. In addition, there was much more sexual content in the stories of the men who had been on the wobbly bridge. Several variations on this same experiment have confirmed the results: danger is related to sexual arousal. A perceived danger and sense of threat to our power is a brain aphrodisiac.

Whether or not the female brain is as responsive to the danger delusion awaits further research, but my guess is that the less-testosteronized female brain is more sexually reactive to safety and security than danger and demand. One husband said, "My wife gets all turned on and talkative when she feels comfortable and safe. When I'm comfortable, I fall asleep."

Place or Passion?

The brain is not only turned on by cuteness and threat. The brain is also "place-oriented." Men and women who meet one another in dangerous or anxiety-producing situations are more likely to interpret their feeling of arousal as sexual attraction to that person. When the danger and mystery of the dark lounge (where inhibitions are decreased by alcohol) become replaced by the cold pillow of morning, PCR, or postcoital remorse, results. In the thousands of couples I saw in my clinic, there was a consistent negative correlation between excitement and danger during courtship and the duration of the marriage. Postcoital remorse or perhaps a "postcourtship remorse" is a major risk to today's marriages.

One psychologist patient of mine illustrated the problems of confusing arousal to danger with arousal to a person. "The next time I date somebody, our first date will be someplace light, quiet, and restful where we can see and talk to each other. I want the woman to be the stimulus I respond to and not the place, the situation, or my own brain's chemicals. We are looking for love in all the wrong places. They're too exciting to think, so you can't really be sure what or who is really attracting you. You don't go to bars to think. With the loud music, sometimes I don't know if I'm being turned on by a good beat or a good person. I'm not going to let the place or the pace determine things. Instead, I'm going to learn about the person I'm with. If you are going to date, you shouldn't 'go out.' You should both 'go in' to each other and learn about each other at some place where you're both not out of your minds and can't hear yourselves think."

We usually court or date to find someone to love forever. If we are distracted by physical beauty, succumb to biological attraction to cuteness, or think that a place makes the person, we will experience post-cuteness remorse. If we succumb to the psychochemical temptation of danger and high arousal—similar to the hormones of sexual intercourse—and mistake it for love, we will experience postcoital remorse. Both factors can combine to result in post-courtship remorse, blocking our ability to find the thinking person's love necessary for a miracle marriage. All of these PCRs are forms of love sickness that leave us with the mere illusion of loving and the thoughtless brain's delusion of fulfillment.

Discovering the Treasure of Love: Passion Versus Compassion

When I lecture to "re-mind" people that loving is a way of thinking and not just feeling, I emphasize the differences between the brain's selfish Me passion and the mind's spiritual Us compassion. I often use two love stories to illustrate my points. I share them here as samples of personal journeys along the way to loving; both illustrate the power of the collective open mind over the Selfish Old Brain.

The first story is about my great-uncle Heinrich Schliemann—the father of archaeology. He discovered the legendary cities of Troy and Mycenae, the Treasure of Priam, and the Mask of Agamemnon. He has been the subject of several books, films, and documentaries. Most historians consider him, along with Freud, Marx, Nietzsche, and Wagner, to be one of the five best-known Germans of the nineteenth century.[7]

The story of the love between Heinrich and his young Greek wife Sophia is described in several novels and in a more scholarly work entitled *One Passion, Two Loves,* by Lynn and Gray Poole. The Pooles say that "Heinrich had his odyssey and his Penelope."[8] Heinrich was consumed by his lifelong personal goal of uncovering the splendor of Homeric Greece. During his quest, he met Sophia. She was thirty years his junior, but her beauty and grace attracted Heinrich's love much as the lost majesty of the city of Troy attracted his intellect. She was on his mind as Troy was in his brain.

Sophia became his necessary love partner—a part of a union much stronger than Heinrich could ever be alone—and she would help him make the miracle he so longed for. Because Heinrich's caring for Sophia and their love transcended his selfish focus on finding the elusive legendary city of Troy, their compassion served as a foundation for the passion that motivated and directed him in his historic odyssey.

Heinrich Schliemann suffered setbacks, disillusion, doubt,

scorn, ridicule, and even the fear that Troy might only be a vanished myth. Through it all, Sophia was by his side until the power of their love together—their miracle marriage—helped them uncover the ancient glory that was Troy. In the tradition of the Great Marriage Myth, their merging had made a forceful whole that made Heinrich and Sophia complete and helped make the world more complete and comprehensible at the same time.

Heinrich had two loves—his passion for the glory of Greece and his compassion with his dear Sophia. His "passion" and romantic suffering was for the discovery of his Greek treasure, but his "com-passion," or shared suffering, was with his wife. His compassion was for his marriage and being able to live his dream with Sophia even as they struggled together to fulfill the passion for solving an archaeological mystery. When Heinrich stooped to place the golden crown of Helen of Troy upon his beloved Sophia's head, he knew he was part of a miracle of love. He knew that his passion had been fulfilled because of his compassion with Sophia.

I chose this love story because, although its lessons teach of the Great Marriage Myth, the story itself is pure myth as well. Like many love stories, this love myth contains the greater myth of Us over Me, of a selfish brain succumbing to the power of two loving minds. It holds all the elements of a lasting and generating love able to make miracles for two and for the world. In fact, my great-uncle's relationship with his wife and many of his exploits in the field of archaeology are part fact, part fiction, part scandal, and part history.[9] It is said that Heinrich often ignored and neglected his wife and exaggerated or misunderstood some of his discoveries.

Schliemann remains a figure whose life and works are still the subject of high-level academic conferences to untangle the great myth from the great scandal. Unfortunately, as scholar William Calder points out, "Archaeology is the only discipline in ancient studies which to attain its end is required to destroy its evidence."[10] Much of the Schliemann factual legacy will be left to scholars and historians, but from deep within our minds—our consciousness, imagination, and faith—we can choose to find within this old story the elements of the Great Marriage Myth to guide our own love.

It is often the novelists who have a clear view of the great myths of our world. They found within Heinrich and Sophia's arranged marriage and turbulent relationship the golden threads that weave the great myth of miracle marriage.

The Treasure and Light of Compassion

Here is the second love story I use to teach about learning to think of much more than Me. This is the actual report from one of the Silver Survivors about the couple's own miracle of shared, compassionate loving and how their merging made a wonderful miracle. As you read this story, remember to look for the Great Marriage Myth lesson of high morality and High Monogamy— "Us for others" over "Me for myself."

"We've cried together for hours," said the wife looking tired and drawn, but at the same time confident and secure. "My husband and I have suffered. God knows how we have suffered. Our dream has been to save our daughter and save ourselves at the same time. My daughter was born blind and retarded. The doctor sort of suggested that we not feed her and let her 'pass on.' We cried together and agonized together. At that terrible moment, and after eight years of marriage, I think my husband and I finally fell in love. My husband's career, my painting and art career, our passion for our individual goals diminished. We became One at that moment—we became married for a higher and shared purpose—and we began to make a miracle together.

"Years of mutual suffering followed, but we knew together that we would fulfill our dream. Every day, we drove our daughter to therapy, taught her, held her, and urged her on when she came so close to giving up. We fought together against the schools and those who discriminated against her and those who so viciously and sometimes unknowingly blocked her way to life. God challenges you with a handicap, but it's people who cripple you. We loved her together and always believed together. When one of us was ready to give up, the other brought us both up. Our minds became one mind in our pondering of our daughter's return to health.

"I remember watching the silly talk shows with people talking about how they could not find love and how they suffered so and were so passionately in search of the love and the lover they needed. I remember how bad I felt for those people, because I thought they would never really know what love is. They were looking for love for themselves, and they were suffering for and thinking only of themselves. They didn't know that love doesn't come for you but from you. Their suffering was selfish passion and not a shared suffering of compassion. Oh, how my husband and I suffered, and we still suffer together for much more than just ourselves.

"Our daughter is twenty now, and she is our treasure. We can't begin to count the hours of pain and torture we have been through to discover our treasure, but everyone came to see our miracle—everyone came to see our Jeanne get married. She works full-time now. She lives on her own, and she has found someone to love and who loves her. My husband and I seemed to be getting married again through our daughter's miracle. You couldn't hear the minister sometimes because of all the crying in the church that day. Everyone held hands, and we all got married again.

"These two hurt young people were marrying one another. Our daughter's husband has been in a wheelchair since birth. He is barely able to move his arms. One blind, one almost unable to move, yet here they were making a marriage partly because their parents' marriages were miracle makers.

"The young lovers were trying to light a candle together to symbolize the birth of their marriage. They wouldn't listen to anyone who said they couldn't do it. They wanted to light a candle as part of their marriage ceremony, and they took about twenty minutes to find it with their trembling hands. My daughter couldn't see and our new son-in-law's hand shook terribly. We all suffered with them as they tried to light that candle. They would get close, burn themselves, then one would try alone and then the other. But finally, they took the long lighter together in their joined hands. My daughter offered her more steady hands to guide them, and our son-in-law offered his eyes to show them the way. Somehow, they found that candle. It flickered on, then off again. We all gasped, but suddenly and like a miracle, they seemed to will that candle to light. The glow filled the church and our souls. Everyone stood and cheered through their tears. But the struggle and suffering weren't over. They're never over, because real love is real suffering together forever.

"The lovers moved toward yet another candle and struggled for several more minutes to light it. They were better at it this time, because they had already begun their own miracle merging of making more than just the two of them by their marriage. I don't know if you can feel it when I describe it, but the suffering and compassion of all those years filled that whole church with light and love. And then, the most miraculous thing of all happened.

"As my husband and I sat crying with joy and pride for their marriage and ours, and as our son-in-law's parents joined us in our tears, our children turned toward us. They each took one of the candles and our daughter pushed her new husband's wheelchair toward us as he seemed to guide her without words. They went first to our new in-laws and with their newfound joint efficiency handed a candle to them. Then they came to us, and as my husband and I took that candle in our hands, we felt the power of their miracle marriage and our own."

The mother and I cried together as she related this story to me. These parents' miracle marriage had given birth to another miracle. They had learned to think of Us in its broadest sense. That is what miracle workers do and are for—to make more miracles. They had silenced passion for self to make a powerful One of compassionate and generating love. Their suffering together to make this miracle created a power life of love, truth, and joy not only for themselves but for those around them. In the tradition of High Monogamy and the miracle marriage, they had helped to bring more joy to the world.

Lessons in the Logic of Love

Learning to love and learning to be moral are simultaneous processes. When we learn how to be moral, we learn how to think and care about other people and other things beyond ourselves. Both high morality and High Monogamy require us to silence the Selfish Old Brain so we can keep our mind on the survival of everyone instead of just ourselves. When we learn how to love, we learn a moral concern for someone as a part of ourselves. The Great Marriage Myth of High Monogamy advocates a higher morality than the Me Myth of Low Monogamy because it focuses on the welfare of Us rather than what's good for Me. What follows is a course in learning how to think lovingly by learning how to think morally.[11]

Love Logic Step 1: Detecting and Controlling Our *Eros* Love Seizures

The first and most primitive form of loving is called *eros*. This is the love of romantic passion written about by psychologist John Lee and many others who have researched the nature of the evolution of loving.[12] It represents self-fulfillment and the search to find the right partner to please the self. This type of loving is like a seizure that grips the entire psyche; the partners become smitten, or love-struck. In India, the god of love is represented as a big, vigorous man who shoots his "arrows of agony" into the heart to cause a love seizure. In our culture, it is Cupid who serves as the archer. The first step in learning to think clearly and morally about loving is to be able to recognize the symptoms of *eros* love seizures. One must learn to avoid, control, and move beyond them, and to recognize less mature loving when we are doing it. Here are the ten major symptoms of a "love seizure," or what one of the Silver Survivors called cupid-itis.

- Dizziness
- Light-headedness
- Distractibility
- Giddiness
- Tightness in the chest
- Heart palpitations
- Preoccupation with thoughts of the loved one
- Moodiness
- Jealousy
- Fixation—feeling that lover "fills a void"

Psychologist Dorothy Tennov described the nature of the love-seizure posture. She referred to *eros* love as "limerence" and an almost convulsive process of being love-struck and then falling "head-over-heels."[13] When Shakespeare wrote that "love is blind," he was referring to another characteristic of the "love seizure"—the complete loss of objectivity that takes place in *eros* love. As I described earlier, the brain's addiction to arousal clouds our consciousness and destroys our rationality, resulting in our submission to cuteness and coitus rather than caring and cognition. One Silver Survivor summed up cupid-itis by saying, "Cupid makes you stupid."

Researcher Kenneth Pope describes the "swooning, falling, and disorientation" of the great *eros* lovers of fiction and verse.[14] Some *eros* seizures result in lovers' becoming clumsy and disoriented. One of my patients referred to her "love bumps" from constant banging into tables and chairs while being distracted by thoughts of her lover. Another patient referred to himself as a "love-a-leptic" because he "seemed to space out and swoon away" when he thought of his lover. Here is an actual clinical account of a love seizure from one of my young college students:

"He really knocked me off my feet. He was what I have been looking for all my life. I could see nothing but him, and I felt faint when he was around me. My heart pounded, and I giggled and just sort of stared at him like I was in a trance. He's on my mind constantly, and I get depressed when I don't see him for a while. If he found someone else, I don't think I could take it. He makes me what I am and fills my every need. I can't even think in my classes sometimes because he's on my mind." The pangs of passion of this young student are characteristic of the emotionally and physically crippling power of *eros* love, and the passion or suffering it causes.

Passion-Potion Poisoning

Popular songs refer to a "love potion" as a powerful elixir of ecstasy capable of totally and involuntarily consuming and overwhelming a person with feelings of love and lust. Researchers have shown that this "love potion" is a form of physiological addiction to our own brain's psychochemical hyperreaction to a love object. When exposure to the brain's idea of the "right" lover takes place (a cute person in a dangerous and mysterious place), some people fall into full love seizures. Unlike rational love, which helps us *both* become a more complete whole, a love seizure deludes us into thinking that another person *makes* us feel complete. If one thing or one person seems necessary for us to feel complete, dependency results. Marrying because both partners want to grow together is different from one partner marrying because he or she can't make it alone.

Psychologists Samuel Peele and Allen Brodsky write, "When constant exposure to something is necessary in order to make life bearable, an addiction has been brought about, however romantic the trappings. The ever-present danger of withdrawal creates an ever-present craving."[15] *Eros* loving, then, is a selfish suffering that results in an overwheming seizurelike state of such magnitude that its sweet agony becomes bitterly addicting.

Eros love is, in fact, a psychochemical high. The lover in seizure becomes addicted not so much to the partner as to his or her own biochemical internal reactions craved by the selfish brain. In effect, the brain falls in love with itself. This is a psycho-chemical reaction similar to an amphetamine high. The brain manufactures its own amphetaminelike substance called phen-ylethylamine in response to *eros*, shutting down production when romantic love ends or post-cuteness, postcoital, or post-courtship remorse sets in.[16] Like the junkie without his fix, the affected person feels a profound sense of emptiness when the brain loses its source of passion potion.

In studies of women who reported disastrous love affairs, re-searchers have found that the victims often go on chocolate binges or junk-food orgies.[17] Chocolate has a high concentration of phenylethylamine, so these women may be seeking to make up for the sudden withdrawal from their affection amphetamine high by finding something to eat. A common addicted lover's statement is indicated by this woman's comment: "I could just eat him up, I loved him so much. I wanted to gobble him up, take him in, and digest him."

Drugs that inhibit the breakdown of phenylethylamine (called monoamine oxidase inhibitors) have been—along with psycho-therapy—successful in helping those women who were severe love junkies, women compulsively driven to sell their bodies and souls to find more *eros* loving. It appears that while men are more responsive to cuteness and danger, their brains also seem less responsive to phenylethylamine. As you will read in Chapter 9, the natural template of the brain is female until testosterone enters the system during "sex week" or the sixth week into pre-natal development. Because the male's brain is more highly tes-tosteronized than the female's, their brains differ in many ways. One difference is that the male brain predisposes men to use and play with things rather than to engulf and care for them.[18] To be maternal may be seen as to be engulfing with protective love, possibly providing one explanation of the difference in the nature of mothering and fathering. (One mother said, "Men are better at Little League than at a little love.") Gender differences in sensitivity to phenylethylamine may explain this patient's report. "When I break up with my boyfriend, I eat everything in the house. My boyfriend goes out and plays an angry and aggressive game of racquetball. He hits and I eat."

Love and the First Stage of Morality

Psychologist Lawrence Kohlberg has developed one of the most comprehensive theories of moral development.[19] He suggests that we learn right from wrong as we learn how to think. He says that our morals are based on how we conceptualize our world and our relationship to others. I have found that lasting love and moral-logic development seem to go hand in hand. High moral development requires a well-developed sense of "Us over Me" and altruism over selfishness. Moral thinking is thinking about life collectively rather than individually and being able to care for others as much or more than we care for ourselves. For each loving style, I will illustrate how one of Kohlberg's moral stages corresponds to that style and how love and morality are one and the same.

The *eros* stage of loving corresponds to Kohlberg's first stage of "premoral" reasoning. This stage is characterized by an attempt to avoid punishment and pain, and to enhance and protect the self at all costs. It is the morality of the impulsive young child behaving so as to avoid a spanking. The "passion" of *eros* loving is also a defensive, insecure state motivated by the morality of saving the self and avoiding punishment or abandonment by the lover. Like the child complying with parental rules to avoid physical punishment, the *eros* love style is one of clinging and even cowering to the lover in order to avoid the challenge and pain associated with further self-development. The orientation of a marriage based on this type of love and prelogic is one of avoiding anticipated emotional pain and childish attempts to avoid emotional rejection.

This woman's statement illustrates the relationship between *eros* loving and the premoral stage of morality: "Our marriage is based on love. We idolize each other and would never go against each other. He is my everything and I am his everything. I would do anything he wants, and he would do anything I want. We live for each other. The crisis of a lifetime would be our splitting up. He makes me whole, and without him I would fall apart. It would be the worst punishment I could imagine if he would leave me. It's only logical that we should be together." The "parental compliance" nature of this marriage is clear and characteristic of what one Silver Survivor called "the erocity thinking error" of mistaking strong emotions for logical loving.

The sexual style of *eros* love is based on an intense sexual magnetism that is quick to ignite and even quicker to extinguish. "I love the hell out of him when we make love," said the wife. "I'm not taking any chances that he won't love my loving. I can't believe how hot I get him. He couldn't find anyone hotter." Sexuality in this relationship is a sex of "good behavior" and being a "good" lover. It is making love to impress and control the lover and to avoid the loss of love.

The first step in learning to think lovingly is to be sure we are thinking about and not just succumbing to love. We must realize that our brains are prone to fits of *eros* and be alert for those times when we are having a love seizure rather than seizing the chance for a more mature love.

Love Logic Step 2: Getting Serious About Each Other

The second love style is called "*ludus* loving," from the Latin meaning "games, sport, pastimes." It is a teasing, meaningless, nonserious, testing type of love characteristic of early courtship and marriages that fail to mature. The thinking behind this loving style is about keeping all relationship options open and looking for the best deal while keeping the *ludus* lover as a backup or a love insurance policy.

If the person thinking about love "ludicrously" is married, he or she attempts to "give to receive" and maneuver for the best marital deal by seduction. One wife said, "One little wink and I can get him to do anything I want, even to happily wrap himself around my little finger." There may be infidelity because the marriage is not taken seriously. The affair may be conducted almost mischievously, as if one should try to get away with whatever one can. Like home for the misbehaving child, the marriage becomes a safe place to return to when an affair ends or the risk of getting caught becomes too high. If the affair turns out successfully, a new relationship starts and the old one is cast away.

The *ludus* love style corresponds with Kohlberg's second stage of premoral reasoning, which is based on seeking the best and most rewards. Persons at this stage think about making deals, doing favors, and negotiating for caring. They move beyond stage 1 morality of doing things to avoid punishment to attempting to behave in order to get the "right" or "best" deal. "I'll clean my room if I can watch cartoons" is the childhood equivalent of *ludus* loving.

The sexual style of the *ludus* lover is more fun and games than commitment and intimacy. This husband's statement illustrates this sexual recreation: "I do her, then she does me. The more turned on I get her, the more turned on she will try to get me. Foreplay is really 'for me,' if you get my point. If I keep her happy, she won't want to go somewhere else for loving and she won't be watching me as closely—if you get my drift. Once I finish pleasing her, I can sit back and get all I can get." If this man's statement sounds immoral, it is because his type of loving is an immature, childish way of thinking about relationships.

Step 1 in learning mindful loving is to learn to see love as a way of thinking about your relationship—a volitional choice of concept rather than an emotional reflex. After learning to be aware of the impulsive nature of the brain's style of loving and seeing *eros* seizures as symptoms of thoughtless lust rather than contemplative loving, the next step in learning the logic of love is to conceive of your love as serious and deserving of your commitment. This is done not because of fear of punishment or the gamesmanship of getting the best of someone, but because your loving relationship becomes the most sensible, important, and central part of your life. A miracle marriage is something we think about not with fear or guile but with the most profound respect.

Love Logic Step 3: Making Friends with Our Lover

Storge love is from the Greek word meaning a respectful and protective kind of love. It is a way of thinking about love that emphasizes regard for the lover's feelings and thoughtfulness about what might be done and said that would make the partner feel better. *Storge* loving is an appeal for acceptance and approval. "What could I do that would please my spouse?" is the primary thought of the *storge* lover. There is little concern about or fear of punishment, and the *storge* lover does not try to manipulate his or her partner. *Storge* loving is a more solid, stable, slowly evolving, reflective loving that grows with the development of companionship. There is no feeling of being love-struck or head over heels. Instead, both *storge* lovers often have difficulty identifying when they actually began to love rather than just like one another. *Storge* loving can withstand crises, but it is not dramatic or intense. It is a relationship made more for problem solving than for miracle making, but its strong adaptive skills are precursors of miracle marriage.

This Silver Survivor illustrates the dynamics of *storge* love thinking: "We had worked together for two years. We respected one another and often went to lunch together. Neither one of us can tell you when we changed from severe like to severe love, but we love each other now and have for twenty-seven years. We never really dated each other. It is more like we aged and thought our way into each other."

Kohlberg called his third stage of moral reasoning "conventional morality." It is based on doing right or wrong to gain the approval of others so that the person can think well of himself or herself. It is a morality not of favors or negotiation but of the search for self-esteem. It is not based on conforming to avoid punishment or to get rewards, but on enhancement of self-image and social reputation by treating someone else nicely. Being accepted and seen as good is reward enough.

The *storge* love style is represented by caring lovers who try to be good friends to each other and wish to be seen by spouses, in-laws, friends, and neighbors as "good husbands" and "good wives." This statement by a Silver Survivor illustrates the third stage of love logic: "I don't buy flowers for my wife because I expect her to buy them for me or because I'm afraid she'll get mad at me if I don't. I buy them because it's what a good husband does. It's just the kind of guy I want to be."

The sexual style of *storge* loving is one of comfortable physical intimacy without tumult and adventure. It is a sex of predictability and closeness rather than challenge, variety, and experimentation. One Silver Survivor husband put it this way: "We don't have a sex life of fever, folly, and friskiness. We both just enjoy sex together like a very good and balanced tennis match in which nobody is keeping score. We just rally and volley until we feel complete—love, set, and we're usually well matched. She's a good lover and I'm a good lover. We're a well-matched set."

Step 3 in learning the logic of love requires incorporating the realization that loving is a chosen way of thinking and not involuntary emotional reaction. Higher love logic goes beyond personal rewards to reflecting and caring deeply about one's marital reputation with one's spouse and one's marriage. One miracle-making husband summarized the first three steps of love logic this way: "First, I had to start thinking about love instead of trying to do it because I felt it. Then I had to take my wife and our marriage seriously and not just as a place to get what I needed. Then I had to start thinking less about what I thought of my wife and more about what my wife thought of me."

Love Logic Step 4: How Not to Be a Love Maniac

The fourth style of loving is referred to as *mania* love. This is the roller coaster of loving, with one or both partners either climbing a mountain of ecstasy or sliding down into a valley of despair. *Mania* refers to madness and agitation and "manic" means to be driven by strong urges, so *mania* loving is a process of sudden starts and stops motivated by an almost insatiable need for attention from the lover (love addiction). This is the common love style depicted in modern movies and plays. The following comment from a *mania* lover illustrates the upheaval of this type of love.

"We have a stormy kind of love. We can feel it when a love storm front is moving in. The atmospheric pressure in our marriage changes. We are in and out of love like a revolving door. It's a combination of the movie *War of the Roses* and the play *Cat on a Hot Tin Roof,* where they try to destroy each other, and *Love Story* where they cherish each other. It's like loving in the tundra at one time and the tropics at another. Sometimes it really tires us out." This loving style is one example of the confusion of danger and arousal with love that I discussed earlier in this chapter. Whereas *eros* love is one-directional until it burns itself out, *mania* can be up-and-down until it tires itself out.

Kohlberg's fourth moral stage, a second phase of what he called conventional morality, corresponds with *mania* loving. This stage emphasizes a moral thinking based on rigid conformity to "the law." Strong guilt and struggle with authority are characteristic of this stage, and *mania* loving also involves a love-power struggle over who is loving the most and best at a given time and who is "laying down the law" or living up to the "way love should be." Adolescentlike arguments often result from conflicting concepts of the right way to love, who is loving the wrong way, who doesn't show enough love, and who broke what love law.

One *mania* lover reported, "Hell, we don't have a loving bond, we have a bondage love. We tie each other up emotionally, try to escape, and then tie each other up again. We cross-examine each other, present evidence, and declare a guilty party for the crime of lack of love. I tell her she commits manslaughter, and she says I commit womanslaughter. We're always catching each other in marital misdemeanors."

The sexual style of *mania* loving is one of "hot and cold" sex. The most bitter arguments are followed by sexual making up, while lack of conflict often results in a decrease in sexual activity. The postcoital remorse syndrome is frequent and often takes the form of postcoitus combat. Sexual sulking may occur, with one or the other partner holding out sexually because of a current battle in the relationship or in an attempt to make his or her point.

This wife's statement illustrates the hot and cold sexuality of *mania* love: "Sometimes we have the most wonderful, romantic, and hot sex in the world when we are in our close phase. But when we are not feeling close, we can use sex as a weapon. Hot love means hot sex, and cold love means cold sex."

Step 4 in cognitive restructuring about love—or an Us mind mastering the Me brain—is to transcend the legalistic logic that leads to confrontation and replace it with thought about a higher moral law. Once we have learned to think about love and to think about ways of mutual gain rather than avoidance of punishment, we have made major steps toward higher monogamy. When we seek to enhance our own loving reputation rather than find faults in our lover, we can move on to the fourth step of learning to think in terms of Us.

Love Logic Step 5: The Pragmatics of Loving

Pragma love is practical, well-thought-out loving based on careful consideration of who would be a good loving partner. This is a cerebral love style that can evolve into the inclusion of one or more of the other more emotional intense love styles while still remaining a rational loving. There is much verbal discussion of "the state of the relationship," as if the couple were outside their interaction looking in. The couple often talks much more than they touch and sometimes seeks objectivity and detachment from "the" relationship as a means of "nonemotional" evaluation. "Getting emotional" is seen as a sign of weakness.

One Silver Survivor speaks of her *pragma* love as the start of their long-lasting relationship. "What would you expect from two accountants? We talked and talked, and we thought and thought. I had a mental checklist, and I'm sure he did, too. It was like making an investment in intimacy. We had a relationship plan before we had a relationship. It worked out well, though, because we've moved on now to a much more emotional closeness. But you know us. We still talk and act like accountants, but we feel like lovers."

Kohlberg's fifth moral-reasoning stage is called postconventional morality. It relates to conformity based on earning the respect of the community at large and enhancing the welfare of that community. This is a morality of honoring contracts, individual rights, and following established democratic principles for the good of the whole. The *pragma* lover guides his or her loving by the formation and honoring of the couple contract and tries to do the "right thing" because of the implied contract of the relationship or marriage. This Silver Survivor illustrates the combination of fifth stage moral thinking and the step 5 style of *pragma* loving:

"A marriage is a contract. People can talk all they want about love and passion, and these things are vital, of course. But a marriage is a legal commitment too, and it is a personal contract of the highest order. We wouldn't have much of a world if people just went around voiding contracts because they didn't get their way."

The sexual style of *pragma* loving is also intellectualized. Sex in this type of relationship is one of tolerance and patience and often involves discussion of technique, timing, and turn taking. One Silver Survivor wife said, "You have to be realistic. Some nights, I just don't want to have sex, but I will please my husband in some way. Sometimes he does the same for me. If one of us isn't getting enough sex or the right kind of sex, we talk about it openly. Neither one of us is sexist, and we believe in a completely equal and democratic approach to our marriage and our sex. There isn't any silent minority in our sexual life together.

We both speak up, and sometimes we can talk ourselves into some pretty good sex and explain away those times when sex isn't so good."

Miracle marriages often include a strong sense of contractual obligation in addition to their sense of mutual respect and intimate merging. Lasting marriages "spiritualize" their legal connection, while marriages in trouble try to legalize, defend, and enhance their own contractual position.

Step 5 in learning love logic requires consideration of a marriage contract as important and enduring not because it protects each partner but because to break the contract hurts society. Nietzsche once said that the human being is the only animal that can make and keep a promise. Thinking about love as a contractual commitment isn't unromantic, it is rational and logical. Such thinking allows the marriage to reflect on the welfare of the community and not just the Me. By doing so, such mutual thought contributes to the welfare of the whole world.

Love Logic Step 6: Sharing Thoughts of Joy

Agape loving derives from the Greek word meaning "reverential love." This is the love of a miracle marriage, because it is a total merging of minds through which our lover is not "on" our mind but "in" and "of" it. He or she is not just "in our thoughts," but helps make us think. The lovers become our cocognizers.

They do not demand of one another, but they are demanding of their relationship as a place of growth, where both partners can produce joy and love as a team. *Agape* lovers engage in High Monogamy, so they are almost never unkind to each other because to be so is to be unkind to the most important part of their life—their marriage. Both partners also work to be kind to their children, family, friends, and the world in which they live.

Agape love is seldom impatient love, but the lovers often feel impatience with those who would use marriage and loving for their own fulfillment rather than for the improvement of the world. *Agape* love is less *passionate* because there is less suffering for and of the self, but it is more *compassionate* because it represents the silencing of the self for the welfare of the unit. It is a shared commitment to the task of spreading joy, growth, truth, and harmony.

Does *agape* and compassionate loving sound just too unrealistic, too difficult, and too dramatic to be possible? The author who coined some of the terms describing the various love styles listed here, psychologist John Lee, also wrote that he never found an unqualified example of the *agape* love.[20] He felt such loving was only an ideal—a miracle—and therefore very rare indeed.

Although I agree that such loving is a miracle, I do not agree that it is as rare as Dr. Lee or other love researchers think or as difficult to attain as these psychologists propose. This loving awe is what the Great Marriage Myth is all about—a merging of minds, a process of thinking logically and morally together. It is being in awe of the power of merging minds and souls rather than overcome with love chemicals. This is the loving that is taught by the ten love laws you will learn in Part II of this book.

Kohlberg's corresponding sixth stage of moral development is the second phase of his postconventional morality. It involves the merging of a sense of what is right or wrong *for the self* with what is right or wrong *with the world*. Kohlberg sees this as the ultimate Us morality that goes far beyond thoughts of Me. It involves responsible planetism instead of protective nationalism. It is a morality of principle and of saving the world, and it is a pledge of allegiance to the Earth. It is standing with someone else against injustice and lies, and replaces these with caring and truth. Because it is morality with the purpose of spreading more joy, truth, and love through the world, it is the high morality of High Monogamy.

The final step in learning how to think lovingly is to stand not only for our own marriage but for marriage as the great myth by which we will guide our life. When we think on this High Monogamy level, we think as the great scientists do—about the laws of wholes and not parts, about forever and not just now, and about the planet and the universe and not just our local living. We think about not only our marriage but the meaning of all marriage and not only about individual people particles but infinite waves of energy. Once we know how to rediscover the Great Myth of Marriage, we learn what *agape* loving truly is, and it becomes a realistic objective.

A Love Wish

Perhaps the highest-level morality and highest-level loving are seen as ideals rather than realistic goals because we have become mentally, morally, and lovingly lazy. Our SOBs, or Selfish Old Brains, are demanding masters who do not surrender easily to a higher purpose than their own survival. High Monogamy requires cocognition much more than it requires mere cohabitation, and the miracle marriage manual you are about to read shows you how to think as One.

The sexual style of *agape* lovers is a metaphor for the highly moral miracle marriage. Here is description of the sexuality of a miracle marriage as offered by one wife Silver Survivor married sixty years! It provides a good review of learning *agape* love and an initial insight into the laws of loving you will learn in the miracle marriage manual in Part II:

"Neither one of us has ever said the words 'I'm coming' when we have sex. We watch the films and hear the comedians when they deal with sex, and they always say "I'm coming" or "Oh God" followed by the word "Baby!" No wonder there's a population problem today if everyone is going to be getting God's attention and then asking Him for a baby every time they make love. They should be yelling out 'love' instead of baby and maybe God would make them love instead of pregnant.

"Us two eighty-year-olds are still making love, and we're no prudes. But when we make love and are fulfilled, each of us usually says the weirdest thing. We say it because we've raised three kids to happy, healthy lives, and we even had to save two of their lives. We've cared for all four of our parents. One of them had Alzheimer's disease and another was bedridden in our home for ten years. We've had our careers, we never missed a vote in one election, and we volunteer together at the halfway house twice a week now. We feel like our marriage was never just our marriage—it seemed to be for everybody. Even from the first night we made love, we always said the same kinky thing when we were completed. You'll laugh I know, and my husband will be embarrassed that I told you, but we each always say, 'Oh God, I'm joining!' "

PART II

A Miracle-Marriage Manual

The supreme human law is love.

—*Saint Augustine*

The following ten chapters present a course in making a miracle marriage. Each is a mini-semester in the application of the laws and principles of lasting love introduced in Part I. But this is not a course in marital survival. It is a love map that requires difficult decisions, work, time, and emotional, physical, and most of all mental energy. To think is to create, and when we think lovingly, we create love. To love is to make miracles, but only a lasting and rational love has such power.

We all must decide if we are capable of the experience of love or representatives of the infinite energy of love itself temporarily manifested in human form. Low Monogamy relates to the first option, and High Monogamy relates to the second. As you learned in Part I, High Monogamy is sometimes difficult, but it leads to the ultimate miracle—learning how to love someone for life and beyond.

Most of the following chapters end with five specific Home Love Assignments or techniques for putting each law of lasting love to work in your own relationship. You have read in the first section of this book that High Monogamy requires a new way of thinking. Much of the love work involves less talking together and more mental reflection, contemplation, and meditation as a marriage. The following list is offered to remind you of the ten laws of lasting love to be explored in Part II:

5

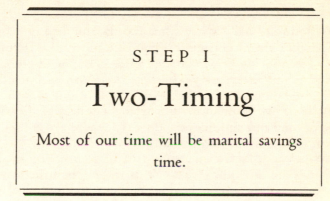

STEP I

Two-Timing

Most of our time will be marital savings time.

LOVE LAW ONE: THE TWO-TIME LAW

New science has shown that time is relative, dependent on our perceptions, priorities, and choices. We make all the time we have, and we only have the time we make. A miracle marriage begins with two people who agree to make their marital time together—otherwise known as MIMs, or marital investment minutes—their number-one priority over all else, no matter what the demands of daily living may be. The commitment to Two Time is based on the premise that even though time is relative, it is forever running out on us. If we hope to find love, we must first find the time for loving.

Sacred and Profane Time

Samuel Johnson said, "When a man knows he is to be hanged in a fortnight, it concentrates his mind wonderfully." He meant that we often squander our greatest gift—the time of our life—until something makes us aware of its preciousness. Sometimes too late, we become aware of the sacredness of our moments. A miracle marriage begins with a shared awareness of the divine nature of time and an understanding that there are at least two kinds of time—sacred and profane.[1]

"Profane" time is known to most of us as "real or absolute time." It is the time our clocks tell us rather than the time we make for ourselves and our loving. We want to know "the" time so we as individuals can be "on" it, "keep" it, and "use it" well. This is a clockwise time of mechanical worldly measurement; it is profane because it comes from swinging pendulums or vibrating crystals rather than from our developing spirit. Profane time is always cyclical, a product outside us to be spent, used, and reused as the same minutes seem to come around again. The hands on our watch go around and around, so we wrongly assume that time is a renewable and recyclable resource, but in fact our time is really moving on and running out.

When Albert Einstein was only twenty-six years old, he demolished the 300-year-old idea of absolute time and made the idea of time more "sacred" by making us understand it as something we ourselves could influence. Because of Einstein's work with relativity, we were no longer outside the temple of time—we were as much a part of time as time was a part of us. His theories of special and general relativity showed that time could be made to dilate, speed up, or slow down, depending upon the movement and location of the time teller in space—a "space time" that is everywhere around, in, and of us. Einstein helped us see time as relative to where we are in our own life space.

A minute on a hot stove seems like hours, while hours with our lover may seem like minutes. By extension, we can make our time meaningful and not limit the meaning of our life by mechanical absolute time. But there is one serious flaw in this relativity theory. No matter what our perceptions of time, we still get old!

Time Will Come and Take Our Love Away

Scientist Sir Arthur Eddington wrote, "The great thing about time is that it goes on, but this is an aspect of it which the physicist sometimes seems inclined to neglect."[2] Einstein's relativity theory gave us the freedom to see time our own way, but a notion of truly sacred time requires that we also remember that our life, unlike the life of atoms and electrons, has an arrow pointing forward to the future.

There is no direction of time in the controlled laboratory experiment and when scientists measure the movement of particles and energy waves. The quantum world has no time flow. Things and events just "are" and "happen," and explanations of quantum events do not involve the notion of clockwise. Newton's laws of planetary motion work just as well if we film them and show the film backward. The principle of relative time neglects, as Dr. Eddington pointed out, that time moves on. The real lesson in learning to make our time sacred depends not only on realizing that we are free to see our time in our own way and to make time a loving time for two, but also on always remembering that our physical chance to love will end.

William Shakespeare wrote in his Sonnet 64, "Ruine hath taught me thus to ruminate: That Time will come and take my love away." The first step in this miracle-marriage manual requires that we learn to choose to live not by solo seconds separate from our love life but in merged moments cherished as limited and ultimately ending here on earth. We live in this world by going forward in a series of Nows from an irretrievable past to an uncertain future.[3] A miracle marriage involves making the choice to share moments in this time travel rather than spending time selfishly. It values every moment as One moment. Profane time is always clockwise, but sacred time is made by the couple wise enough to know that our spirits are only passing through these aging bodies and not confined by their destiny.

Profane time is a personal time based on the Me Myth of getting everything the self can get out of every measurable and absolute minute. It is a particle or individual time based on one person trying to use all the time he or she can. "Profane time and Personal time both start with P," said one Silver Survivor, "and that's one way I remember how selfish profane time is. Sacred time starts with S to stand for 'shared time,' and moments shared are the truly sacred times of our life."

To learn the first step in this miracle-marriage manual—the making of Two Time—we must employ the relativity of time by seeing as much of our living as we can from the point of view of Two and Us rather than Me and Mine. Our time together here is short. Don't wait! Make plenty of time to love each other now.

Now Is the Moment

The Hawaiian Wedding Song begins with the words "Now is the moment of sweet Aloha." Literally translated, it means that now is the time for *a* meaning "love," *lo* meaning "land or earth," and *ha* meaning "spirit," or *now* is the only time we have to love here on earth. A miracle marriage learns how to grasp the Now because it is not limited by guilt from the past or dreads for the future. We can make our nows together by selecting mutual memories to experience and share in our present instead of ruminating alone about individual guilt regarding the past or fears of failure in the future.

A miracle marriage can help its members see, as scientist Ken Wilbur writes, that there do not have to be boundaries to our shared Now when we realize that "past as memory and the future as expectation are in [the present] and not around it."[4] Time relativity teaches us that time is not "behind" us and the future is not "in front of" us.

Looking for Then

I have noticed that when I ask my patients about their past, they often look off to their left. Perhaps because we read from left to right, or perhaps because many past memories are stored in the brain's right hemisphere, we tend to set the past "out there behind us or slightly to our left." I have also noticed that when I ask my patients about their future, they tend to look up and to their right as if their future is to their right or slightly overhead. Perhaps because we are taught that Heaven is in the future or because our brain's left hemisphere is where anticipation and planning functions are located, our eyes look off to our right. In both cases, our eyes reveal that we seem bounded by the past and future rather than free to create from them a loving Now.

When I asked my Silver Survivors' group about their pasts or futures, I noticed two things. First, their verbal response reflected an Us orientation and not a Me orientation. They had chosen to make their time relative to the two of them rather than basing it on one or the other of them. I also noticed that when I asked about the future or past, the twenty-five couples always looked directly into each other's eyes as they answered. They had all learned the first step in this miracle-marriage manual—that individual guilt and pride and personal fear and anxiety can be overcome by creating a relative new Now based on the loving couple rather than the striving and time-driven self.

Dr. Wilbur writes, "All guilt is a state of being lost in the past; all anxiety is a state of being lost in the future."[5] When we go beyond the simple cliché of a selfish "living for now" to make a true merging of two selves, we learn to see guilt and fear as signs that we are limited by individual feelings about an absolute time somewhere outside us and behind or ahead of us. Miracle marriages construct their Now together by living intensely together as they relish their shared past and wonder at the present promise of their future.

Loving in the Two-Time Zone

We learn lesson 1 of this miracle-marriage manual when we are able to make Two Time by celebrating our past together rather than focusing on our individual shortcomings of days gone by and by remembering that every Now moment is a source for making meaningful mutual memories. Two Time is also achieved when we think of our Now as challenged by what we can yet achieve together rather than what we must do or might fail to do as individuals in the future. When we feel guilt and fear, we should be alerted that our self has not yet been silenced enough to free us from the profanity of personal time. When one of us feels guilty and anxious, both of us should start thinking more about our loving now and less about our selfish pasts and futures.

When we make a miracle marriage, we move to a new time

zone of shared time rather than personal time. We learn how to find union with God through the spiritual completion and consummation we experience together. Philosopher Meister Eckhart wrote, "There is no greater obstacle to union with God than time." He meant that the personal or profane selfish view of time limits us from our spiritual potential, while shared time is a sacred time that brings everyone health and happiness in the couple-created Now.

Misery Moments That Stop Your Clock

Every one of the Silver Survivor couples has experienced at least one tragic or near-tragic moment in their lives together that taught them to value Two Time over One Time. They call these occurrences "misery moments" when something frightening and terrible seemed to stop their selfish clocks and reset them to a shared Two Time.

"Did you ever hear someone say they're going to 'knock your clock off'?" said one Silver Survivor husband. "When I sat trapped in my car after our crash, that really knocked my own clock off. I saw my wife outside crying and banging on my window. I couldn't tell the difference between her screams and the wailing of the sirens coming. I could smell gasoline. We thought I was going to blow up right in front of her. We had been driving to work like we always did. I was driving and talking on the car phone, and she was sipping coffee and reading the paper. We were totally absorbed in our own separate worlds. And then—wham! We're hit head-on. Rushing along with rush hour to keep to a deadline, I almost ended up out there dead on the highway dividing line. . . . 'God,' I thought then, 'we're going to blow up together before we've had enough time together.' Right then I promised myself to make time to love my wife and she said she would never allow the world to tell us what time it is. It's our time now, and this miserable moment really knocked our clocks off and brought us to our sense of the sacredness of our time together."

I hope this book will save you from having to experience a misery moment like the couple above before you begin to learn to tell Two Time. Time is on your side if you make the time to be at your partner's side. While working with the Silver Survivors,

I wrote a brief summary of some ways you can reset your emotional clock from Me Moments to Shared Seconds:

HOW TO RESET YOUR EMOTIONAL CLOCK TO TWO TIME

- Remember that what your time together means is up to both of you, because time is relative to you and not absolute.
- Remember that even though your time is relative and determined in its nature by your perceptions, it is nonetheless flowing toward the end of your physical existence. Let the arrow of time point you toward enjoying one another as often as possible and making your MIMs, or marital investment minutes, your number-one priority.
- Remember that your feelings of personal guilt and fear are symptoms that you are still in the Me zone and bounded by living in your personal past or for your personal future. Try to put more time into your Two by living, feeling, and appreciating your togetherness at this moment.
- Remember that "Now is the moment of sweet Aloha." Love in the Now by bringing to your mutual Mind the joys of your shared past and the wonderful expectations of your shared future.
- Remember that you are both spirits sharing your human experience and not humans having a spiritual experience. It's a short time here on earth, so enjoy as much of it as you can by validating the experience with and through one another. Remind each other often that the time for earthly loving is quickly passing.

What Time Is It in Paradise?

Some years ago, my wife and I traveled to a remote Tahitian island far off the tourist track. In this paradise, the crystal blue ocean water and warm clear tropical air were exactly the same 82-degree temperature. A gentle breeze barely bent the palm trees and gently rustled their large leaves. There seemed to be no time at all here other than the alternating of sparkling sunlight and velvety starlit nights. Because the profane time of modern society had passed this paradise by, we were among the first group of white faces the lovely people of this island paradise had seen.

As my wife and I walked along the beach, the children ran and danced around us. One little girl ran up beside me and in a giggling voice said, "What does that do?" She pointed at my ever-present wristwatch as the other children clustered around us.

"It tells the time," I answered, handing her my watch for closer examination.

The little girl gently took my watch and pressed it to her ear. "When does it tell it?" she asked. "I only hear ticking."

"You have to look at it," I answered, starting to feel foolish at bringing "my" time to this timeless place.

"Does your blood flow through it so it can tell your time?" she asked. "I saw you look at your time teller and say to your wife that it was time to eat. Does it read your body and tell when it is time to be hungry or time to make love?" The other children giggled and ran off along the beach. "Does it tell you how much time you have to live?" continued the girl quietly and with awe— even fear—in her voice. "How does it tell you your time?"

"Actually, I guess I tell the time by looking at my time teller," I said, beginning to laugh at my own ridiculous explanation. I realized that I could not describe the time I was allowing to guide my entire life, and that I had actually begun to think that my watch *was* my time. Even in paradise, I wasn't making my time or even taking it. I could not be here Now when my time was being kept for me and therefore from me.

"Do you want to keep my time teller?" I asked the now quiet and reflective child. "Oh no," she said suddenly and handed my watch back to me quickly. "I don't want time to tell me anything." She ran off to join the other children as I slowly, shyly, and with a sense of embarrassment and surrender put my watch back on my wrist. My wife reached over and pulled the stem on the side of my watch so that the second hand no longer moved. "Let's tell our own time, OK?" she said.

How My Wife and I Discovered Eternity

When my wife and I faced my near-death from cancer years after our trip to Polynesia, we learned the lessons of sacred time together through our own moments of misery. As I lay with a tube down my throat, gasping at the air around me as if I were drowning, my wife and I had a misery moment that taught us about the meaning of shared sacred time.

There was no night or day in this fearful place called "intensive care." There were machines everywhere with digits telling the time, but there seemed no time to tell. As I lay helplessly waiting for the next medical report, I seemed trapped in a hellish eternity interrupted only by the flurry of nurses and doctors trying to save a life or the ceremonial removal of those who had died. One evening, as my wife and I cried together, a doctor was busying himself with one of the pieces of equipment next to my bed. He was setting the time on one of the machines to measure out intermittent doses of medication to be released every four minutes. "This will burn pretty badly during the time it is on," he said.

"How much time?" asked my wife, still choked by her tears.

"Oh, I could never tell you that," he answered awkwardly as he assumed his practiced doctor-philosopher stance and gazed up and to his right. "We all have to die sometime. All any of us can do is focus on now. I can't even tell you if he'll live through the night."

My wife had become used to the hurried responses of some of the medical staff, and her next comment was quiet and measured. "No, sir," she said without looking up. "I mean how long does he have to be on that machine? I'm asking about the machine's time, not his. How much time on that machine?"

Embarrassed, the doctor responded, "Oh, I'm terribly sorry. I didn't mean to upset you. He needs to be on it for exactly twenty-eight minutes. I'll keep the time for him." He looked at his watch to determine when he should return to turn the machine off, paused a moment as if ready to talk to me, and then turned and left my bed.

"He's right, you know," said my wife, tightening her hand around my own. "All we ever really have is now. Let's not miss this Now no matter how bad it seems. Let's not let this cancer steal our Now." We embraced, we cried, and the Nows of our loving through our moments of misery helped to save my life.

My wife brought pictures of our past together and we reflected on our courtship, our wedding, and the birth of our sons. My wife brought pictures of our home on Maui, where, as I described in Chapter 1, the demigod namesake of that island is said to have snatched the sun to control time. I wrote notes, my wife spoke to me, and we enjoyed the Now of our shared anticipation of a future we would not surrender to cancer cells or cataclysmic forecasts from medical timekeepers and takers. We touched whenever we could and tried to communicate by looking into each other's eyes. We made our Now as free as we could of regrets of our personal pasts and fears of the future. We learned that hope depends on a boundary-free and shared Now that contains little guilt and fear. Hope is not a blind faith in a personal future. Hope is less "mind over matter" than keeping the mind on what really matters—the miracle of marriage.

We learned the ultimate lesson of the first step in this miracle-marriage manual—that it is the relative or shared Now that is eternity. We commonly think of eternity as a very, very long time stretching billions of years into an uncertain future. Eternity seems so long or so incomprehensible that we feel we are not a part of it. My wife and I learned that the eternity of loving is not everlasting time together but acute and constant awareness that time ends and the Now is what matters. Now is a relative moment made more valuable because of the irretrievable nature of our passing time together. My wife and I learned that the Two Time of our Now is true eternity. I hope this book will teach your marriage the same lesson.

A Two-Time Telling Technique

"We've come up with what we think is a great idea to help your readers learn what you mean by the Two-Time love law," said one Silver Survivor. "My wife and I each bought a watch. These watches have two separate faces so we can set two entirely different times. You should see people look at these things. One of the faces is set by what we call the WIM, or world investment minutes. That's the clock time of our day-to-day living. The other face is set for our own marriage's Two Time. We each stop and start the Two-Time clock only when we are spending time with each other. Just looking at two watches at once helps remind us of us. It's really a gimmick, but it helps us focus on us. Each new year we start again, and in just a few weeks we can see how many marital investment minutes we have put in compared with world investment minutes. Today is February 6, 1986, at 7:40 P.M. WIM, or world-investment-minutes time, but it's January 11, 1986, at 11:20 A.M. MIM, or marital-investment-minutes time. Of course, WIM time will always be far ahead of MIM time, because of work and sleep and other obligations, but this Two-Time telling technique helps us keep track of *our* time and not just *the* time."

The Silver Survivor couple above illustrates how difficult it can be to make time for MIMs in our world. Although it is popular to *say* how important family and marriage are, most of us spend comparatively little of our time in these two areas of our lives. My patients seldom complain of having too much time to spend with their families. To make a miracle marriage, we have to learn to put our time where our love is and to make time for two *before* we make time for everything else. All of the next nine steps in the miracle-marriage manual depend on first investing the time necessary to make a miracle.

A miracle marriage does not make time stand still, but it will not stand still for a thievery of its time. If either partner in a miracle marriage is becoming stressed or pressured, feels guilty or anxious, is consumed with work and career, is overinvolved with parental obligations, or is rushing to too many individual recreational pursuits, he or she is falling into the time trap of investing an excess of WIMs and insufficient MIMs.

Coconspirators for a Marital Miracle

I almost died during my recuperation from a bone marrow transplant for treatment of cancer. A virus attacked my lungs, and I was quickly strangling to death. I gasped for air, but my lungs were like cellophane and could barely hold oxygen. Learning not to breathe is not easy. "Let the machine breathe for you," yelled the nurse as I struggled against the restraints on my wrist put there to stop me from tearing the tube from my throat that seemed to be choking me to death.

My wife was at my side throughout the crisis, and I soon noticed that, even though I could not let the machine breathe for me at its own mechanical rhythm, I could feel my wife breathing in and out. She "inspired" me to breathe in Our rhythm, and I matched my breathing to hers instead of struggling to match the mechanical metronome attempting to force me to breathe its way. Our miracle marriage had made a miracle. A few days later, and much to the surprise of the doctors, the tube was removed, and I survived the lethal viral pneumonia—almost always fatal in transplant patients.

Later, when the tube was removed from my chest, my breathing was still difficult. When my wife was allowed to visit, however, my breathing became more regular and easier. I noticed that I breathed much more slowly and deeply when my wife was with me, and that I would automatically begin to breathe in sync with her. Since that experience, I have observed what I call the phenomenon of "marital conspiracy."

Conspire, in its literal sense, means "to breathe together."[6] French scientist-priest Pierre Teilhard de Chardin referred to the power of a "conspiracy of love," and my own experience and clinic observations indicate that spouses in miracle marriages begin to breathe together. They breathe much more slowly and deeply when in each other's presence than when they are alone or with others. I suggest that Two Time influences the synchronized, slower breathing pattern that evolves between longtime lovers—a form of a miracle metronome ticking by the cadence of the couple's own "conspiracy."

The rhythmization of breathing is a basic yoga technique, and some practitioners of this art report a respiratory rate much slower than that of most of us. Observers have noted that, in a meditative state, some yogis breathe once for every ten breaths taken by the average person.[7] In vital living time (based on the number of inspirations and expirations), some yogis actually live at one-tenth the life speed of the rest of us! While the yogi typically practices this breathing alone, the miracle marriage seems able to live at its own unique life rate, and the couple conspire together to make their own time.

I now ask couples working toward a miracle marriage to try this conspiracy assignment themselves. Practice slowing your breathing in synchronization with your spouse, and you will see tangible evidence of the relativity of time. You will be making a marital metronome that yields much more vital time than the relentless ticking of mechanical clocks. You will feel the same comfort and safety I felt when I was dying and my wife gave me "real inspiration" to replace the failing artificial respirator. You will feel connected in time and place so that your Now will be more easily shared. Most of all, instead of having your breath taken away by a hurried, demanding, and selfish world, you will feel fresh air being breathed into you by the power of your shared love.

A MIM Quiz

To help you learn this first love law of Two Time, the quiz that follows will measure your MIMs (marital-investment minutes) and help you discern when you are on Two Time instead of One Time.[8] Each question should be reflected on and discussed with your spouse or with the person with whom you are considering making a miracle love. You may wish to talk about each item, but remember also just to react together beyond words and sit together in quiet mutual reflection, or what I call "couple con-templation." If you will make the time to just "be" together in consideration of these items, you may find—as the Silver Sur-vivors did—that you will not need many words to communicate deeply and profoundly about this and the other quizzes offered throughout this miracle-marriage manual. In each case, I have included an illustrative comment from a Silver Survivor to show how he or she made his or her own marital Two Time:

TWO-TIME TEST: MAKING MIMS

1. Is your first response to a work assignment, an invitation to a party, or the opportunity to go to a concert or sports event to think about your MIMs rather than your own personal work or recreational schedule?

"When someone calls to ask me a favor," said one wife, "my first thought is about what this means for us and our schedule and not just me. I think first if I want us to do it or if I want to spend MIMs on this."

2. *Do you use the word "I" or "we" when accepting an invitation or planning an activity, trip, or project?*

One Silver Survivor husband said, "Ever since we dated and have been married, we both always say 'we' instead of 'me.' Even at work when I talk with colleagues about my life or my interests or what's going on or politics, I tend to say 'we.' I notice that some people tend to say 'I' as in 'I put the money down on a new house' rather than 'we' put the money down."

3. *Does the time you spend away from your spouse seem to be different from the time spent with your spouse?*

"I can't wait to get back together with my spouse, even if all we do is sit at the table quietly and read the paper," said a Silver Survivor wife. "Time with my husband just flies by, and there is never, never enough of it. The drive home from work seems to take forever, and sitting and talking with other people seems to get in the way when I really want to spend time with my husband. When I'm with him, it's 'our' time, but when I'm with other people, I seem to be on 'clock' time."

4. *When your spouse asks you to do something with him or her, is your immediate response to do it in order to find some time to be with your partner instead of feeling that the request represents "just another time pressure"?*

One husband said, "When my wife asks me to go shopping with her, it's an invitation to be with her. The other guys think I am a complete wimp for loving to go shopping with my wife. I hate shopping. No . . . first I hate buying and then I hate shopping, but I love being with her and having time together. Even if it's mall time, at least it's MIM time, too."

5. *Are you and your spouse in the same time zone, feeling like going to bed and getting up at about the same time?*

"We are each other's alarm clock and snooze alarm," said a wife. "We will be sitting in the family room and in the middle of a TV program we are both watching. Then, together, we feel like going to bed. I don't mean necessarily for sex. Even if we don't each feel like it's time to go to bed or to get up, we do it anyway to stay on our Two Time. If we wake together before the alarm goes off in the morning, one of us pushes the snooze alarm button, and we can roll over, go back to sleep, and wake up together again without the alarm. I know couples where one is tired when the other isn't or one is ready to get up when the other wants to sleep, but we have managed to make our own shared sleep chemistry instead of giving in to our selfish ways of time."

6. *Are you and your spouse "seasonally" in tune, feeling energized around the same time of the year and more tired or "laid back" during other seasons? Or is one of you full of energy in the fall while the other feels more energized in the spring?*

"We are fall people. That's our season," said a husband. "It wasn't that way when we got married. I used to be spring and she was winter. She loved to ski and I loved softball. Now we go to college football games, get cider and doughnuts, walk in the fall colors, and love fall together. The other seasons are good too, but fall and to some extent summer are when some of our best MIMs occur."

7. *Do you and your spouse feel sexually "in sync," usually desiring sexual intimacy on the same day or night and at about the same time?*

"I was sure he was faking it," said one wife. "He seemed to always be ready for sex and want sex whenever I did. It was too good to be true. Now we have what we call our 'sex-cadian rhythms.' We go weeks without a lot of desire for sex, and then we go into these sex peaks when we both want it a lot. We don't have sex to make our marriage better. Our marriage makes us want to have better sex."

8. *Are you and your spouse on the same working schedule—feeling like getting things done, cleaning, sorting, and filing at the same time—*

rather than one of you being ready to work while the other has to be coaxed or feels guilty that he or she is not ready to get things done?

"One of the great parts of our marriage is our shared laziness," said one wife. "Early in our marriage, I would feel guilty when he would get going on a project and I preferred to sit on the couch. We each had to work when we didn't want to, give in to the other person's way, and try to get energized rather than just follow our own individual energy pattern. Now we can get energized and lazy together. We go on house attacks when we clean like crazy, and then we sit back and let the work pile up for another attack. Like my husband says, we love work—we can sit and look at it together for hours."

9. *Are you both "owls" or "larks" (both night people or morning people), instead of one of you being an A.M. person and the other a P.M. person?*

"I really think there should be a law against owls marrying larks," said one Silver Survivor. "When I saw the movie *War of the Roses,* where the lawyer says that the only thing he could think of that made a good marriage is that cat people should marry cat people and dog people should marry dog people, I thought that maybe he had something there. But I really think you both have to work to either become A.M.-ers or P.M.-ers together. We just were not that way at the start, and we had to work toward being one way or the other instead of some compromise that made both of us unhappy. We are both A.M.-ers now, and I could never live with a P.M.-er."

10. *Do both of you value punctuality and time to the same extent, instead of one of you always being ready early and waiting for the other who seems "time blind"?*

"We really couldn't care less if we're on time," said the husband. "I used to be ready an hour early and stand outside the bathroom door making repulsive noises to try to get my wife moving. I gave in. I get ready by her schedule. Since I'm so fast, I wait until she says the magic words 'I'm almost ready.' Then I start getting ready. I still beat her, but we're closer to our own Two Time. Instead of hurrying up to wait, now I wait and then hurry. I always hurry anyway, so instead of getting mad at her I use her almost-ready time as my starting time."

The twenty-five Silver Survivor couples averaged a score of 9 on the Two-Time Test, while a control group of twenty-five couples who were separated, going through divorce, or recently had divorced averaged 3.2. To score nearer to 10 on this quiz requires making the constant effort to silence the selfish sense of time in favor of an evolving Us time and to learn a new Our way instead of trying to get your own way. The owl and lark can unite to fly together in a new time that is far beyond compromise.

The challenge of learning this Two Time is great, but the miracle of High Monogamy far transcends the mediocrity of Low Monogamy. If your score on this or any of the quizzes in this manual seems low, remember that I am speaking of a miracle and not mere survival. Miracles are never easy.

Marriage, like time, can be "used" to serve many purposes for the unsilenced self, and many Low Monogamists keep different and individual schedules. People in Low Monogamy often find a degree of self-fulfillment and security in their sense of time, but High Monogamy is a different and far more difficult love challenge. A low score on this and the following quizzes in this miracle-marriage manual is an indication not that you have a "bad" marriage but that there is much more you can do if you choose to move from Low to High Monogamy and go for the miracle of Us.

The Couple's Cop-out: The Quality-Time Mistake

Perhaps the greatest danger to lasting marriage is the "quality-time-versus-quantity-time" dimension of the Me Myth. "We try to spend some quality time together every weekend and take at least two trips together a year for even more quality time," said one psychiatrist husband. "Do you also plan some inferior time together?" I asked. "Or do you only have time for quality time and nothing else."

I was not joking. Popular psychology has provided the perfect couple cop-out by suggesting that "it is not the quantity of time you spend together that counts but the *quality* of the time." It is easier to make the most of the time you put in than to make the constant effort to put in more and more time in your marriage. Quantity of time is as important as quality time, and a miracle marriage depends on total MIMs as much as it does "good" MIMs spent doing "the right thing" or meeting perceived marital obligations.

As you learn together about Two Time, remember that you have been well trained in the following seven time lessons of the Me Myth of Low Monogamy. I have followed each lesson with the contrasting lesson of the time of a miracle marriage:

Me Myth: Communicate your own ideas and represent your self assertively to demand "time for yourself."
Miracle-marriage lesson: Your first effort should be to save as much time as possible for your marriage.

Me Myth: Be yourself and invest your own time wisely.
Miracle-marriage lesson: Be together and make time to live life together wisely.

Me Myth: Put in quality time because no one ever has a sufficient quantity of time to put into their marriage.
Miracle-marriage lesson: Quantity of time is the first prerequisite for making the time we need for loving time.

Me Myth: Guard your own time; do not let anyone steal it from you.
Miracle-marriage lesson: Give your time freely to your marriage.

Me Myth: Your time is your own to do with as you please.
Miracle-marriage lesson: Time is ours to use in loving and joyful living together.

Me Myth: It is a personal sacrifice to share your time.
Miracle-marriage lesson: Love is sacrificed when we spend most of our time on ourselves.

Me Myth: Don't waste *your* time.
Miracle-marriage lesson: All time is our time, and time spent loving is never wasted time.

My data indicates that couples who embrace the quality-time concept are much more prone to divorce and experience marital distress than those couples who put in a lot of distressed time together. In fact, couples with too much time on their own and too much of what they call quality time together reveal that there must be a great deal of low-quality time they are attempting to counterbalance and a lot of their time they have chosen to spend elsewhere. You can't manage time unless you can manage your marriage.

Familiarity or a great deal of time together does not have to breed contempt unless the self is so assertive that it refuses to be silenced for the good of an Us. When the ego will not give in, time together can become an annoying obligation or result in a conflict of lifestyles that blocks self-fulfillment. Couples who brag that they almost never see each other or live a country apart seldom make a miracle marriage. They may succeed at their career but fail at love, because they learn only how to make "some time" for two rather than to make Two Time. Couples who spend hours and hours together dealing with problems, suffering through crises and "misery moments" as a unit, and trying to cope with life's challenges as a team are the couples who transcend Low Monogamy and achieve a miracle marriage.

This wife and mother of two severely retarded children illustrates the impact of quantity time spent in a marriage. Her commitment also raises the possibility that the real quality time may be the moments of sharing an ordeal rather than sharing a night out on the town:

"It was probably because of the problems of our two daughters that we have spent so much time together in our marriage. You can't be thinking about 'quality' time when you are busy trying to save two lives together. We did not divide our time into quality versus quantity. We made our own time to help our daughters and still help our marriage. We don't think that absence makes the heart grow fonder. We think that just being near each other a lot, even though we were struggling much of that time, is what made our marriage grow stronger."

Time Talk and the Sound of the Silenced Self

Listen to how your marriage speaks of time. Do you hear, "I'm overwhelmed, I've got to get this done, I've got to do everything, I need some time alone, I need time out, I'm busy, I'm short of time," and other phrases that reveal that the self has not been sufficiently silenced to learn Two Time?

Miracle marriages sound like this: "We're really tired. We've really been through the wringer. We've got to get a rest. We've been very busy." The following statement from a Silver Survivor indicates Two-Time talk.

"You made us practice and practice that Two-Time-talk stuff, but now we see what you mean," said one Silver Survivor. "Even if you try to think a certain way, you also have to learn to talk that way. It doesn't automatically happen."

Popular psychology's tendency to overemphasize self-fulfillment is an obstacle to learning to talk as two in a marriage. The last decades have seen the flourishing of "assertiveness training" and the language of "I."[9] More recent researchers and writers warn of the social tension and pain caused by the rush to self-assertion and fulfillment.[10]

The Lonely Self

Narcissism is primarily a disorder of time perception. Like Kohlberg's first stage of premoral reasoning discussed in Chapter 4, it is spending most of one's thinking time on thoughts of the self rather than in caring for someone else. Narcissism typically masks self-hatred rather than self-love, and the result is a squandering of sacred shared time in favor of the profane pursuit of self-gratification. When we have the feeling that we are taking up the narcissist's time, it has the effect of driving us away from, rather than toward, him or her.[11] Try as he or she might to talk a good game of "marriage first," the narcissist is either unable or unwilling to suffer the ordeal of the silencing of the ego. "My side of the bed, my car, my stuff, my space, my feelings, my life, and my happiness" and expressions of self-territory protection are a typical emphasis of the narcissistic spouse.

Narcissists feel "two-timed" when someone requires them to share rather than take and to sacrifice rather than be indulged. I have often heard self-talk in divorce courts, and you read of such statements in the countercustody battle I described in Chapter 2. "I need time to grow as an individual" or "She wanted too much of my time" are sample comments in such conflict.

Narcissism is based on a "my turn, my time first" orientation.

No marriage can carry the burden of two selfish egos or even one narcissistic ego, because the time commitment demanded by the always needy and insecure solitary ego is overwhelming, tiring, and stifling. Narcissism consumes rather than helps to consummate a marriage. Spouses become objects rather than partners, obligations rather than opportunities, and the lonely language of "my time" is the most obvious revealing characteristic of the narcissist. For the narcissist, self-worth is self-accomplishment, not shared loving.

Unfortunately, almost all of our current psychology rests on the model of the self in isolation and sees health as synonymous with the independent ego. "I am a self to myself, but an object to others. To others I am a thing, a 'what,' and others are objects to me," says leading British Freudian psychoanalyst Malcolm Pines.[12] Therapists still talk and teach about how to have "good object relations" as a means to loving, but in High Monogamy the object is to learn how to silence the self in order to relate.

Another necessary step toward making a miracle marriage is to overcome narcissism and the constant encouragement our world gives to it. In describing psychology's failure to help us learn how to stay in love, author Allan Bloom points out, "The only mistake was to encourage the belief that by . . . going down the path of the isolated self, people will be less lonely."[13] The rediscovery of the Great Marriage Myth depends on going beyond what psychologist Abraham Maslow called "self-actualization" to "Us-actualization."[14] We must begin with ourselves, but we must not end with ourselves. Truth and time begin with two.

HOME LOVE ASSIGNMENTS

1. Make the decision to make your marriage first above all else. Make this commitment tangible by writing it down together and placing your announcement in a place where both of you can easily see it. Talk, reflect, and contemplate together about the simple Two-Time statement "Love takes time, Love makes time, and Now is the Time for Our love." Think together about the fact that there will be no lasting love without immense time investment in that loving. With-

out this step of commitment to making your marriage your priority above all else, little progress can be made toward lasting love.

2. Put in the MIMs, or marital-investment minutes. Do it in order to want to do it more and more, instead of waiting to want to do it. Feelings *follow* behaviors, so you will *feel* like putting more time into your marriage *after* you actually *do* it. Start by spending fifteen additional MIMs a week just being together. Extensive talking and problem solving isn't necessary during this time. Just *be* together an additional fifteen minutes over the whole week and you will have added sixty MIMs per month of miracle-marriage-making time.

3. Carry something to work, to school, shopping, or just around the house that symbolizes a MIM reminder—something that reminds you of your marriage. One Silver Survivor wife wears what she calls her "wedding arrow." She said, "I have a wedding ring, but we've learned that time is moving on, so an arrow reminds me of how important our time together is." I ask some of my couples to cut out a small picture of their spouse and paste it over the face of their watch. It may be frustrating at first when you are trying to live by local or WIM time, but seeing your spouse every time you try to "tell" time brings Two Time to your attention.

4. Spend some "junk time" together. To override the quality-time myth, spend time together cleaning closets, waxing floors, or washing the car. Anybody can enjoy quality time, but the challenge of miracle marriages is to flourish even through the junk times.

5. Each partner should write a brief description of the marriage as you would like it to be five years from today. Be as unrealistic as you wish, but write down and then read each other's view of how your marital future will be and what memories from the past of your marriage you would like to take with you. Do your descriptions seem more like challenges, dreams, or warnings? Are there implied regrets? Remember that the marital Now of eternal love I described in this chapter is free of individual guilt and fear and full of mutual pride and hope. Are you putting in enough MIMs to make meaningful Nows together that contain the best of your memories and the promise of your dreams? Do the

dreams have to wait five calendar years, or can your Two Time make the time to make the miracle of a dream marriage come true much sooner?

The next step in the miracle-marriage manual is to learn how to put the physics principle of uncertainty to work for your relationship. If you have implemented some of this chapter's suggestions on Two Time, you have an eternity of Nows for all of the steps to follow.

6

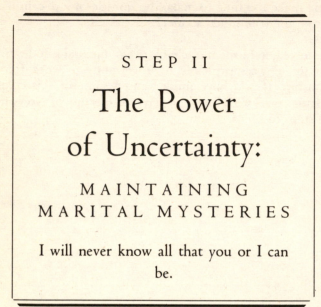

STEP II

The Power
of Uncertainty:

MAINTAINING
MARITAL MYSTERIES

I will never know all that you or I can
be.

*Two hundred million Americans want to leave some
things a mystery, and right at the top of those things
we don't want to know is why a man falls in love
with a woman and vice versa.*

—Senator William Proxmire
Response to a request for funds
to study the nature of love

LOVE LAW TWO: THE CONFIDENT UNCERTAINTY LAW

Just as light is either a particle or a wave depending on how we look at it, all spouses are both individual person and energy in process. There can be no certainty about our self, our marriage, or our spouse, because in looking at one part of our lover or our loving we are not looking at another part. Neither spouse can know the other completely, because as soon as we think we know something about our beloved as a person, we automatically know less about who *we* are. Conversely, the more we know about ourselves, the less we know about our beloved. The uncertainty principle devised by physicist Werner Heisenberg teaches that it is impossible to know simultaneously the position and the momentum of an electron because as soon as we measure its position, we cannot know with any certainty whatsoever anything about its speed. A miracle marriage is aware of this same uncertainty in its process of lasting loving, and it fosters, encourages, and celebrates this intimate indeterminism as the origin of surprise, chance, and free choice. Spontaneity is the spice of lasting love.

The Necessary Uncertainty of Miracles

"Our marriage counselor told us that we had to really get to know each other," said one wife. "She said we should always ask 'why' someone did something so we could get to know everything there was to know about them as a person and feel more secure. I think I am now reasonably certain about who my husband is. In fact, I think I know him so completely that I know him better than he knows himself and even better than I know myself. In fact, I've gotten to know him so well that I'm divorcing him as soon as I can."

This woman's statement typifies another assumption of Low Monogamy or marriage based on the Me Myth: We have been taught by popular psychology that when we finally get to know our self well, we are then free to direct that self's attention to the complete knowing of another person's self. The Me Myth says that once I am certain about where I am going, I can then try to be certain about who is going with me. The Great Marriage Myth says that lovers are forever uncertain about their selves and the self of the partner; we accept the challenge to work at getting a little *closer* to knowing where our "self" is going and who our traveling companion is. The miracle marriage is never sure of the "selves" within but it has complete confidence that the relationship grows through the never-ending process of learning about the evolving Us.

The more accepting and tolerant of uncertainty a scientist is, the more he or she continues to learn about the mysteries of the quantum world. The history of science illustrates that at just the moment we think we have all the answers, new questions arise. Einstein showed that just when we thought we were sure about the absolute nature of time and space, there were new and more challenging ways to understand that time was relative and space curves back upon itself to actually enfold time as its fourth dimension. Just when we thought science could measure almost anything with precision, Professor Werner Heisenberg's uncertainty principle, proposed in 1927, showed that the more accurate we think we are in our measurement of one thing, the less accurate we are in measuring another.

Uncertain People and Confident Couples

To better understand the relevance of Heisenberg's uncertainty principle to everyday living, consider the simple act of measuring the air pressure in your car's tire. The very act of measurement allows some air to escape as you focus your attention on the number on the tire gauge. You may think you are certain about the pounds of pressure in your tire, but you were wrong the moment you did your measurement. Because you wanted to know more and because your self thinks it now had some accurate data, the tire has been changed. Your certainty about the air pressure is less, even though you think you know what the air pressure is. One of my students explained uncertainty of measurement when she said, "By trying to be sure how something is, you automatically make what you were measuring a 'was.' The world is set up to stay a secret." There is a limitation to the accuracy of measurements built into nature, and lasting love is based on accepting and enjoying this guaranteed uncertainty.

A part of the miracle of our evolving world and our evolving love is the experience of constant uncertainty. Nobel Prize winning chemist Ilya Prigogine wrote, "The world is richer than it is possible to express in any single language [one type of knowledge or measurement]. Music is not exhausted by its successive stylisations from Bach to Schoenberg. Similarly, we cannot condense into a single description the various aspects of our experience."[1] The second step in this miracle-making manual is for both partners to be as humble in their uncertainty of one another as they are supremely confident that their marriage thrives because of the natural energy of its constant change.

Absolutely Determined to Fail

The opposite of High Monogamy's confident uncertainty is Low Monogamy's "absolute" marriage. Partners in an absolute marriage often set a goal to get rid of as much chance or uncertainty as possible. They seek to understand everything in terms of clear cause and effect: who does what why and to whom, or who causes whom to be whom and how they are. If something goes wrong in the absolute marriage, then somebody must have messed things up. Either the husband, the wife, or the marriage itself went "wrong." If something goes wrong in the confidently uncertain marriage, the couple is challenged by the opportunity to learn more about the changing relationship and never doubts the viability of the marriage.

Low Monogamists try to follow the way of the Me Myth by trying to be more sure of themselves. As a result, they attempt to impose certainty on and expect certainty from their relationship. Partners in absolute marriages often try to become marital mechanics, attempting to determine for sure who has broken down and why. They trust their individual one-sided assessments and measurements of problems. They attempt to repair the broken partner if possible, or assume or assign blame as quickly as possible. If all else fails, divorce court may be sought as the ultimate authority to determine fault, to assign appropriate punitive damages, or to declare the marriage certainly beyond repair.

When couples come to my clinic in conflict, their certainty fuels the fires of their passionate battles (not compassionate mutual suffering). Both spouses say they were "certain" their view was correct or that they knew beyond doubt who and what was wrong with the marriage. But when the Silver Survivors were interviewed, they were seldom certain of the one way to work things out and were not convinced that their own assessment had validity. "I can just tell you how I felt it," said one Silver Survivor husband. "Neither of us can be sure what went wrong, because we're both part of this thing. It's impossible to measure something when you're a part of it. You can only measure when you're outside, and neither of us would ever let that happen."

Marital Mechanics or Marriage Gardeners?

Many marriage therapists are marital mechanics who seek to repair a part of the marriage. The best example of the marital mechanic is the so-called sex therapist who spends hundreds of a couple's valuable MIMs teaching efficient touching techniques and tune-ups. These sexperts offer maintenance of Low Monogamy and fail to realize that there is a High Monogamy of intimacy that is far more spiritual than sexual. Other marriage therapists are communication specialists (what one of my patients called "say-perts") who seek to make each individual partner a better talker or a better listener. They fail to realize that most of marriage's communication goes far beyond words. Marital problems are products of the natural uncertainty of all of life and living. No marital mechanical expert can show us how to touch or talk our way out of the necessary and evolutional suffering through life's unpredictability and our constant personal and loving transformations.

The marital gardener is someone who realizes how mysterious, holistic, dynamic, unpredictable, and unknown a lasting loving relationship is. The gardener knows that there are many domains of life, and not just the one we happen to be looking at at a particular time. Marriage gardeners appreciate the fact that you can plant a seed, but its growth is never the result of one warm rain. All gardening is uncertain. If it weren't, we would never have to tend to our gardens. Marriage is as uncertain and beautiful as the blooming garden. It requires loving tending rather than the mere sowing of seeds in expectation of certain results.

When weeding or marital adjustment *is* necessary, the marital gardener begins with the assumption that the garden will survive and that weeds are—as native Hawaiian Pete, who tends our garden in Maui, says—only flowers naturally growing in the wrong place. Solving or getting rid of problems that can choke out love's bloom does not have to be associated with blaming the weeds or accusing a spouse of "causing" them to grow. Weeds are as much a part of gardens as flowers, and they are brought on by the same warm rain and sun that brings forth the blossoms and the fruit. Deciding together how our marriage will grow and what naturally occurring parts and problems of that marriage we will keep and which ones we need to prune away together is the way the miracle-marriage garden is kept alive and beautiful.

Why Miracles Happen

Saint Augustine, in *De Libero Arbitrio,* said that human freedom involves two ingredients: chance and choice. These are also necessary elements of the making of a miracle, because without locally or here-and-now uncaused, unpredictable, spontaneous occurrences, miracles could not happen. Miracles are surprising alchemical reactions made by revering the constant mysteries and uncertainties of life.[2]

During my cancer, the more certain my death seemed, the more I felt the possibility of a miracle. The more certain the doctors tried to be about my dying, the less uncertain everything about life and living seemed to be. One of my fellow patients said, "I'm only sure of one thing. You can't be sure of anything. Come to think of it, I'm not even sure of that." Everyone knows that miracles happen, but if life were certain, there would be no need for miracles. Nothing would ever surprise us and remarkable and miraculously startling events would not occur. Because of nature's built-in unpredictability, mystery, chance, and choices, miracles are possible. The more we think we know, the more we do not yet know.

Professor Heisenberg often used the example of the wooden weather house, which reacts to humidity and air pressure. Sometimes the old wooden man comes out and the old woman stays in, and certain weather changes are predicted on the basis of this pattern. Other times, the old woman comes out and the old man cannot be seen, and different weather is forecast. The old man and old woman take turns coming into view, and when one of them is visible and "measuring" the weather, the other is not known and its way of measurement is not known.[3] Miracle loving is the awareness and toleration of uncertain rhythmic changes in the relationship as well as an alternating focus on husband and wife. Heisenberg's wooden weather house does not work if the old man or the old woman stays out all the time. We can be much more certain about which person we are seeing then, and the climate changes associated with that figure, but we will never know about nature's constant changes and uncertainties associated with the less-known complementary figure awaiting his or her turn to appear and help us learn. We can't explore the unknown until we free ourselves of the tyranny of the known.

Measuring Your Uncertainty Quotient

What follows is an exercise to help you progress through the second step in our miracle-marriage manual. It is a test of your marriage's UQ, or Uncertainty Quotient. I have included a Silver Survivor's statement following each item so that you can use this quiz to be sure that you are never sure of your marriage, your self, or your partner.

UNCERTAINTY-QUOTIENT QUIZ

1. Have you learned something entirely new about your spouse in the last several weeks, instead of feeling that you already know all there is to know about him or her?

"The more I think I have her figured out, the more I discover what I don't know about her," said one husband. "I saw her playing Nintendo last night! My wife—the surgeon, the opera lover, the person who has never watched a situation comedy or bought anything that wasn't practical and useful—went out and bought herself a video game and started playing it. I was sure she did it to develop her hand-and-eye coordination for doing surgery. Wrong again!

When I asked her why, she said she spends her day putting people back together so she wanted to explore the complementary side of herself and start blowing things up. Video games were her safe way to do it. I learned never to be so sure of her again."

2. *Have you tried lately to learn something new about yourself and share that lesson with your spouse, instead of trying to stay the same person he or she married?*

"My husband was stunned when he saw me playing video war games," said the physician described by the husband above. "We had a nice long talk. I tried to tell him how much I liked to do stupid things once in a while and was not the cool, calm, collected, careful person he thought I was. Oh, I was that, too, but I'm changing and I have this other side that I've learned about me. I've probably come to see my other side because I live with him, and he helped bring it out. I'm probably the second-best surgeon at our hospital, but I'm beyond a doubt the best fighter pilot on the medical staff. That's what makes our marriage great. I keep learning more about him and me in it. I hate surprises in surgery, but I love them in our marriage."

3. *Have you been surprised by your spouse's reaction to you recently or do you feel that your husband or wife always responds the same way?*

"Last week, I hugged my wife like I always do," said one husband. "Then all of a sudden, she grabs me, throws me against the wall, and lays this big long kiss on me. She always used to give me a little mini-hug back when I hugged her. She knows I'm a hugging type, but all of a sudden she reacts with this hug attack. Sometimes I can't be sure how she'll react to me."

4. *Have you intentionally tried to surprise your spouse pleasantly with some new feeling, fantasy, thought, viewpoint, or reaction to him or her, instead of falling into the same reaction pattern?*

"I was waiting for him this time," said the wife of the husband above. "For years he hugged me, and I sort of hugged him back a little. He would never admit it, but I think down in his little sexist heart he thought men are the sexual aggressors. I really got him this time. As soon as he thinks he's certain how I'm going to react to him, he'd better be ready for something new. I'm going to send him into spouse sex shock!"

5. *Do you feel that you have space to grow, change, and develop in your marriage or are you trapped in roles assigned by society or your own family's traditional patterns?*

"That's how we keep us alive," said the same wife who had planned the surprise "hug attack" on her husband. "We will not let ourselves become one way or see things always the same way. We both are alert to how complacent and patterned we're getting, and even though we need some predictability to feel restful and peaceful for a while, it is also very seductive and all too easy to get too comfortable and stop growing. We both feel that we have no limits, completely free choice, and the opportunity to take chances in our marriage. If you can't take chances there, where can you take them?"

6. *Does your marriage constantly change the "rules" about who does what chores and who has what marital tasks or are you stuck in an earlier established pattern of who does what when in "gender-based" marital roles?*

"I was cutting the grass the other day," said one husband. "My neighbor came out and asked if my wife was sick. I told him she was fine, and he said that he thought my wife took care of the outside of the house. I guess he thought you have to be a marital specialist assigned to lifelong duty in a specific role. We never do that. Nobody has to do any one thing, including budgeting, paying bills, and cleaning. We are constantly 'growing' our marriage, and we do not let marriage institutionalize us."

7. *Is your marital relationship a source of challenge in your life or another place of hassle and stress in daily living?*

"This guy next to me at work says the same thing every night near 5 P.M.," said one wife. "He always says that it's time to go home to the old ball and chain. I'm not insulted. I feel sorry for him, because I don't think he's kidding. When the phone rings at work and it's his wife, he has this sigh and a 'Oh . . . now what?' reaction. When my husband calls, I'm happy, and I can't wait to get home to him."

8. *Have you and your spouse learned something new together in the last few months, such as beginning a new hobby or recreational activity together, discussing a controversial issue and coming up with some new ideas instead of thinking in the same old ways about controversial social issues?*

"When we were first married, my husband went to play golf, and I went to play tennis," said one wife. "Then we saw that the better we got at these things, the further apart we were getting. I don't think you can be a class-A tennis player or a near-pro golfer and still have a miracle marriage unless you also are learning something with your spouse that you put the same amount of energy into. We needed to learn something together. You told us to pick something we both hate so neither one of us would have a head start or more involvement in it. We picked bowling. Neither one of us had ever bowled or wanted to bowl. We didn't even like the name they give the place you do it—an alley. Now we don't bowl at all anymore, but we spent over a year of MIMs learning how to bowl together, and that was the whole point. We were learning together instead of separately. Now, we're taking up bridge. We both hate that too, so it should be perfect."

9. *Are you and your spouse* unsupportive *of one another in that you both feel free to criticize and be criticized and to argue your view strongly whether or not your partner agrees? Or do you keep your opinions to yourself for the sake of peace at any price or because you feel that one or both of you need constant support and cannot tolerate the uncertainty of conflict and change in the relationship?*

"My wife is definitely not supportive," said one husband. "When I come home and complain about my boss, she listens, thinks about it, and then either says she agrees or, like the other night, she says she thinks I might be a jerk this time. She doesn't support me in every situation. She says she supports the marriage, not just me or her. Last night I told her my boss said that I'm too opinionated and judgmental and should moderate myself a little bit. I told her I was ticked off about what he said. She thought a few minutes and then said, 'I think he may be right this time. Just like me, you can be a real pain in the ass sometimes. So chill out, Mr. Pushy. It's better for your health and our health anyway.' She was right, of course. You really need an unsupportive spouse if by support you mean 'my husband, right or wrong.' Real support is supporting your spouse when you think he is right and telling him when you think he's all wet."

10. Do both you and your spouse get your turn to be the focus of things instead of one person being the prime focus? Do each of you get your chance to "come out" of Heisenberg's weather house?

"Early in our marriage, I gave in, gave up, and tried to match my opinions to his," said one wife. "He seemed to be in charge of the marital policy, our opinions, and the state of our union. Now we argue like crazy about a lot of things like sexism, male and female differences, and any and all world issues. We each have our turn to say our piece, reflect, and fight. We're not fighting each other. We're fighting to keep the marriage alive and new."

The Silver Survivors averaged a UQ, or Uncertainty Quotient, of 9.2, whereas a control group of marriages in the phase of separation, divorce, and immediately postdivorce averaged 3.1. The closer your own UQ is to 10, the more in keeping your marriage is with the lasting love law of uncertainty and marital gardening rather than mechanical marital determinism.

The remainder of this chapter describes some of the Confident Uncertainties that led to productive arguments and discussions of uncertainty by the couples in my clinic. The debate over gender differences makes an excellent source of uncertainty challenges because both partners usually have strong opinions in such areas as male dominance, female emotionality, and which gender is more sensitive. After reading about the other sure confusions that follow, reflect together about them to ensure that your marriage is more uncertain than ever!

A Death Benefit? Chronobiological Certainty

"Women live on the average seven years longer than men," said one husband. "See what an advantage they have?"

Throughout the world, it is a fact that men die approximately seven years sooner than women.[4] It would seem a certain female advantage to live longer, and many couples joke about what one wife called "built-in male obsolescence." Even the "advantage" of a longer life of the female spouse, however, is not certain in its implications for a couple and makes for a good practice point for developing your marital uncertainty. I call this the "chronobiological certainty" factor.

Because of lifestyle differences and a built-in male genetic disadvantage, wives are much more likely to become the primary care givers to their sickly male spouses than vice versa. The well spouse is almost always the wife. This gender difference seems to be decreasing in correlation with female achievement of more equal opportunity—opportunity, that is, to kill themselves as quickly as men by being more cynical, competitive, and hostile in the workplace.

Since men die younger, and financial discrimination continues against women with regard to retirement and health care benefits, women are much more likely to have woefully inadequate retirement incomes. Women are more than twice as likely to spend their older years alone living at the near-poverty level or being placed involuntarily in nursing homes. In consideration of these facts, spend some time in your own marriage talking about and contemplating together the "death difference" in couples. Is the wife certainly luckier to live longer, or will she have to live out her years in harsh and lonely circumstances? Consider together how this issue may impact on your relationship as one of the certain uncertainties of life. The process of sharing verbally or contemplatively will strengthen your marriage by helping you both learn more about a part of loving that we often prefer to ignore: how that loving will make the necessary transitions in form and circumstance in our last years together on earth.

Part of your marital miracle may not be made with both of you living in this physical world, so discuss this Confident Uncertainty soon. The Great Marriage Myth teaches that love transcends physical death and lasts forever through the spiritual merging of two souls. But what about the physical aspects of one partner leaving the earth sooner than the other? How does your marriage deal with the uncertainties of this certainty?

The CWMMC View of Loving:
Sociobiological Certainty

Another assumed certainty of male-female relationships is that women have more invested in protecting their marriage than men have.[5] Since most psychological theories have been proposed by CWMMC mental-health experts (Caucasian white male middle-class psychologists), their particular view of loving has become the "therapeutic certainty" of coupling on the basis of sociobiological reasoning. As one research scientist sarcastically commented about this white male dominance of psychological and relationship theories, "Even the rats we study are white."

The sociobiological certainty view of the nature of female and male investment in marriage goes something like this: Men have millions of sperm, and women have only a few eggs. Women carry the children in their bodies, so they can give birth to only a few children in their lifetime, whereas men can have literally hundreds of children by depositing their sperm in many carriers. Men's genitalia are on the outside, so they are more easily accessible to stimulation and available for immediate and easy use. Because women can have fewer offspring, they must invest more in the partnership in which these children are born and must find a strong and skilled hunter or good provider male to support and protect them.

Sociobiological certainty suggests that the "sensitive" man is a new cultural invention. Millions of years ago, when the bear was outside the cave, women wanted a man who was a powerful protector of her investment, *not* a man who would, in the words of scientist Ken Wilbur, "share his feelings, be really sensitive, and cry, and get eaten by the bear."[6] In the psychotherapeutic and sociobiologically based view, marriage becomes a child-protection agency owned and operated on behalf of the insecure female defending her limited opportunity at parenthood. Men can have many offspring and therefore do not have to invest as much in their marriage. It seems "certain" then, that the factors of millions of sperm versus one egg, external versus internal genitalia, and females carrying the children within their bodies have a profound influence on sex roles. According to this certainty, husbands cannot have the same marital commitment as their wives.

But is this view so certainly true? Another way of looking at this same issue of marital investment is that it is men who should be more concerned for their marriage because, for them, parenthood is mere speculation. Because they know that their external genitalia lead them toward sexual adventure and to having multiple partners, men have only trust as a basis for fatherhood. For women, parenthood is biological birthing fact. To be certain that a child is a man's own biological child, the husband must be committed to the marriage from the start to keep track of what he assumes to be his own successful and exclusive impregnation, and to protect and keep an eye on his investment.[7]

A provocative new theory suggests that males evolved as extensions of their own brawling sperm competing for one rare egg.[8] Evolutional biologist Robert Travis writes, "In one sense all male-male competition is just so much sperm competition."[9] Applied to marriage, this theory implies that husbands are struggling to represent their sperm while wives are striving to protect their eggs.

Even if these sociobiological theories are valid, is biology destiny? In the Low Monogamy of the Me Myth, the psychologically accepted sociobiological certainties seem strong. But we are more than sex-cell representatives. We have a mind, a soul, and a spirit too, so we can transcend our biological destiny. As actress Katharine Hepburn said in the movie *The African Queen,* "Nature is what we are put in this world to rise above." The High Monogamy of the Great Marriage Myth offers the hope that the sperm-war and egg-defense scenarios described here are more challenges to rise above our natural tendencies than certainties.

Reflect and meditate on just how "certain" the origins of the "macho versus mother" investment issue in your relationship is and what its origins may be. If you have a lasting love, you will see that marital investment changes by the chance, choice, and challenge of uncertainty. It does not remain stuck with certain evolutional preassigned gender insecurities, because our mind and spirit tell our Selfish Old Brain that we do not have to accept our biology as our destiny.

Is It Depressing to Be a Wife?
Psychobiological Certainty

Another "certain" view of marriage that is also embraced by the CWMMC psychologist has been that wives seem to be depressed much more frequently than husbands. It is a fact that cross-culturally women are clinically diagnosed as suffering from what psychiatrists call "unipolar affective disorder" or depression more than twice as often as men (of course, the diagnosis is most often made by the CWMMC therapists).[10] Data indicate, then, that women are depression-prone.

But is feminine depression a psychobiological certainty? Recent evidence suggests another possibility.[11] All of us get depressed from time to time. Perhaps the *way* we *react* to depression or are allowed by our culture to show sadness determines how we act out our depression. Perhaps we live in a society that is so male-centered that we have decided that the healthiest response to sadness is the male response: keep your chin up, your mouth closed, and your tears to yourself. Women are neurologically wired (because of the lower dose of testosterone at about six weeks of age in the uterus I mentioned earlier) to read their feelings better and are better tuned to and able to express their emotional states.[12] Perhaps they are simply expressing depression as they are better prepared to do by sharing it openly. For this, they are labeled dysfunctional and are sent to CWMMC therapists.

Men, on the other hand, have brains wired by a prenatal testosterone soaking of their neurons.[13] Their brains are made more for solving sadness than sharing it, which may explain why so many women complain that they "just want to be heard" and so many men complain that they "don't know what to *do*" when their lover cries. Since the male brain does not promote sharing sadness, this may cause men to pay insufficient attention to their own sadness until it becomes severely debilitating.

One wife described the gender side of sadness this way: "Men and women both get very, very sad sometimes. But women go for help if their sadness interferes with their loving. Men get sent or are forced to go for help if their sadness interferes with their working. Women try to talk their way out of the blues, and men try to work their way out. We all should learn to love our way out of our sadness together using both the male and female way. We should learn to talk together and solve together." One strength of the miracle marriage that you will read about in Chapter 9, where I discuss the principle of complementarity in loving, is that expressing and solving sadness can be accomplished when both partners transcend their "natures"—making a more adaptive totality that contains both the Adam and Eve brain styles of dealing with sadness.

Another factor that makes the depression difference between the genders even more "uncertain" is the fact that depressed people generally have a relatively accurate and realistic view of the world in general. Current data indicates that pessimism and depression go hand in hand, but that the pessimist is typically accurate in his or her view of their world.[14] Optimism is based on healthy denial and being able to look at the world through at least rose-tinted if not colored glasses. Women are more likely to ruminate about their problems and to be pessimistic.[15] Men are more likely to want to "get on with it" and deny their problems. Again, a miracle marriage builds a strong bridge between these orientations and uses them both for dealing with the uncertainties of life.

One of the clearest predictors that depression is lifting is when depressed people become more optimistic, by beginning to see things *more* unrealistically or begin to believe that others view them much more favorably than they really do.[16] Thus, if men are supposed to be the realists, why aren't *they* the ones who are more depressed while their more "unrealistic" feminine counterparts are more ignorantly gleeful? One wife said, "Women take their sadness out on themselves. Men take their sadness out on the world." The whole issue of depression and male-female relationships is not as certain as we may think.

Consider the issue of sadness and depression in your own relationship—it is certain to occur, but it is uncertain when, on whom, and how it has its effect. Reflect together about whether more serious depression is gender-related or perhaps due to styles of expression by one partner or the other or the nature of your marital interaction itself. These more abstract depression deliberations are best held when both partners are not too de-pressed. If one or both of you are very, very sad, it is best to move beyond the abstract to the concrete, and I will show you how to deal with the sadness of loving in Chapter 8.

Men Work and Women Keep House: Bioeconomic Certainty

Despite the sexual revolution and feminist movement, there con-tinues to be covert cultural "certainty" that men are more nat-urally the hunters or workers and women more naturally the gatherers or housekeepers. Although millions of women are working outside the home these days, there remains a bioecon-omic certainty that *by nature* men would do the hunting and work outside the home, and women would protect the hearth.[17] In studies of more than 800 primitive societies, there has never been an exception to this pattern. Women joining "the hunt" for a paycheck is seen as mere socioeconomic aberration and necessary adjustment to modern times and economic pressures, which draw the natural gatherer out from her cave against her natural destiny.

Again, is this bioeconomic certainty—however modified it might be in modern society—really so certain? Perhaps the issue is not the male's natural hunting capacity but rather the fact that men are much more expendable than women. If ten men go out to hunt and all but one become the prey, there is little effect on the number of children that can still be born to the women in the village. If only one of ten women came back from a hunt, however, the survival and propagation of the group would be severely compromised. In the interest of keeping human society alive, it seems clear that if someone has to "go," it is better to let the men become the hunted. It is the genes' "need" to keep on going that sends the men out to hunt, not some natural or innate hunting skill.

Spend some time reflecting together about the issue of who goes out to work and who stays home. Even if you both work, theorize about various other hunter-gatherer patterns that you think would be interesting and why each of you fills the roles you fill in your marriage. If your marriage has fallen too quickly into a hunter-gatherer mentality, remember that chance, choice, and challenge are much more important to a creative, miracle-making marriage than compliance with a bioeconomic certainty.

Why Are Men in Charge?
Biodominance Certainty

In almost every known society, men continue to hold the most revered and powerful positions.[18] Why are our most expendable citizens placed in charge? Some male psychologists suggest that men are naturally dominant because they are "certainly" stronger and smarter. Other theorists suggest that the issue of a natural male biodominance is much less certain.

Perhaps whoever has managed to gain control of society's most valued resources has gotten the power in that society. Since men were more expendable and therefore did most of the hunting, perhaps they gained control of the most treasured resource of all—meat or protein. Perhaps male dominance is simply an issue of their protein power.[19]

Another possible explanation for male dominance over women is that since men are not able to be sure if a child is biologically theirs, men must secure their rights to their children by first securing their dominance over the women who bear their children.[20] Perhaps male dominance is a manifestation of guarding territory won in a sperm war. Or perhaps all this biodominance theorizing is wrong, and dominance is actually more related to specific relationships than it is to these sociobiological speculations. Who can be certain?

Consider the issue of biodominance certainty in your own marriage. Explore the possibility that dominance may be the result of what is needed within a given marriage more than what is biodominantly natural to a male or female. Discuss whether or not dominance may be the result of excessive submission by one partner rather than aggressive control by the other partner. No matter what, be sure to be unsure about all of this when you are finished talking, and be sure that neither spouse dominated the debate.

Perfidious Faces? Biocommunicational Certainty

Women smile more than men, read faces better than men, and are physically touched more by men than they touch men.[21] Women also tend to be more deceptive in their facial expression than men.[22] In general, women can decode or read deception in body language or facial expression better than men can, while men often miss body or facial language altogether.

Is one gender more perfidious than the other in the way they express themselves with their bodies or faces or the way in which they see, interpret, and use body and facial signs? People in general are better able to mask their feelings by controlling their faces than their bodies, but there seems to be a lot of "certainty" on both gender sides about who is sneakier or has the most leaks in his or her covert communication channels.

Spend some time reflecting with your partner about the body and facial communication channels in your own marriage. Who talks with the face, the body, the voice? Which of you is a better body or face reader than the other and which of you tends to be more of an open or closed book? Once again, if either of you thinks you are certain about the biocommunicational status of your spouse or yourself, talk again another time. Keep in your marital mind that the propensities of the prewired male and female brains do not have to have a "certain" control over the nature of your relationship. The more certain each of you is of "the way it is," the more incomplete your view of the real potential of your mind to make up your brain and for your marriage to find its way.

HOME LOVE ASSIGNMENTS

Here are five home love assignments to help you practice Confident Uncertainty—the second law of lasting love.

1. Draw a "marriage time line" together. Place along this line your plans, dreams, and goals, as well as those of your partner and of the marriage as a whole. Look together for some assumptions you may have made about the nature of

loving and how some of the "certainties" described above may have found their way into your own marriage and limited your options. See if the two of you can't turn some of the "certainties" you find into uncertain challenges for your marriage right now.

2. Write a caricature of yourself. Write one or two paragraphs that exaggerate what you feel to be your personal strengths and weaknesses. For example, describe yourself as a "pushy pessimistic power monger" if you think you tend to be a little too assertive, negative, and demanding sometimes. Have your spouse do the same self-caricature about himself or herself. Exchange and discuss or just reflect for a while about these images. Then, have your spouse write a caricature of you while you do one of your spouse. Discuss differences in points of view, what is exaggerated, what gender assumptions were made, and what should have been exaggerated or deemphasized that was not. The idea is to see how different the spouses' points of view of themselves and of their mates can be.

3. Spend one day in complete marital role reversal. The husband acts as he sees his wife typically behaving, and the wife does the same regarding her husband. Pay particular attention to the body language, facial gestures, habits, and typical verbal statements you have come to see in your spouse. At the end of the day, discuss what you experienced and share what *you* learned about *you*. What patterns in yourself may encourage certain behaviors in your spouse? The idea here is not to blame or mock but to see and learn from a different and less "certain" perspective.

4. Try the Lottery Exercise. Pretend your marriage just won the lottery and that you were set for life financially. How would you and your marriage change? How would marital roles be affected? What parts of the marriage that seemed "certain" would remain when money was no object?

5. What would your life have been like if you had never married? Reflect with your partner about the changes and challenges of your life had you been without a spouse. The idea is not to compare single with married life but to gain insight as to how marrying made your life what it is and how the presence of another person and the total merging with another person has changed each partner. Of course,

you cannot be certain of how things might have been, but the second law of lasting love suggests that you can never be certain of how your life *is* or will be.

One factor that makes lasting love so uncertain is that a true marriage is a merging of two into a dynamic and unpredictable One. The third law of lasting love, a boundary-free One Love, is discussed in the next chapter.

7

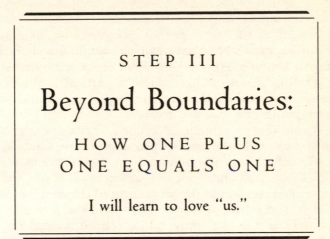

STEP III

Beyond Boundaries:

HOW ONE PLUS ONE EQUALS ONE

I will learn to love "us."

We are fully ourselves only in relation to each other. The "I" detached from a "Thou" disintegrates.
—Walter Tubbs

LOVE LAW THREE: THE ONE-LOVE LAW

The overriding principle of the quantum and cosmic world is unity. All things and energies everywhere are the same stuff. A miracle marriage is above all a total and permanent merging in which two become One, the new "third thing" that energizes each of the unifying spirits.

The Call for Contact

I saw a zebra in the zoo the other day. She was just standing there as if in a daze. Now and then, she would lower her head and take a bite of grass, raise her head again, and chew slowly while seeming to look out to nowhere in particular. She seemed sad to me, and I asked one of the zoo keepers nearby if anything was wrong with this beautiful animal.

"Certainly there's something wrong," she answered. "How would you like to be the only striped horse in the whole world? She's our only zebra right now, and she's terribly lonely. She's lovesick about it all, and you can hear her say it if you listen."

We watched together as the zebra stopped chewing, raised her head high, and cried out loudly. The sound was a combination of dog bark and donkey bray, and it echoed around the zoo. "That's her contact call," said the keeper. "All animals have it, but zebras are some of the most loving animals in the world. She is crying out for love. She won't feel happy until we find her a mate. She's incomplete now, and she is telling the world." As if to accentuate her keeper's words, the zebra shook the silence with another contact cry.

Do Zebras Fall in Love?

Are animals capable of love? All evidence points to the fact that they are. Famous animal researcher Harry Harlow referred to love as "affectional ties" or the tendency of animals to try to be together with other animals. In terms of the third law of lasting love—Oneness—animals try to merge and stay with other animals above and beyond their biological drives toward random repro-duction.[1] Harlow proved that affectional ties exist in monkeys between infants and their mothers, between monkey siblings, and within heterosexual affectional systems. Research on Man-yara elephants showed that these huge beasts take considerable time from their sixteen-hour-a-day consumption of more than 300 pounds of food and drinking more than 50 gallons of water to touch, rub against, clean, and help one another.[2]

Any pet lover has felt profound "oneness" with his own dog or cat, and stories of animals being involved in miracles of saving human lives are common. If you have a pet, do you think he or she can have a broken heart or feel lonely? Most of us would respond in the affirmative.

"I fish for hours alone just off the coast of Florida," said one Silver Survivor. "This has never happened when I fish with a friend, but very often when I am alone for a long time in my boat, a dolphin will come up beside me, snort, and stay with me for almost an hour. It's like they think I'm alone, so they pair up with me." This story illustrates the fact that there is indeed something within the nature of life that drives it toward what researchers call affectional ties and what I call Oneness.

The Healing Herd

In the nineteenth century, Charles Darwin's work on evolution brought animals closer to humans by showing our evolutionary ties to early primates. In the next century, Sigmund Freud helped us see how close humans are to animals by showing that we share many of the same needs that lower animals have—including the need for contact comfort, sex, and bonding. We all "herd" and try to become One with others. Human beings differ from other animals only in our greater capacity to think and worry about our Oneness with others, but all animals share the same biological imperative for merging.[3] There is something comforting, safe, and healing about being within the herd. Although the spirit has its human experience, it prefers to do so with other spirits having the same experience.

Separation signals physical ending. Only when death seems certain does the weary old dog seem to separate from his family, limp to a corner in the house, curl up on his blanket, and wait to die. On a recent visit to the Hawaiian island of Lanai, I was snorkeling in the clear warm ocean of Manele Bay when I noticed a dolphin floating slowly just beneath the surface a few yards away. I watched for a few minutes and then swam to shore. A local Hawaiian said, "I saw you watching that dolphin. He is dying, you know. Dolphins always swim in pairs, but when they get ready to die, they swim away and wait in the warmth of the sun filtering through the water. Then they quietly die and float alone out to sea." Love and connection are processes of our physical living, but death is a transition of the loving spirit. While we're here on earth, we are driven to be together.

The instinctive drive toward Oneness is illustrated by the following things. First, zebras react in herd or group fashion when danger is sensed. They immediately and automatically form a semicircle facing the danger. The whole group then watches the predator or perceived threat intently, and they all keep moving their "caution circle" to maintain a 100-yard safety zone (the zebra's safe fleeing distance between themselves and the perceived danger). When the safety zone is breached, the herd flees together. Zebra stripes make them stand out as individuals, but when the herd moves quickly as one, these same stripes result in a blur similar to quickly flipped pages, which makes it difficult for predators to single out one zebra. The isolated zebra is an easy target, and usually just stands still for the kill as if disoriented and helpless. Zebras, like us, react to threat as One or they do not survive.

My next story comes from the other end of the life continuum. One evening just after one of the Silver Survivor couples had left my office, I heard what sounded like a gunshot. It was very late, and I was alone in the office. I cautiously went to look out the window and saw the couple that had just left. They were clinging to each other and backing toward their car. I could see the shadow of a large figure near a street light, and the couple saw it, too. The man and wife kept clinging, looking, and backing away. The figure quickened his pace toward the couple, apparently encroaching into the couple's safety zone. The couple quickly joined hands and sprinted to their car.

As I dialed hospital security, I kept looking out of the window. The dark figure came closer, and I could see that it was one of our hospital guards trying to show his identification to the couple. I later discovered that the shot I had heard had nothing to do with my couple, but they had reacted by creating their own "couple caution circle." When threatened, they had become One.

Safety in One

My wife and I formed our "couple caution circle" when I was struggling against cancer. When doctors would approach my bed with news of my progress, my wife would join with me in mutual embrace. The reports were seldom good during the early phases of my illness, and one day a doctor brought particularly frightening news.

He was a doctor new to the bone-marrow transplant unit, and his fear and insecurity were often translated into his seeking a safe "doctor distance" from his patients. Every time he entered my room, my wife would scurry from her chair near my bed and sit beside me on the bed. On this day, the doctor looked at his ever-present clipboard as he murmured, "It doesn't look like you are going to make it."

Before I could ask a question of this shadow of doom, my wife stood up, handed me my robe, adjusted the four intravenous tubes and bags attached to my body, and said, "Let's get out of here. This man is a risk to your health." As my wife helped me to struggle toward the door, the doctor approached us. "Stay back," demanded my wife. "Stay away from us."

As we walked together through the hall of this sad, sick place where I had lived and suffered for more than two months, the doctor attempted to catch up with us. "Keep going," said my wife as she pushed the intravenous stand with one hand and held up her other hand to warn away the approaching doctor. "We're going to talk to someone who really knows what is going on. Don't come any closer to us," said my wife protecting our "couple caution circle." The two of us moved as One as we fled to the safety and hope of a doctor who did not confuse diagnosis with verdict. I could never have made that walk toward wellness alone, and throughout my illness and miracle cure, I learned that Oneness is the same thing as wellness.

Do You "Have" a Marriage or "Are" You Your Marriage?

To learn about the "third thing" that comes from lasting love requires that the boundaries we create between the self and others be destroyed. Our world sometimes seems to be a massive collection of boundaries between what we see as opposites. We feel more that we "have" a body than we feel that we "are" our body. The self/not-self boundary is clear. The body seems more "mine" than me, we "have" sex rather "being sexual," and we divide the question of where we are going with our life from the question of whom we will go with.

Almost everything we deal with daily is viewed as divided into opposites: good versus evil, beauty versus ugliness, pleasure versus pain, strong versus weak, and smart versus stupid. These are only some examples of how our Selfish Old Brain creates brain boundaries that help it make quick either/or decisions for survival. The mind can tell the brain to think otherwise by teaching it that lasting love is *not* a process of maintaining barriers between two selves but of demolishing personal boundaries forever. Low Monogamists *have* a marriage or are *in* one. High Monogamists *are* their marriage and constantly work to create one.

The Naturalness of One

It is peculiar that our brain is so consumed with keeping things separate, because nature itself knows nothing of such boundaries. As scientist Ken Wilbur writes, "Nature doesn't grow true frogs and false frogs, nor moral trees and immoral trees, nor right oceans and wrong oceans."[4] Wilbur goes on to quote Henry David Thoreau, who said that nature never apologizes because nature does not see boundaries or opposites, and therefore never sees what we humans see as "errors." Wilbur writes, "There might even be smart bears and dumb bears, but it doesn't seem to concern them very much. You just don't find inferiority complexes in bears. I am afraid that Nature is not only smarter than we think. Nature is smarter than we can think."[5] I suggest that, since we are all One with nature, we can use our mutual minds instead of our selfish brains and learn to apply nature's way of thinking to live and love without boundaries.

The miracle of lasting love is that we begin to love our spouse not because he or she loves us, makes us feel secure, or is an image of ourself but because our husband or wife actually *becomes* us. Christ did not teach us to love our neighbor as we love ourself but to love our neighbor *as* ourself. A lesson of the third law of lasting love—One Love—is that we must silence the individual Self to discover that we are capable of being One with another person.

The Dual Nature of Waves and Particles

One of the strangest features of the quantum world is the duality of particles and waves. Science writers Peter Coveney and Roger Highfield point out an ironic sidelight to research into the Oneness of waves of energy and lumps of particles by noting that physicist Joseph J. Thomson had earlier received the Nobel Prize for showing that matter is made up of particles, which we now know as electrons, while his son received the same award for demonstrating that electrons display properties of waves.[6]

New science has shown that, contrary to the brain's bias for boundaries, things are never truly separate. Photons, or particles of light, behave like waves or particles depending on how we choose to see them. Shine a photon through a single slit and it behaves like a particle shining at a specific point, but shine a photon toward two slits and record the pattern of interference and the photon behaves in terms of its wavelike capacity.[7] Any separations we try to make in our world are merely matters of mental convenience.

Even Einstein was perplexed by this strange Oneness of matter and energy. Although he himself had discovered the particulate or particle nature of light (the photon), he wrestled until his death with this complex feature of nature. He wrote, "All these fifty years of pondering have not brought me any closer to answering the question What are light quanta?"[8] Scientists today, however, believe that everything that "is" is One and of one stuff.

People in marriages are particles and energy moved into One. The Me Myth emphasizes our particlehood, but the Great Marriage Myth emphasizes our simultaneous particle *and* energy nature and the possibilities of our joining as a powerful new One—what some scientists call the "onta."

Onta Love

Physicist Henry Margenau uses the term *onta* (Greek for "being") to describe individual elements that merge with one another to become something much more than the sum of the two. He calls these onta "entities that defy ordinary intuition."[9] In our see-

and-touch world, we find it easy to contemplate particles and individual people, but we have great difficulty in thinking about something that is not one thing or another with some boundary around it. Onta, however—like a miracle marriage and all the stuff in the universe—are energy and particle connected forever.

Physicist Niels Bohr stated that "all being is unity."[10] This phrase may sound mystical, but it summarizes the findings in physics that shook the scientific world to its roots. Put individual heart cells in a petri dish, and they beat their lonely rhythm until the energy of other individual heart cells joins them in the dish to throb in mutual rhythm. As you will learn in Chapter 11, where I write about couple chaos, things have a way of falling apart to fall back together again as One, but the process of change does not mean that things truly separate.

The "identities" of onta are represented by their atomic number or other mathematical symbols that help describe their general individual behavior or spin—their particle personalities. When onta merge, however, they form something entirely above and beyond the total of these numbers or the sum of their "particle personalities" as individual onta. We are individual and system, and even when we or electrons are behaving like particles, we are not as certainly separate as our behavior and perceptions would lead us to believe.

Werner Heisenberg's law of uncertainty reminds us that when we look for particles, we find particlelike behavior but know little of the wave of energy. When we look for waves, we find wavelike behavior, but we forget about particles. Everything in the world, "naturally" including us, is One potentiality. We have the potential for using who we are as individuals *and* how we are together to make our miracle marriage. Paradoxically, the individuality of the onta is maintained and even enhanced through the merging and the new Oneness.[11]

To illustrate the scientific concept that all being is unity and miraculous manifestations of both our particlehood and wavehood, Dr. Margenau describes the example of neutrons and protons—quantum stuff—separated in space. When not merging, the neutron is neutral in its charge and the proton is positive. When these onta merge, says Margenau, "their identities disappear, their properties merge, and a distinction between them becomes impossible. But they are still 'onta.'"[12]

Like the totality of the eclipse of the sun described in Chapter 1, the moon and sun merged into One onta of unique light and power that could be felt billions of miles away from this cosmic union. Just at the moment of the merging of the images of the sun and the moon, a flash of light appears at the top of the shadow of the moon and a glowing ring circles the moon's image. Astronomers call this phenomenon the "wedding ring" effect because the sparkling light near the top of the totality seems to be a magnificent diamond perched upon the glowing circle of light that surrounds the moon. When my wife and I observed this cosmic wedding ring, I thought of our One Love as a bonding in which the "and" in the equation is loving and the result is a miracle One of lasting love that saved my life.

A Test of Your Own Onta Factor

To work on step 3 in making a miracle marriage, take this test to assess your own onta loving. After each question, I have included Silver Survivor statements to help you see how these miracle marriages created and maintained their bonds and demolished all barriers between their souls.

THE ONTA, OR MARITAL ONENESS, TEST

1. Do you feel that your marriage has become an entity beyond the combination of two personalities?

"Our marriage is much more than the two of us," said a Silver Survivor. "It is much stronger than our total combined strength and much more resilient than our personal coping ability, and seems to have more power than just two people together. Even so, we seem to be able to be more ourselves than ever because of our marriage."

2. Do you feel a balance between who takes care of whom instead of one partner feeling like a parent or caretaker for the other?

"You see a lot of marriages where it seems like either the husband or wife is the caretaker and the other spouse is the caretakee," said a Silver Survivor. "In our marriage, we shuffle back and forth between who is taking care of whom at any given time."

3. Do you feel that the more you are together, the more together you feel? Or do you feel that the closer you get, the more aware you become of the personal differences between you?

One husband said, "One of my friends always says that familiarity breeds contempt. In our relationship, my wife and I feel that familiarity breeds commitment. We seem to get closer and closer the more we are together."

4. When you have sex, do you feel as if you are "sharing sex together" instead of doing it to or for one another?

"I think a lot of people in the old days had sexless love," said one wife. "They seemed to think that sex was not a part of love. Now you see people having loveless sex. In our marriage, we don't work on trying to come together when we have sex because we are already together and our sex is a celebration of already being together instead of trying to come there. Sex for us is a Oneness thing and not a 'to' thing."

5. Do you feel that your marriage is held together by hope and happiness rather than by fear of rejection or by a sense of helplessness, insecurity, and uncertainty about your own ability to make it alone?

One wife said, "I have a friend who is in what I call a 'hate affair.' She seems trapped in her marriage instead of growing in it and with it. I know that a love affair never lasts, and hot romance burns itself out, but I think hate affairs can last forever because the spouses are too afraid to try to learn to love forever. They are individuals trapped, tied, and tangled up together instead of being voluntarily bonded together as One. They stay together out of insecurity and fear of rejection rather than out of growing love and respect."

6. Do you do things for your spouse because it makes your marriage stronger? Or do you do them because it makes you feel that you have behaved like a good husband or wife or because you feel you owe something to your spouse?

"We don't do things for each other," said a husband. "We don't try to behave and be good little spouses. We do things because it makes Us grow together. I'm not trying to outdo my wife or other husbands by being the best husband, but we do work to make our best marriage."

7. Do you feel equal to and with your spouse, as if either you or your spouse can be stronger, more effective, or better in some way?

"My best friend spends hours telling me how much smarter her husband is than she is," said a Silver Survivor. "She really seems to feel like she got the best deal in the marriage and that her husband sort of got stuck with her or tolerates her as a maid or something like that. She'd better realize that if she keeps trying to convince him that she got the best deal, she may succeed, and he'll go looking for a better deal for himself."

8. Do you sometimes feel that you are so much a part of your spouse and your spouse a part of you that you aren't sure where you start and where he or she leaves off? Or do you feel that there are distinct and well-guarded individual boundaries?

"It sounds almost mystical, but there doesn't seem to be any space between us anymore," said a husband. "I feel what she feels, and she feels what I feel. We can just look at each other and, faster than the speed of light, we know how we each feel and how our marriage feels."

9. Do people sometimes comment that you and your spouse seem to look and act alike?

"We didn't see it until we were watching a videotape of our last vacation with our friends," said the wife. "Everybody said how much we looked alike. Now that we notice, I think we do look alike to some extent, although we were not at all alike in looks when we married. I guess becoming one flesh might be more literal than we think."

*10. Can you sense how your partner feels or thinks even at long
distances from each other, instead of feeling out of touch with each other
when you are physically apart?*

"We are so much a part of each other that we are One
no matter where we are," said the wife. "I travel all the time
on business, but I never feel really far away from him. There
is a bond that keeps us together that distance doesn't affect
at all."

The Silver Survivors' average score on the Onta, or Marital
Oneness, Test was 9.8. The control group averaged 1.4. This
was one of the most significant differences between miracle marriages and relationships that were failing. This was also one of
the highest of the ten test scores earned by the Silver Survivors.

Attachment to Hate Affairs?

To achieve the Oneness of the onta factor, the One-Love Law,
it is important to realize the difference between bonding and
attachment and what can go wrong when attachment rather than
true bonding takes place. A bond is based on reciprocal, reflective, and mentally mature loving and giving, and on a sharing
that makes two people into a unit of one. An attachment is uni-
directional and based on less thoughtful and immature dependence, taking, and the fear of autonomy or independence.

A newborn baby "attaches" to the mother. The child *must* have
the mother in order to live, initially gives little back to the mother,
and is totally needy. The child does not decide to attach. It just
happens. When Low Monogamists describe their love, they often
say "it just happened to them." One reason that nature saw to
it that children have the neotenic or cute face I described in
Chapter 4 is to be sure that the mother and father will not
abandon this initial one-way attachment because it demands so
much and gives so little. Nature sees to it that parental attachments to children and childish attachments to parents "just happen," but High Monogamists *make* their love happen by contemplatively and volitionally deciding together to bond.

Since childish or childlike behavior tends to elicit parental behaviors from others, some spouses trapped in an attachment

rather than a bonded marriage tend to regress to a childlike dependency. An attachment marriage is more a place of refuge than of personal growth.[13] One or both spouses sometimes relive their childhood conflicts with their own parents through marriage and resort to strategies they wrongly think worked for them before as a child. If our spouse becomes automatically attached rather than thoughtfully bonded to us, we often form a hate affair with him or her, because of our own frustrated needs for an adult with whom we can share and think about life.

Paradoxically, the parent-child attachment marriage is one of the longest-lasting relationships, proving that it is not the length of marriage but the miracles it makes that really matter. In the hate affair of attachment, both partners tend to struggle for a lifetime, with one person feeling overwhelmed and parentized by the other, whereas the regressive spouse spends his or her marital life in fear of abandonment coupled with childlike resentment of his or her dependency.

Four Causes of Marrying Your Parent

Spouses who regress to behave as children in their marriage and in effect "marry their parent" typically have experienced one or more of the following problems in their childhood and reenact it in the patterns within their marriage. All of these problems are major obstacles to the Oneness of lasting love:

• Exploitation: Having had his or her own childhood exploited and robbed of its innocence and natural dependence by a parent who came to interact in a childish way with his or her own child, the exploitee, now grown and married, is exploited once again by a spouse. I describe the child in this situation as suffering from the Carthage Complex, through which one child in a family is symbolically "sacrificed" or is made to give up his or her childhood because one or both parents never gave up their own. One child in every family in the ancient city-state of Carthage experienced the ultimate exploitation by being killed or sacrificed for "the good of the gods."[14] Such spouses will do anything in order to solicit parenting from their husband or wife as a means of reclaiming their lost opportunity to be a child. One wife said, "I feel like I wanted to fall into my husband's arms, but I'm afraid

I fell into his hands. I became his child instead of his lover, and I did chores for him rather than made a marriage for us."

• Abuse: Because of actual verbal or physical abuse as a child, the abused spouse has overlearned the role of helpless victim. Spouse abuse is a complex and multifaceted issue related to several causes, most of which have much more to do with the abuser than the abused. One contributing influence to such abuse is the surrender learned by the abused child as the only strategy available when confronting the torture of abuse by an all-powerful parent.

• Neglect: Some children grow up with parents whose philosophy of parenting is one of expecting their children to be "seen and not heard" or whose own narcissism is so strong that children are only an artifact or accomplishment in their marriage rather than a part of their Oneness. Like the parents in the custody battle I described in Chapter 2, some parents assume that the children will grow up on their own so long as the parents provide for them. The child learns that he or she lives as a temporary visitor in the home, a necessary adjunct but not a key part of the family system. The neglected spouse also regresses to this pattern in his or her own marriage, deferring to the husband or wife in all matters and living parallel to but not really "with" the spouse. One wife said, "I have spent my life on my husband's arm. I only wish I could have been in his arms."

• Deprivation: The neglected child may be spoiled by materialistic indulgence, but the deprived child is even more alone. He or she learns very early to be last, to get less or sometimes almost nothing, and to go without the basics of life. Diet and general health suffer, and such a child fails to thrive. When such patterns are carried over into adult life, the deprived spouse often experiences health problems and deprivation of the basic necessities, while the depriving spouse indulges himself or herself. "I would see a picture of my wife and me," said one husband. "We're the same age, but she looked tremendous and very young, while I looked drawn, tired, and old enough to be her father. I tried to give her everything and all of me, and I think she took it."

When one of the partners "regresses" to survive in a hate affair, he or she has usually found someone to marry who too easily falls into the trap of parenting or reinforcing whichever of the four regressive patterns of exploitation, abuse, neglect, or deprivation the spouse falls into.

The Danger of Marrying Your Child

Some spouses deal with their own childhood family conflicts not by regressing to the childhood role in the marriage but by assuming the pseudo safety of total control, becoming the parent rather than the partner of the husband or wife.

When your own childhood has been one of isolation, insecurity, fear, and vulnerability, sometimes the only "safety" seems to be found in being the parent who appeared to have such power over your own life. You deal with these conflicts through the compensatory seeking of power rather than continuing to submit to it.

Hate affairs flourish when the "parents" and "regressors" find each other, attach to rather than bond with each other, and struggle through their married life with the nagging sense that they have done all of this before but can do nothing to untangle themselves from these corrupt family ties. When author and humorist Erma Bombeck joked of "family ties that bind," she was more insightful than she herself may have known.

Marriage Between Consenting Adults

The Oneness of a miracle marriage is composed of two consenting adults who are able knowledgeably and maturely to give their consent to be adults and grow together to be more than they can ever be as individuals. The key characteristics of miracle marital bonding are as follows:

• A marital avenue for transcending childhood developmental disadvantages instead of integrating them pathologically into the marriage. This transcendence is made possible because *both* partners invest extensive MIMs in their marriage, tolerate with patience and understanding the uncertainty that all of us bring to marriage, and are willing to make a new One that overcomes the disadvantages that may have come from childhood. They learn from each other's problems and discover new ways to protect each partner from the guilt of an isolated individual past and fears of a lonely future.

• Developmental maturity of both spouses, who have each been able to set aside, overcome, correct, or work through their childhood conflicts and are prepared to grow with and not under the protection or control of the spouse.

• A reciprocity of caring behaviors and responsibilities in the marriage.

• Mutual protection of each other, giving and taking from each other, and seeing of the spouse as equal to oneself in skills, personal strength, and coping mechanisms.

• A balance of benefits within the marriage, with *both* spouses deriving advantages from and suffering sacrifices for the marriage.

• A marital avenue for transcending childhood developmental disadvantages rather than integrating them into the marriage in a parent/child hate affair.

The miracle marriage is made up of a bond between adults who are aware but go beyond the children within them by consenting to help each other grow into a new caring and productive adulthood together. The spouses in the miracle marriage form a Oneness that brings more joy and love to their own children and to the world in general, instead of being consumed by one or both partners' needs to relive the past. One husband who overcame a childhood of conflict in and through his marriage said, "I know they say that he who does not remember history is sure to repeat it, but I think that he who cannot forget parts of it and start making a new history is doomed to constantly live in it."

The Marital Mask

One of the most surprising findings in my study of the Silver Survivors was that the spouses in these marriages had come to resemble one another physically. The resemblance was often far more than a subtle one, so I decided to test my theory that marriage causes a merging and Oneness *even in physical appearance!*[15]

I asked ten of my medical students to match pictures of spouses

I was working with in my clinic. I blocked out the backgrounds of the pictures to hide any clues of connection. I also included pictures of complete strangers, of spouses who had been married for only a few years, couples having marital problems, and my Silver Survivors. All ten students matched all of the Silver Survivors perfectly! They were less successful with the couples who had been together for a shorter period of time and least successful in matching pictures of people in marital distress.

While the effects of similar diet and exercise have some impact on the facial similarity and posture of spouses together for years, these factors are not the central cause. My work, and the work of other researchers, indicates that spouses who stay together learn a silent empathy and mutual mimicking of one another's emotional expressions so that their faces are sculpted by one smile or frown wrinkle at a time into a "mutual marriage mask."

After years of doing marital therapy, I began to study the faces of the couples during their first visit. I could see "marriage merging" on the faces of some and only unique differences on the faces of others. Some couples "looked married" while others "looked separate." This third loving law of Oneness has a most profound effect—even a physical effect—on the partners of a miracle marriage.

HOME LOVE ASSIGNMENTS

You are now three steps into your course in making a miracle marriage. As you continue to practice your love assignments, remember that this course in marital miracles takes time. You will have to invest MIMs. Be patient as you progress through this manual and tolerate the uncertainty of learning more and more about becoming One togeher.

1. This assignment may seem a little strange at first, but give it a try anyway. Sit in silence in a completely dark room with your partner. Try to feel the presence of your partner and sense how he or she is feeling and thinking. After a few minutes, and still in the dark, talk about what you felt. Discuss the extent to which you could "feel" and "sense"

your spouse and the degree to which your feelings were similar or complementary.

2. Set aside time each day to spend a few minutes thinking about your spouse. Agree on a mutual time to "maritate," or meditate about your marriage. Write down what you felt and thought, and discuss later what you wrote with your spouse. You may be surprised to note how many similar thoughts and feelings you both had. You may also learn that, as with meditation, you can practice your "maritation" and develop your Oneness together.

3. Talk with your partner about the degree to which each of you has contributed to your new marital One. What unique individual characteristics from you or your spouse have become a part of the marriage? What characteristics of the spouse have each of you taken on?

4. If there were only one *major* difference between you (and there are always more than one, and they all seem major at one time or another), what could you and your spouse agree that difference is? Talk this issue over and take your time. Talk and "maritate" together several times, and allow yourselves to be uncertain as you search for the one key difference. It is the process of looking, not the final discovery of a difference, that can teach you both about just how much Oneness there is in your marriage.

5. Every morning before you get out of bed, spend just one minute in a silent embrace. Reaffirm your oneness together. Celebrate your participation in the miracle of one person joining with another person to make One miracle love.

8

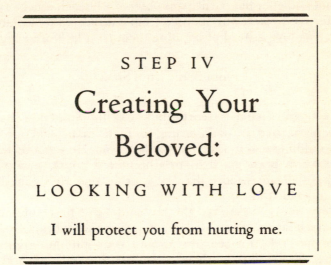

STEP IV

Creating Your Beloved:

LOOKING WITH LOVE

I will protect you from hurting me.

"You would not even exist if it were not for me,"
Jehovah reminds Abraham. "Yes, Lord, that I
know," Abraham replies, "but also you would not be
known if it were not for me."

—*Hebrew legend recounted*
by physicist John Wheeler

LOVE LAW FOUR:
THE LOVE-LOOK LAW

Through our chosen way of seeing and sensing our spouses, we help to evoke who and how they are. We do not create our partners, for they are God's work, and they are responsible for being all they can be, but how we see our partners depends much more on who we are than how they are. Husbands and wives are not audience but participant observers in each other's epoch of life. We protect our spouses from hurting us by looking at them *with* love instead of berating them *for* a lack of loving.

From "Stud" to "Spud"

"My husband's name is George, but I call him Spud now. Before we were married, he was a caring, energetic man," said one wife. "He couldn't seem to keep his hands off me. He was a real stud. Since we've been married, he's become a couch potato and watches ballgames more than he watches me. He's gone from stud to spud."

"Very funny," answered the husband. "But have you looked at yourself lately? When we got married, you were beautiful. You would never let me see you without your hair just right and without sexy clothes on. Now, you wear that old robe and you do your hair for everyone but me. If I've gone from stud to spud, then you've gone from doll to drudge."

As destructive, insulting, hurtful, and infantile as the above argument may sound, it is an all too common illustration of how spouses assume a point of view that fails to protect the other from marital pain. Instead of working to look for love, it is easier to watch for flaws. The postmarital change in our spouses is due more to our *way of seeing* each other than to what we actually see. It is due more to projections and reflections of our own personal image—a falling out of romantic illusion and into loving reality—than to actual changes in our husband or wife.

Romantic Ghosts and Marriage Monsters

Husbands and wives who came to my clinic frequently reported what they saw as serious postmarital conversion in their spouse. Spouses complained that their partners began to change soon after marriage and started to behave more negligently than they had during courtship. "What happened to the man or woman I married?" was a common lament.

Major reasons for the experience of "postmarital reality remorse" are the romantic illusions and perceptual distortions that led to marriage in the first place. We marry a romantic apparition and end up seeing a marital monster. This happens because we tend to marry when we are young, pretty or handsome, and making our best effort to look the best we can and put our best personality features forward. Unfortunately, we also typically marry when we are emotionally immature and intellectually at our stupidest, most shortsighted, and most impulsive. Perhaps if we all waited until we were about forty-five years old to marry, we would be less infatuated with images and more mature in our expectations of a lifelong mate.

Author Judith Viorst writes, "Infatuation is when you think he's as gorgeous as Robert Redford, as pure as Solzhenitsyn, as funny as Woody Allen, as athletic as Jimmy Connors, and as smart as Albert Einstein. Love is when you realize that he's as gorgeous as Woody Allen, as smart as Jimmy Connors, as funny as Solzhenitsyn, as athletic as Albert Einstein, and nothing like Robert Redford in any category—but you'll take him anyway."[1] The fourth law of lasting love teaches us that we should look with love and logic instead of lust and infatuation. It instructs us to be more aware of how loving and lovable we are instead of how lovable a partner seems to be.

The Me Myth of Low Monogamy teaches that if we see love, we can believe we are loved. The Great Marriage Myth teaches that how we see is who we get. If we first *believe* we are loving and loveworthy, we are more likely to see our partner as loving.

Focusing the Projector
Instead of Adjusting the Screen

The fourth step in this miracle-marriage manual—learning to look *with* instead of *for* love—suggests that it may not be only the partner who stops trying to be the best of all spouses. Like the scientist making observations, we become a part of the experiment in love.

The scientist knows that his or her observations always alter what is observed. Likewise, the very fact that we observe our partners changes them. When we begin to look more judgmentally at our spouse and to blame him or her for our feelings of romantic letdown, we usually see what we are looking for—a far-from-perfect person who was never, as Judith Viorst suggests, as beautiful and brilliant as we fooled ourselves into seeing. If we fall in love with our own illusions, the monster we will be frightened by is created by the reality of the real demands of real loving and living.

Certainly some marital partners do change drastically after marriage and begin to disregard their appearance and ignore their spouse's needs. More often, however, changes are a result of the *looking of the observer*. It is the projector or person projecting his or her point of view and not the image that creates what is seen. Science's discovery—that the act of observation not only influences but physically alters what is observed—destroyed forever the possibility of the uninvolved, passive, objective observer. When we apply science's lesson to our loving, we realize that if we look *for* love we may never find it, but if we look *with* love, we project that loving to our partner.

Collapsing into Love

The Love-Look Law is suggested from the work of Nobel Prize winners Niels Bohr and Ilya Prigogine. Bohr's quantum theory said that the transformation from a plethora of potentiality of wave and particle is accomplished by a "collapsing of wave function," or the act of observation causing energy to become particle.[2] Aristotle foresaw this remarkable breakthrough of quantum thinking when he discussed the duality of "potentiality" and "actuality."

The Love-Look Law says that when and how we look at our lover collapses all his or her potential into a present actuality, and it is our looking that causes this collapse. This collapsing is a form of "falling in love." Since Low Monogamy is often based on emotional impulse and involuntary submission to strong biological and evolutionarily based drives, falling in love is associated with the Me Myth. Since how we view our spouse is a matter of our own free choice and our point of view is based on our awareness that we will tend to see "how" we look, it is more accurate to refer to High Monogamy as "jumping in love."

Chemist Ilya Prigogine called the power of the observer the rule of "the participant observer." Everything from an observed atom to a plucked flower is changed in its "potentiality" and made a "present particle" rather than "passing potential" by the act of our observation. By looking at, assessing, and judging our lover, we merge with whatever or whomever we are observing. We cause our spouse to collapse into our view of him or her. We project the image we see.

A Watched Spouse Never Shines

The proverb "a watched pot never boils" refers to the fact that when we keep an eye on something and expect something to happen, the act of our constant vigil seems to prevent the expected event from taking place. In marriage, when we keep our expectant or critical eye on our partner instead of attending to being the type of lover we hope to be loved by, our observation prevents change from happening! Our spouse cannot shine when he or she is eclipsed by the shadow of our gaze.

A remarkable consequence of quantum theory is that time actually stands still while a quantum system is observed. The center or nucleus of an atom can be unstable and undergo radioactive decay. This is where radiation comes from. But when an apparatus is set up that constantly watches or measures what is happening in the atom's nucleus, the atom remains in an undecayed state. It remains a singular-particle "pot that never boils." The constant observation stops time for the atom and prevents change from taking place.[3]

In our marriages, the more we adopt a critical posture, watching for changes in our partner rather than working to make changes in ourselves, the more we are actually paralyzing our relationship and preventing the changes we hope for.

How to Look with Love: "In-Sight" and "Love Glances"

The look of love has two characteristics. First, we should develop our "in-sight" more than our "out-look" and work constantly to *be* the partner we would want to love us. By so doing, we are more likely to elicit exactly what we wish for. The power of observation is not based on visual acuity and objectivity but on the awareness that observing alters and helps create what is observed.

The second aspect of the look of love is never to look too long *at* our partner. Instead, we should take brief love glances and then turn away to allow other potentialities of our partner to emerge and our own viewpoint to develop and mature before we look again. We should use these love glances in place of critical glares and then look back within ourselves while our partner's potentialities are allowed to continue unimpaired by our paralyzing gaze that can—as happened to the atom under constant vigil—freeze our partner in a static state.

The Look That Can Stop a Clock

As one more example of the power of the observer, consider the fact that just looking at a clock can stop it! Science writer Itzhak Bentov described an almost unbelievable exercise that illustrates the power of observation on what is observed and how even time can be stopped by keeping our eye on it.

Patients who learn through biofeedback to put themselves in a deeply meditative state (producing theta brain waves) and watch the second hand of a clock discover that the second hand will come to a complete stop under their gaze! As remarkable as this phenomenon may seem, it has been repeatedly documented.[4]

You can try to verify this effect by your own experiment. Sit quietly with your muscles relaxed. Be sure a watch or clock with a clearly visible second hand is nearby. Close your eyes and visualize the most relaxing scene you can imagine. When you feel completely relaxed and totally in your imaginary scene, slowly and slightly open your eyes and look at the second hand. If you are truly relaxed, you will notice that the hand seems stuck or moving sluggishly along. If you become shocked by this phenomenon, the hand will immediately return to its normal pace.[5]

Time is relative, so on some levels the second hand was continuing to move. But because of the nature of your observation, time for you had stopped until you were shocked back to another relative reality of time kept by the spring in your clock or the vibrating crystal in your watch. Observation had actually stopped one type of time that is no less real than the swing of a pendulum.

One of my Silver Survivor couples tried a variation of this visual-time-stopping experiment that illustrates that the effect can be shared with someone else. "We sat together looking at the second hand on the clock on our family room wall," said the wife. "We each put on a pair of earphones and listened to one of our favorite pieces of music by the composer Yanni, called 'Reflections of Passion.' We particularly enjoyed the piece called 'Secret Vows.' We were both stunned when we discussed later how we both noticed that the second hand seemed to move for both of us in coordination with the changing rhythms of Yanni's music!"

Four Tests of Your "Us-Sight"

Physicist John Wheeler said, "In some strange sense, this is a participatory universe."[6] This is not to say that there is not an objective world, but we also create our own worlds because we become a part of what we see. Chemist Ilya Prigogine wrote, "Knowledge is both objective and participatory."[7] The fourth law of lasting love, the Love-Look Law, requires us to learn that, no matter how negative or positive the life dramas that seem to unfold before our eyes, we are never separate from what we see. We are not the audience of our life and loving. We are the actors in our love epic.

On one level of reality, the positive or negative actions of our spouse take place separate from us. As psychologist Fritz Perls was fond of saying, "You are You and I am I." People do act immaturely and behave aggressively and abusively. A spouse may yell, scream, and throw things. You have the choice, however, of *how* you will see such behavior and how you will mobilize the power of your observation. Here are four questions you should ask when your quick glance reveals something that you did not want to see:

• Can I look with tolerance? Can I look beyond the behavior I didn't want to see for the signs of the potential for love that I wanted to see and for what I myself can do to increase my chances of seeing it?
• Can I look with forgiveness? Can I keep looking back again and not be frightened off by contrasts I seem to see with what I had hoped for in our loving? Can I keep in mind that a new

point of view can help create a new role for my lover in the drama of our loving?

• Can I look with optimism? No matter how destructive the behavior I see seems, can I still look back in at me to see how I can be even more of what I want instead of angry and despairing at what I've seen?

• Can I look with creativity? Can I avoid looking critically and judgmentally and put my power of observation to work to compose a continuing and evolving love epic and new roles in that epic for myself and my lover?

The following is a statement by one of the Silver Survivors that illustrates the application of the four questions above: "I've learned how powerful my observation is, and I know that how I am affects how he is and can be. That doesn't mean that he doesn't just plain behave like a complete ass sometimes. I used to watch his temper tantrums and almost keep a scorecard against him to prove my point about what a fool he could make of himself. These came in handy for later arguments. But then I learned to look beyond what I saw, to look for love, to look away and allow time to pass and his good points to come out. I tried to make the supreme effort to learn from what he was doing in order to teach him by example." The spouse who tries to be an objective or detached observer can end up watching the marriage deteriorate and detach from him or her even as the evidence is being collected. The real miracle happens when you use the power of observation to enhance the power of your love.

The Philosophy of a Miracle Marriage

Philosopher Lawrence Cahoone writes, "Human beings create, think, and become individuated, independent creatures only with and through a context of meaningful relations to other human beings and to non-human beings."[8] Observation is always an interactive process. We do not watch our world being made. All philosophers have taught that through our consciousness, we create the world.[9]

Saint Augustine wrote of tiring of his aimless seeking to find God somewhere outside himself and discovered that "I found Thee not, because in vain I sought without for Him who was within myself." The third law of lasting love, the law of One Love described in Chapter 7, also taught that we look in vain for love if we look outside ourself for loving. Our lover is part of us, created by us, and made of and with us. One of our most profound powers to make a miracle marriage comes from the philosophers' and physicists' lessons that the seeker finds what he or she seeks and discovers only what he or she creates. Miracle marriages are made when both spouses become marital "sensitive sensors" rather than marital "critical censors."

Two Painters of One Portrait

Psychologist Dana Zohar writes, "We bring our world and ourselves into being through a shared, creative response to the world and to each other. In a sense, we *are* our relationships."[10] When spouses talk about a husband, a wife, or a marriage as if these elements were outside them, they fail to see their power to be a part of their marriage and to study and learn within it.

We can protect our partner from hurting us by beginning with a loving point of view and by acknowledging our part in creating the image of our spouse and our marriage. We are always coartists in the painting of the portrait of our love and not art critics of one half of the picture. If we don't like what we see, we should wonder as much about how *we* are as how our lover seems to be.

Psychologist Carl Jung wrote, "If things go wrong . . . I shall put myself right first. We are not only the passive witnesses of our age, and its sufferers, but also its makers. We make our own epoch."[11] One of the Silver Survivors paraphrased Jung's words as follows: "You can choose to wait and watch until you can say 'look! . . . love!' or you can take responsibility for how you see your loving and your lover and first say 'love!' . . . and then 'look' with love."

A VITAL VISION TEST

To help you with your fourth step in this miracle-marriage manual, take the following loving vision test designed to measure your awareness of your participation in the creation of what you see in your marriage.

1. Do you look openly, receptively, and nonjudgmentally at your spouse or do you look for problems and flaws in your marriage or your spouse?

"I never have to ask my husband to look at me," said a Silver Survivor. "Some wives I know have to practically sound a horn to get their husband to look, but when we are going out for the evening, my husband always tells me how he sees me. I can't remember asking, 'How do I look?' I always feel like he is looking at me for the first time."

2. Do you "sense" your spouse with more than just your eyes— hearing, feeling, smelling, tasting, and emotionally tuning in to your partner? Or do you take the "what I see with my eyes is what I'm getting out of my marriage" approach?

"When I look at my wife, I see her with more than my eyes. I see her with my heart and through my heart," said the husband of the wife quoted above. "I didn't marry bone and flesh. I married her, and I want to see all of her."

3. When you look at things together, do you join together in a new common viewpoint—each of you seeing something or an aspect of something you might not see as an individual, rather than each of you seeing only what you would see alone?

"He taught me to see," said the young blind wife I described in Chapter 3 who lighted the marital candles with her physically impaired husband. "I think I see him better than most wives who can see their husbands. I use his eyes for my own view of the world, and I see with our love. I really think your eyes can blind you, and you can have better vision if you don't depend on your eyes. If you are used to depending on your eyes, you start to get lazy in how you look. When people say that they don't look so good, I think they might mean that they are not seeing what they could see if they would look with their hearts instead of their eyes."

4. Are you an optic opportunist, looking for the good, the beautiful, and the wonderfully unique about your spouse rather than a perceptual pessimist looking for defects and imperfections?

"One key choice you make in a marriage is what you are going to look for," said a Silver Survivor. "You can look for beauty or you can look for a beast. I hear about a lot of marriages in which the husband or wife is creating a marital monster out of the spouse and looking for every negative he or she can find. Sooner or later, we all get the face we deserve. Either by frowning and causing our own wrinkles or by looking for and then creating the flaws we see in our spouses, we get what we deserve."

5. *Do you take good glances rather than looking with long, critical, and valuative stares at your spouse?*

"When we had our first child, I remember that I loved her so much that it bothered me when I saw her doing something bad like being a brat with another child or picking at her nose. It just didn't fit my romantic image of her. Then I learned just to look away and not take such long and critical looks. If you look long enough, you'll always find something you don't like even with someone you love. Now I do the same thing with my husband. I look quickly for the good. When I see him doing something I don't like or that doesn't fit my loving image of him, I just look away. Quick looks are less likely to leave lastingly bad impressions, but a quick glance that confirms my love seems to make me want to look again. I call these my forgiving glances."

6. *Without looking at your spouse right now, could you describe in detail exactly what he or she is wearing, including color, style, and pattern?*

"My sister was surprised the other day," said one wife. "She was having coffee with me, and we saw my husband pull up in our car coming home from work. I decided to show off and tell her, without looking, exactly what he was wearing, including tie color and color of his socks, shoes, and cuff links. I hit it perfectly except for the tie. He had spilled soup on it before a meeting at work and had bought a new one to wear. I feel like my mother. She used to be sitting in the kitchen when I was leaving for school. When I came home, she could say at a glance, 'Where's the scarf you had on this morning?' I guess when you really are a part of somebody else, you see a lot quick."

7. *When you look at your spouse, do you look for the special beauty and attractiveness unique to your partner or do you look "comparatively," using some external standard of size, weight, height, or other cultural beauty criterion?*

"I think your marriage is in real trouble if you have to compete with the bathing suit models in *Sports Illustrated*," said one wife. "If I thought for a minute that my husband compared me with those young kids, I would give up. He loves to look at beautiful women and I love to look at beautiful men, but that's a lot different from the beauty we see in each other and project to each other. It really turns me off when I hear women telling me how a woman should look to keep her man."

8. *Do you look at your spouse with a fresh outlook, without confirming what you have seen in the past and without assuming that you have been looking at your partner for years and already know exactly what you will see?*

"When I was looking in the mirror the other day, my husband came up behind me and started looking with me," said the wife. "He ran his hands over my face as we looked. We didn't talk, we just looked. I felt like he was looking at me for the first time, and it was a very special moment for us—a MIM well invested."

9. *Do you work at creating a pleasing visual image of yourself for your partner instead of taking the marriage relationship for granted and saving your "sprucing up" for strangers and friends?*

"Why do we work so hard to look great for people we don't love and take a beauty break when we are around those we do?" asked another Silver Survivor. "You can't dress up all the time, but you can both put the effort into looking good for your spouse. I noticed one day that when the doorbell rings, I have a straightening-up reflex. I always quickly comb my hair and adjust my clothes. The mailman never catches me at my worst, so I try to present at least my minimum mailman look for my husband."

10. Do you look in unbiased fashion for a variety of moods and feelings when you look at your spouse instead of just looking for the mood or feeling you want to see or are afraid you might see?

"I can feel my wife scanning me sometimes," said the husband. "It's like Dr. McCoy in *Star Trek* when he scans somebody. Dr. McCoy scans vital signs, but my wife scans for vitally good signs. She can find something good or special no matter how rotten I think I look or how bad I'm feeling."

The average score of Silver Survivors on the vital vision test was 9.2. The control group scored 4.3 (higher than on some of the other tests, perhaps because couples in distress begin looking at one another—sometimes for the first time).

Perceptual Protection

The best protection you can give your spouse is to protect him or her from hurting you. You do this by beginning with the assumption that most people do not hurt other people *intentionally*. We hurt people by failing to pay enough *attention* to others' feelings. When we look critically for our partner's *intentions* and fail to look with loving *attention* to our spouse's potential for loving, we only hurt our marriage.

In my work with couples, I asked them to begin with the assumption—true or not—that neither partner intends to hurt the other. Although both partners were feeling pain, we assumed that it was accidentally inflicted by the spouse, and that if the intent was indeed to inflict pain, they could have done a much better job.

If you look for love in your partner and agree together to look with love at one another and to remain perceptually open to all that your spouse can be—instead of seeing someone who wants to hurt you in some subtle way—the marriage can become a place of mutual protection rather than a competitive, critical appraisal system. When you see a changing wave of loving energy rather than a particle person who is static and fixed in his or her annoying ways and hurtful habits, you begin to see your partner's potential for love and not just the pain he or she may seem to cause.

Saying "I'm feeling hurt" is much more constructive to a marriage than the words "You're hurting me." When you say what you are feeling, you have the power to play an active role in making changes. When you say what someone is doing to you or how he or she is "making" you feel, you become powerless to create change, and your marriage will be haunted by the ghosts of your past as a couple and monstrous images of your future. Ralph Waldo Emerson warned us to "Be present in the present," and miracle marriages loving together in keeping with the fourth law of lasting love see the Now of their marriage as something they are constantly creating together. You are much less likely to be hurt by someone you are looking at with love in your eyes and who sees the hope of future potentialities, acceptance, and forgiveness reflected there.

Ping-Pong Peeking: Eye Calling

As one final example of the power of the Love Look, consider what the Silver Survivors refer to as eye calling. One husband Silver Survivor described eye calling this way: "The participant-observer principle of lasting love means that by looking at my partner, I also affect not only how but how often she will look at me. I don't have to ask my wife to pay attention. I can 'eye' her to." The Silver Survivors call this alternating perceptual style Ping-Pong peeking. When one spouse looks at the other, there is something about the looking that elicits a looking back.

"His looking at me is just like a 'message-waiting' light inside me," said one wife. "I can feel his eyes and sense when he is looking, and I will look back. He does the same thing with me. Sometimes we laugh about it when he looks, then I look, then he looks, and so on until we seem to have sent a ton of messages without talking. It's like perception Ping-Pong."

This wife's statement reflects the tangible power of creative observation. All of us have experienced the sensation of feeling someone's eyes on us. Like the quarks in quantum physics, we are reacting to the influence of the observer and feeling the tangible force of being observed that can change us from particle person to a wave of loving energy.

I noticed that the Silver Survivors usually got one another's attention not by calling out the spouse's name but simply by looking in their direction. Eye calling is a simple thing, but it is further evidence that the look of love can help you cast a loving eye on your marriage.

HOME LOVE ASSIGNMENTS

1. Try the eye-calling exercise with your spouse. When you think your husband or wife is not paying attention to you, call him or her to you with your eyes. I promise you that it will work, and you will have proved the power of the fourth law of lasting love and one of the key laws of physics—the law of the participant-observer.

2. Play perceptual Ping-Pong with your spouse. Sit across the room from each other and look at each other. You will notice that a visual rhythm will automatically emerge between you as the power of the observer shows itself again. Without changing the focus of your eyes and just looking into each other's eyes, you will sense that something within both of you causes your partner to seem to be looking "at" you for a while. Then the looking switches, and you will feel that you are looking at your partner. There will be a rhythmic alteration between who seems to be looking *at* whom. You also will notice that you begin to send messages about feelings back and forth without talking. If you discuss this exercise together later, you will both notice that you've become much better at this means of communication.

3. One of the exercises often used by the couples in my clinic is called eye-balling. The word "balling" has been used as a crude slang expression for sexual intercourse. The couples modified the term and used it to refer to my assignment requiring them to set aside some private quiet time at home and lie nude together in bed with only a candle or soft light burning. I ask them to look eye to eye while they embrace

and sense and express their sexual and sensual arousal with their eyes, not their hands or bodies. I asked the couple to refrain from making physical love after this exercise so that the assignment was not experienced as a form of sexual foreplay or titillation but as a means of seeing and knowing the partner beyond the urgency of physical arousal.

4. The next time you go to a museum or travel to some new place, use your spouse's eyes to see. Close your eyes and have your husband or wife describe what he or she is seeing. Have your spouse tell you what he or she sees in looking at a painting, a sculpture, or some feature of nature. Then allow your partner to borrow your eyes and describe what you see.

5. When your spouse is not aware of it, try to study him or her. This isn't easy, because you may end up eye calling, but if the other person is distracted by reading or by some other activity, take a good look. Don't look just to see how your spouse is; look to see all he or she has been with you and still can be. The power of the observer and the power of the Love Look is seeing the potential in one another to create loving by projecting love's image to your spouse and your marriage. Don't look out! Look in!

STEP V

Complements of Love:

MARRY QUITE CONTRARY

I will celebrate our differences.

We have to forgive each other our halfness. That's where we start, and we work up from there.
—Ken Wilbur

LOVE LAW FIVE:
THE COMPLEMENTARY-LOVE LAW

COMPLEMENTARY LOVING: Men and women are two different ways nature expresses the components of its wholeness. New physics teaches that everything in the universe exists in complementary pairs, each of which is necessary for the existence of the other. Just as waves and particles are two different but complementary ways of expressing one quantum reality, maleness and femaleness are the complementary parts of nature's "real" whole person. Lasting love does not depend on men becoming more like women and women becoming more like men. A miracle marriage is made from understanding, accepting, forgiving, and then celebrating our halfness and making a powerful new whole of the halves that each of us contributes.

Why Are Most Marriages Heterosexual?

Throughout history, marriages generally have taken place between men and women. Men seldom marry men and women seldom marry women. Beyond mere procreative imperatives, is there any other reason that we usually marry heterosexually?

"Are you crazy?" answered one of my male medical students when I posed the above question in class. "If I wanted to marry a man, I'd just marry myself," he continued. "I'm hard, women are soft. I'm flat where they go out. They're just the opposite of me and that's what I like about them."

Even though the class laughed as this male sudent continued his homophobic tirade about male-male marriage, the student had raised a key point about the fifth law of lasting love—Complementary Love. Most of us accept biological or physical complementarity in the form of sexual attraction between the sexes, but we seem to stop short of seeing that complementarity goes far beyond this male's final chauvinistic statement: "Men have a pole and women have a hole. It's a perfect fit, and it's just the way nature intended it to be."

Low Monogamy maintains barriers between gender-based biological and procreative differences as both spouses remain half people, living their lives beside each other. High Monogamy of the Great Marriage Myth celebrates the central gender differences by merging the complementary natures of men and women in how they think, feel, behave, believe, and love.

Most marriages are heterosexual because the two genders are halves of nature's whole. Although it is possible that two men or two women could form a miracle marriage of their own complementarities, it is less likely that they are naturally opposite enough to make a sufficiently enduring and dynamic whole.

Opposite but Never Separate

The universe is a massive collection of contraries. Good versus evil, inside versus outside, light versus dark, positive versus negative electrons, high versus low, long versus short, life versus death, pleasure versus pain, and an infinite number of opposites are nature's template of life. We assume that Heaven is where all the positive sides of the opposites of life await us—where joy, peace, security, and love are. Hell is where despair, suffering, fear, and pain wait for the failed human spirit. We define all progress as movement *away* from negatives and toward the *positive,* yet all of the progress of modern medicine, agriculture, and industry toward what we have deemed to be the positive side of life has not seemed to make humanity much happier.

We assume that because the nature of things is that they exist in complementary pairs, one of the pair is automatically better than the other. We flee from one of the pair and rush madly toward the other, and as a result we lead unhappy and one-sided lives. Our technological progress toward one side of nature's opposites—the world of stuff—has resulted in what some social commentators call the Age of Anxiety or the Time of Melancholia. We have almost all of one side of life and almost nothing of the other—the spiritual—so we find ourselves spiritually suffering in great technological comfort.

We are afraid of death, so we try to sap all we can out of life. We are afraid of illness, so we jog until we injure our knees and eat fiber until our bowels lock in order to stay well. We are afraid of loneliness, so we do almost anything to find someone to be with—if only for an evening of sexual passion or in a series of failed marriages matched to our career, childbearing, and aging needs. Low Monogamy is well suited to the pursuit of one side of life's complementary pairs, because it maintains the boundaries between opposite Me's rather than making the miracle of a new One Us capable of "looking at love from both sides now."

Our depression and melancholia rest with our difficulty in merging nature's opposites and continuing in vain to establish one "opposite" as "the only way to be." Nature and evolution have seen to it that differences that do not make a difference do not survive. Without death, life could not exist. Without darkness, there could be no concept of light. Without femaleness, there could be no maleness. We can combine our differences and break down the boundaries between the genders by realizing that we are naturally complementary halves of one loving whole.

Hopping over the Bundling Board

In rural colonial America, courting men and women were allowed to occupy the same bed for the night, so long as a two-foot-high board was placed between them. This piece of wood was called the bundling board, and it seldom served to be an effective barrier. An entire generation of "bundling board jumpers" was created when this wall of love was erected. As poet Robert Frost suggested, there is something about nature that doesn't tolerate walls and barriers.

Nature created opposites, but never boundaries. There are no natural permanent walls in the universe. The lessons learned when the world tried to divide Germany with a wall between East and West Berlin demonstrated that, try as we might, we cannot overcome nature's way of oneness. East and West may be opposite directions, but they are not separable places.

Einstein's relativity theory taught us that rest and motion are opposites that become One. Planck's quantum mechanics revealed that particles and waves are opposites, but that they are both aspects of one reality. Just as waves and particles can become a One in which "each is both," our maleness and femaleness or yin and yang can merge into a miracle.

Kipling's claim, "East is West, and West is West, and never the twain shall meet," reflects the orientation of the Me Myth that there is a boundary between you and me, and the I and the Thou. "Boys will be boys" and "Isn't that just like a woman" are statements that reflect our failure to see that nature's opposites are presented to us as challenges to create wholes and not as permanent territorial maps demarcating life's polarities. Everything that "is" exists interwoven with everything else. The fifth step in this miracle-marriage manual requires that we learn that lasting love is the process through which the "twain can meet."

A Coincidence of Opposites

Physics teaches that we can no longer speak of an object being located in space or happening in time, but only of a space-time occurrence. Where, who, how, and when we are all merge into a union of opposites or what physicist Ludwig von Bertalanffy called "the coincidence of opposites."[1] Through the merging of the natural coincidence of opposites, all life is created.

My wife and I were watching the waves off Maui today. There is a beautiful white-sand beach that sparkles against the deep blue ocean at a place the locals on Maui call Dig Me Beach. This is a place where people go to be seen or "dug" and to "strut their stuff" in a man-woman courtship ritual. The women walk in pairs, talking softly to one another in their "dental floss bikinis," pausing every half hour or so to pose strategically on their blankets. They act as if it were mere coincidence that they are at Dig Me Beach so near their counterparts. The men walk in larger and louder groups. They flex their muscles, push, shove, and wrestle with one another. They roughhouse in the surf as if the women pretending not to watch were there only to get a sun tan.

The two groups so opposite in their styles appear separated from one another by an invisible beach bundling board, but the barrier is an illusion. One surfer told me, "The guys show off on their surfboards, and the girls pretend they are surf-bored, but we know each of us is here. That's why we're here." No matter how separate the wrestling warriors and watching sand maidens remain, they slowly but surely move toward one another. By the time the sun begins to set at Dig Me Beach, many pairs of pushers and posers have merged into matched couples of surfers and sunners.

My wife and I noticed how like the waves these young people were. The powerful waves that crash to the shore are another form of naturally occurring coincidental opposites merging into a meaningful One. Each wave is a single event that expresses itself by its combination of crest and trough. There could not be a wave to watch and wonder at or to surf in if two troughs or two crests combined. Two sames could never make the miracle of a wave. There could not be the miracle of lasting love if there were not sunners and surfers—females and males trying to navigate through life together. Two sames make more of the same. The combination of two complementary opposites makes the miracle of a new One.

The fifth law of lasting love—Complementary Love—is that men and women are created with certain major sexual differences. Lasting love depends on finding ways to accommodate each other's genuine differences creatively instead of trying to dismiss, overcome, ignore, or diminish them.

Induced into Our Gender

Popular psychology's attempts to diminish the basic differences between the genders have failed, because we just can't help it—we differ by far more than the distinction between our genital insignia. To paraphrase a cliché of the old American West that "men are men, and they smell like it," the complementary law of loving says that "men are men, and women are women, and both genders love like it."

Author James Thurber said, "I love the idea of there being two sexes, don't you?" God saw to it that the complementarity of a two-sex system is set within us during our development. The "inductor" theory of neonatal development states that the template of our gender is "induced" by a chain reaction passing from gene to hormone to brain. We are all conceived naturally female. Some of us stay that way, whereas others of us are induced to differentiate into the "complementary female" known as the male.[2] We all start out female, but if an XY (male or Adam) chromosomal pattern is present, the brain of the growing fetus reacts more intensively to the effects of the testosterone that impacts on all fetuses in the sex week, or about six weeks into prenatal development. The chromosomal XX (female or Eve) pattern results in a less testosterone-reactive brain, and the relay race of chromosomes to hormones to brain structure to gender loving style is under way.

Actor Alan Alda jokes about male behavior patterns being due to "testosterone poisoning." He says that the symptoms of this poisoning include tear deficiency, potbelly, spindly legs, and a tendency to sleep on couches.[3] Within Alan Alda's humor is much truth, for the testosteronized brain of the male is significantly different from that of the female.

Sex Stew

Because of the differing testosterone reactivity, a different love map becomes inscribed in the minds of adult men and women.[4] The sex hormone testosterone acts like a "sex stew," in which our brains simmer through their early development. This stew continues to brew in the form of a masculinizing hormone produced in adult men by the testicular cells of Leydig and in the adult female to the adrenal glands. For the XY Adam fetus, the impact of this hormone at about six weeks can divert the naturally female fetal brain to a male mind, and nature's "couple's coincidence of opposites" continues through life.[5]

Early medical models saw the brain as an electronic machine or switchboard. We now see the brain as more of a soggy computer, functioning by way of the misting of neurochemicals over, around, and through the neurons or brain cells. This magnificent organ weighs less than 3 pounds and in the mature adult constitutes only 8 percent of our total body weight, yet it is the most complex of all nature's creations. How the brain functions determines much, but not all, of how we live. You read in Chapter 4 how the mind can tell the brain how and what to think. Nonetheless, how the brain is oriented toward the world determines a great deal of how we are oriented in our loving. Testosterone is one of the most powerful psychochemical mind mists, and it predisposes the Adam or Eve fetus to think and love in opposite ways.

Alpha and Beta Minds

The male mind thinks in terms of objects, manipulation, and power. One Silver Survivor summarized the male mind pattern as "M for mechanistic, A for aggressive, L for lust, and E for ego." The female mind thinks in terms of people, responsiveness, and caring. The Silver Survivor described female thinking as "F for feeling, E for empathy, M for meaning, A for altruistic, L for listener, and E for effacing." Although this Silver Survivor was overgeneralizing and exaggerating (one-sidedly) the opposites of male and female cognition, she was essentially correct.

Because some women "think like men" and some men "think

like women," I refer to the typical testosteronized male-mind thought style as "alpha thinking." The term "alpha" has been used by zoologists to refer to the dominant, aggressive, manipulative, powerful animal in a group—usually but not always a male. I refer to the female mind thought style as "beta thinking," or the less dominant and less aggressive pattern of thinking and behaving. Men are often alpha thinkers because nature made them that side of the male-female opposite arrangement. Women are more often beta thinkers because nature made them the other side of the female-male "coincidence of opposites" template. Because of factors we do not yet understand (possible in-utero factors resulting from stress, disease, drugs, etc.), some Adams (XY) think in the beta fashion and Eves (XX) think in the alpha fashion.

In a sense, we all have half a mind—either alpha or beta—and the challenge of a lasting relationship is to make this pattern work for instead of against our love. As you work through this fifth step in this marriage manual, remember the lesson from Chapter 5's Two-Time love law that nothing in nature is absolute. What we define as "male" or "alpha" thinking can, to various degrees, be found in wives, and vice versa. Your own marriage may have an "alpha female" and a "beta male." It is much more typical, however, for the Adam fetus than the Eve fetus to have its brain stewed in testosterone. Perhaps it was nature's plan that giving us opposite ways of thinking would cause us to learn not to think as one but as two together.

Sex and the Single Hemisphere: Half a Brain

Just as everything in nature exists in opposites, the cerebral cortex, or the cap on top of the brain where we do most of our thinking, has two opposite sides to its wholeness. Among other things, the left side specializes in verbal and listening skills, interpersonal relationships, interpretation, and finding meaning in the world. The right side specializes in doing, using, manipulating, fixing, and feeling. Both genders draw from both sides in all that they do and think, but they do so in quite opposite ways.

Boys (or alpha thinkers) show earlier right-hemisphere de-

velopment than girls, and this in part explains their cradle preference for things over sounds and space over people.[6] Girls (or
beta thinkers) have a more developed left hemisphere, in part
explaining their general superiority in verbal skills and listening
over boys' preference for doing and manipulating.[7] Girls' brains
are wired for discussion and conversation and boys' brains are
set up more for doing and controlling.[8] Because of their "testosterone poisoning," men have a built-in brain bias for compartmentalized thinking, hearing and interpreting feelings less
effectively, and being consumed more with carburetors than
caring.[9]

Because of their less developed corpus callosum (the part of
the brain that helps our left and right hemispheres communicate
with each other) boys' or alphas' brains are made to function one
hemisphere at a time—what some women or betas may experience as a half-witted approach to life. They have trouble putting
their right brains together with their lefts and their feelings together with their mouths. Their genitals seem to have a mind of
their own, because the part of the brain controlling genital response is dissociated from caring, consideration, and caution.
Their ability to know "why" they do what they do or the effect
it has on those around them is not as developed as the female's
sensitivities in these same areas.

Because women or beta thinkers have a more well-developed
corpus callosum, or "brain connector," the left sides of their
brains usually know and can interpret what their right brains
are feeling. What a woman "does" is strongly influenced by the
right hemisphere. The typical alpha thinking of the male is more
segmented and feelings are more easily distanced or forgotten.
The typical beta thinking of the female is more holistic and tends
to blend the feelings from the right side with the facts from the
left.[10] Men sometimes have feelings about what they are doing,
but women more often try to do what they are feeling.

As far back as the nineteenth century, German psychologist
Gustav Fechner proposed that splitting the hemispheres of the
brain would result in two separate human beings. Surgery that
accomplished just this (called commissurotomy, because the com-
missures, or connections between the hemispheres, are severed)
was first done in the early 1940s as one means of controlling
severe epilepsy. This surgery is still performed in rare cases

today, and studies of approximately 300 patients who have undergone this treatment reveal that their left brains have no "idea" what their right brains are experiencing.

Alpha and beta thinking patterns are two opposite mind personalities that can be combined into a marriage of One mind that unifies both male and female thought styles. The alpha style is more "particular" or segmented and partialistic in its approach to life. The beta cycle is one of waves of energy and emotion.

The right brain is very, very "stupid." It is made for processing without reflection or contemplation. Australian physiologist Sir John Eccles writes, "I don't even know if you could assign it the attribute of having an attitude. There is a distinction between mere consciousness, which your average dog and cat have, and the world of language, thought and culture of human consciousness."[11] Alphas, who have less of a connection between their left and right brains and are more right-brain–oriented to begin with, are coded to be a little more "stupid" or less humanly conscious than the betas, whose left and right brains work better together.[12]

The Male's Overgrown Clitoris

The testosterone effect that occurs at about six weeks into prenatal development reaches from head to groin. The natural Eve (XX) assembly instructions for female genitalia can be altered by testosterone during the prenatal sex week.[13] In almost all cases, when the natural XX Eve chromosomal pattern is present, a clitoris develops as an organ to enhance sexual pleasure, and labia and vagina are fashioned for sexual pleasure and a birth canal.

The XY Adam assembly instructions allow testosterone to do a form of neuro-transsexual surgery on the alpha's or testosteronized fetus's genitalia. What would have been his tiny clitoris grows to an immense size. Unlike the female, who is free to use her clitoris for pleasure only, the male experiences the development of a huge clitoris-penis, which must serve the quadruple duty of ridding the body of waste, carrying sperm, receiving pleasure, and symbolizing alpha or dominant status among his alpha-mates. One of my beta-Eve medical students stunned her male classmates by pointing out, "Women just have this clitoris thing tucked away waiting for pleasure. We can use our clitoris, but men are used by their penis. Men don't have anything like what we have. Our clitoris comes out when, where, and with whom we want it to, but a man's penis just hangs out there all the time. I've never heard a woman called a 'big clitoris,' but I've certainly heard many men referred to as big—well, I don't want to say it in public. I think Freud and his men have clitoris envy and vaginal awe."

In the testosteronized male, his "ovaries" drop down in the form of two spheres to be carried in a sack formed by the sealing of his labia. In effect, the scrotum is a sealed vagina with millions of immature half-eggs with tails developing inside. The penis sits on top of the entire modified apparatus working overtime at several jobs.

Combining the single-hemisphere alpha-Adam brain and his overgrown clitoris with a beta-Eve's whole-brained approach accompanied by a sex organ made only for pleasure at its owner's demand, we have either God's greatest hoax or His greatest challenge to make these differences complementary instead of devastating. If we can learn the lesson of complementary loving, we can break down the boundaries we ourselves have created between nature's necessary opposites to join in a remarkable and adventurous journey of love.

The Two Pornographies

One example of contrasting alpha and beta styles is their respective pornographies. Typical male-oriented (alpha) pornography, with its focus on anonymous sex and orgasm, treats women as sex objects to be manipulated and used. Women are exploited for their bodies and their subservient indulgence of any male sexual need. Their unique and personal worth as individuals is ignored.

Women's (beta) pornography—in the form of popular romantic novels—sees men as success objects, who rescue, protect, and indulge women with diamonds and furs. The covers of these novels show muscular men in protective postures with women clinging to their hero's glistening bodies. These success studs have "taken their woman away" from all danger. The man's personal and individual worth is disregarded in favor of his skills, strength, and stamina. Both alpha and beta forms of pornography are exploitive, because they do not value the woman or man for their own unique merits or for their unique human dignity.

Men's pornography is much more visually explicit, but women's "novel pornography" is much more widespread. Success-object novels are purchased by the millions, but sex-object novels do not sell nearly as well. Men have their adult peep shows, but women have their soap operas. The two opposites of pornography reveal how each gender brings its own negative side to the relationship between the genders. Realizing how alphas or betas bring their politics to their loving is an important step toward helping each person find his or her missing half.

Alpha and Beta Equals Omega

Take the following test to discover where you and your partner are on the alpha-beta spectrum. By breaking down the barriers between the natural opposites of alpha and beta styles of thinking and loving and contributing the strengths of each of our respective loving styles to our marriage, we can make a new complementary whole called Omega Merging. Omega is the last letter of the Greek alphabet and often is used to represent a final holistic merging. Like the onta, or the dualistic Oneness I described in Chapter 7, omega represents a merging of alpha and beta complementary loving styles into a loving totality.

In taking this test, it may be helpful for you to ask your spouse to classify you while you do the same for him or her. On a piece of paper, write the numbers 1 through 30. Next to each number, write either an A (for alpha-style thinking) or B (for beta-style thinking). Remember two things as you assess your loving style. First, men are usually alpha and women are usually beta, but the style that has evolved from your own childhood or from within your own relationship may not comply with this pattern. Answer on the basis of how you are in your relationship and not how you think you should be. Second, this test is based on opposites and averages, and each item is exaggerated in its contrasting opposites. Everyone is unique and would probably fall somewhere between the two poles for each item. The forced-choice nature of this test is intended to facilitate awareness of the "necessary differences" that make for meaningful marriages and not the relegation of a spouse to a personality type.

Count up the number of alpha and beta characteristics to see which way you tend to lean on this scale of couple complementarity. Just by being a man or woman, you automatically score either one alpha or one beta point on No. 23.

Silver Survivors' marriages were characterized by the fact that one spouse leaned strongly to the beta side on the above test, while the other was much more alpha. It was not always the Adam who was alpha or the Eve who was beta, but the Silver Survivors arranged themselves into alpha-beta omega couples with one partner contributing the alpha half and the other contributing the beta half.

The control group of failing marriages was characterized by two alphas, two betas, or a failure to form a holistic omega point that acknowledged, forgave, and integrated alpha-beta differences into a strong unit. A key difference between the control group and the Silver Survivors was that the miracle marriages saw the opposite sides of this test as "marital menus," from which each spouse brought his or her own source of nurturance to the marriage, while the failing marriages saw the test as two columns from which each partner drew evidence of the other's weaknesses and flaws. "Look at all we can bring to our marriage" was the approach of the High Monogamists. "Look at how different and separate we are" was the approach of the Low Monogamists.

Omega: The Golden Mean

Aristotle believed that beauty and love were attained by striving for what he called "the golden mean." He was referring to the principle of "nothing in excess." Through this philosophy, he was anticipating the quantum physics principle of complementarity, which holds that nothing is complete alone or in and of itself.[14] Walling oneself off from a lover by clinging unresponsively to too much alpha-tizing or beta-tizing creates barriers to a marital omega point.

Philosopher Pierre Teilhard de Chardin wrote, "Nothing is precious except that part of you which is in other people and that part of others which is in you. Up there on high, everything is one."[15] His message illustrates the two necessary tasks of High

THE ALPHA-BETA TEST
OF COUPLE COMPLEMENTARITY

ALPHA	BETA
1. Emotionally stoic	Emotionally hypersensitive
2. Physically numb and unresponsive to touch	Overly demanding and needful of physical touch
3. Distracted and oblivious to surroundings	Hyperalert and overreactive to surroundings
4. Undersensitive sense of smell	Hypersensitive sense of smell
5. Hyporeactive to sound	Hyperreactive to sounds
6. Poor memory for details	Nitpicking about details
7. Thing- and gadget-oriented	Person- and relationship-oriented
8. Poor reader of subtle cues, seems oblivious to signals	Oversensitive to slightest clues and cues
9. Bases decision on self-needs and self-enhancement	Overly accommodating and self-sacrificing
10. Overly intolerant	Overly forgiving
11. Seldom confides in others	Overly open and trusting
12. Poor memory for faces, good for names	Good memory for faces, poor for names
13. Misses the hidden meaning	Too alert for hidden meanings
14. Domineering, controlling	Too compliant
15. Overly cynical	Overly naïve
16. Resists comforting and nurturing behaviors	Childlike dependence on parentlike behaviors
17. Visually stuck: "sees it = believes it"	Flight and fantasy: "believes it = sees it"
18. Present-oriented—practical, pragmatic	Past- and future-oriented—impractical, romantic
19. Passionately assertive	Compassionately a pushover
20. Likes sex	Likes sensuousness
21. Lights on during sex (never shy about body)	Lights off during sex (very shy about body)

ALPHA

22. Realistic and unwilling to dream and pretend
23. Male
24. Hostile
25. Overly competitive
26. Projects blame to others
27. Sees things as always changing for the better
28. Wants to take action rather than listen

29. Says things once, and that's it
30. Eternal optimist and denier of problems—realist with a "don't worry, be happy" orientation to life

BETA

Lives in a dream world

Female
Passive
Always compromising
Takes things too personally
Sees things as staying bad or getting worse
Just wants to be heard rather than doing something about a problem
Ruminates and goes on and on
Eternal pessimist and seeker of problems—superstitious with a "if you're happy, worry" orientation to life

Monogamy related to the fifth step of Complementary Love. First, we must learn to accept the fact that we are all half-people in search of someone else with whom we can become (not be made!) whole. Second, we must work on our own to diminish those areas in our loving where we are taking too opposite an orientation to daily living. We must be willing to suffer a silencing or softening of the extent of our alpha or beta nature to facilitate the merging of opposites.

Low Monogamists "passionately" cling to who they are as individuals, no matter how opposite from their partner they seem. High Monogamists "compassionately" choose to suffer with someone else to fit their opposites together, by working at modulating their nature and accepting the nature of their lover.

Time Is on Our Side

As we age, male levels of testosterone decrease and female testosterone levels tend to increase. It's as if nature feels that we have had our chance to wrestle with the opposites of life, so she gives us a reward for enduring the silencing of the self and learning a lasting loving. We are given the chance in our later years to rest from the hard work of making our miracle to enjoy it more fully together. The diminished hormonal effect associated with aging is not overwhelming, and basic differences remain, but there is something peaceful in the long-lasting marriages that go far beyond surrender. One argument for sticking it out in a marriage when we seem too opposite from one another is that time will temper our hormonally based brain differences.

I learned from the longest-lasting marriages in my study that a major part of the law of Complementary Love is learning the difference between surrender and submission. Submissiveness implies that we give up our unique individuality "for" and "to" someone else. Surrender implies that we "give in with" our partner to the natural differences between us to allow the differences to make a stronger whole.

Each of us carries half of the values of the human race.[16] Men, or alphas, know about "going somewhere" and are driven by a passion in their quest of accomplishment. Women know about "being there" and show a compassion and caring about everything and everyone. Submission is "giving up" to one or the other of these opposite orientations and is the way of Low Monogamy and Me. Surrender is giving in to and for a new relationship containing two people growing together. Low Monogamy requires only submission for its survival, but a miracle marriage requires the ultimate act of love—the surrender of the self for the good of a new Us.

HOME LOVE ASSIGNMENTS

1. Retake the alpha-beta test in this chapter several times over several weeks. Score yourself, score your partner, and have your partner score you. Discuss how permanent the patterns seem to be and where and why any changes seem to be taking place.
2. What would the two of you agree is the biggest difference between you regarding the alpha-beta scale? Which of the

thirty items of the alpha-beta test reveals the biggest disparity in point of view or behavior in your marriage? Discuss whether the difference is a strength or weakness and whether or not you would like to accentuate or minimize that difference.

3. Since your marriage has the purpose of enhancing the world as well as each of your lives, discuss your feelings regarding whether the world in general seems to be becoming more alpha or more beta in its approach to people, politics, and the planet. How does your marriage fit into the alpha or beta nature of your experience of the world at large?

4. How much of your own behavior has influenced your spouse toward alpha or beta characteristics? Discuss how each of you tends to alpha-tize or beta-tize the other by your actions or inactions in your marriage. For example, one alpha Silver Survivor said, "I really never saw the value in this meditation stuff. I'm a doer, not a thinker. My husband is the contemplative type, and I've noticed that I'm getting a little more that way than I used to be. He meditates for an hour and I'm a minute meditator, but I can see him in me. I'm becoming more beta-tized, and I think he's getting a little more alpha-tized."

5. If you were forced to classify your marriage, discuss together if your marriage "omega" point or Oneness seems to lean more toward an alpha or a beta orientation. Your view of this will change over time, so put in some MIMs to take stock of the alpha-beta nature of your loving to be sure it is heading in the direction of surrender for the relationship rather than submission to your spouse. The fifth step in making a miracle marriage involves trying daily to make the natural opposites of two lovers into one complementary omega unit by taking the following steps summarized by the letters in the word OMEGA:

● O—Be *Open* to seeing your own alpha or beta nature. Your partner may see your style more clearly than you do, so listen to him or her.

● M—Try to *Meet* your partner halfway by not establishing barriers because of your differences. Forgive the faults and incompleteness in the Me in one another, because that Me was designed to be only a half.

• E—Try to *Empathize* with your partner's style because he or she can't help it. The unique and opposite characteristics of your spouse were largely given to him or her before birth and strongly reinforced during childhood. Rather than lay guilt upon a partner, let that partner know you know he or she can only bring half to the marriage. The other half is your responsibility.

• G—*Grow* together to complete each other's halfness rather than criticizing each other for what comes naturally. As one Silver Survivor put it, "I think of it as the 'seven-year hitch.' It takes at least seven years of marriage just to know who's alpha and who's beta and to what degree. Then you can begin to really start to put your halves together to make a whole marriage."

• A—*Affirm* your partner rather than blaming him or her. Work together to use the opposites that each of you brings to the marriage instead of trying to be someone you will never be or expecting such an unrealistic goal from your spouse. Remember that the law of Complementary Love asserts that opposites are necessary for the making of wholes. Lasting loving is always a matter of choices. In the case of complementarity, you can choose to accommodate one another's half or to attempt together to transcend your individual halves to make a new whole. Low Monogamy only asks that each spouse accept, accommodate, submit, or perhaps attempt to fake being someone or some way he or she is not naturally designed to be. The Great Marriage Myth asks each spouse to transcend his or her natural differences by first accepting them, then forgiving them in each other and in themselves, and finally learning how to celebrate the miracle of nature's way of giving us the two halves of a miracle and the love to put them together.

STEP VI

The Quantum Leap of Love:

COMING TOGETHER ANYWHERE

I am with you anywhere, anytime.

Whatever it is, it avails not—distance avails not, and place avails not.

—*Walt Whitman*

LOVE LAW SIX: THE TRANSCENDENT-LOVE LAW

Lasting love that comes from the union of two souls transcends space and time. It is not bound by our bodies, diminished by distance, or blocked by barriers of any type. Miracle love is never local or restricted by the see-and-touch world. Miracle love is unmediated, unmitigated, and instantaneous in its effect.

Grace and Grit

As the oxygen mask was slipped over my face, I heard someone in the operating room say, "It will take a miracle to save him." Sitting hundreds of feet away, the miracle maker was already at work. Through the concrete walls and faster than the speed of light, a healing energy burned through me, an "always fatal" virus was destroyed, and I was saved.

Stories of medical miracles often tell of personal grit, the healing power of the individual's mind, and a positive attitude. In my case, it was more grace than grit that saved me. I had given up after two cancers, two chemotherapies, total body radiation, and a viral pneumonia had sapped every ounce of my energy. Through the grace of the love of my marriage, however, nothing as local or here-and-now as a virus could stop my miracle.

My wife sat with one of my sons in a dark waiting room down the hall from the operating room. She sent the healing power of her love to me through walls, metal, flesh, and bones to spark instantaneously the immune cells in my body to demolish the invaders of my body. Until the revolution in scientific thought in the early 1900s, it was assumed that immediate action-at-a-distance, or effects that were faster than the speed of light, were impossible. The greatest scientific minds in the world, however, showed that nonlocality, or such spontaneous and nonphysical effects, were not only possible but commonplace. The sixth step of this miracle-marriage manual shows you how to use the power of what science calls nonlocality and I call the grace of love to work miracles.

Local Lust or Limitless Love

"You really think you know how powerful love is when you first become infatuated with your lover," said one Silver Survivor. "You are overwhelmed at first, but it is just like the preview of coming attractions at the movies. It's a flash of some of the spicy parts of loving, but it is far from the whole picture itself. Lasting love is like a powerful full-length film. It has fast-moving parts, slower-moving parts, tears, and laughter, and causes a range of feelings. And the best films transform you in some way forever, and that's what lasting love does."

This wife's statement illustrates that romantic love—the love of Low Monogamy—is local. It's an immediate, here-and-now, lustful intensity limited by time and space. When the person we are infatuated with is not with us, we pine for him or her and feel completely out of touch with that person. When our spouse in a lasting love—the love of High Monogamy—is not physically with us, we can still feel, see, and communicate with him or her. Lasting love is "super love" that travels faster than the light from the sun can find its way to our eyes, and it was the power of such love that showered my operating room with a healing light that saved my life.

This is why the infatuation of the Me Myth—me wanting you here now—is but a mere glimpse of the true grace and power of the miracle love of the Great Marriage Myth: the capacity for Us to be together always and anywhere. Low Monogamy depends on the physical presence of our lover at this moment. High Monogamy love transcends all the boundaries of space and time and is not restricted by miles or minutes. If you are wondering how anything could be so powerful that it transcends the bonds of time and space, you have only to consider one of the most significant scientific discoveries in the history of the world.

Love Isn't in the Air — It's Everywhere

In 1964, a scientific discovery was made that altered forever the limits of our consciousness and our loving. You have already read about how applications of the relativity theory show that we can make our time individual or mutual or for doing or for loving. You have learned that the uncertainty principle can be interpreted to mean that love's uncertainty makes for wonderful loving mysteries. You have seen that the unity of everything in the universe suggests that two persons can become an inseparable One. You have discovered the power of the observer to alter what is observed and how the look of love creates loving. You have considered the fact that everything in the universe exists in complementary pairs of opposites each of which is one-half of a loving miracle. In a mathematical proof that shocked the most open-minded scientists, an Irish physicist proved that "immediate action-at-a-distance" is possible and what is local is really only our narrow perception of our everyday life.

Physicist John Stewart Bell's mathematical theorem provided the key that frees all of the energy behind these findings to do what seems impossible by our here-and-now mechanical standards. He showed that when one member of any quantum pair—two electrons spinning in space—is interfered with, its partner is also altered at *exactly the same time*.[1] Change the spin of one, and the spinning of the other is instantaneously reversed at the same time no matter where it is. Bell's theorem was so astonishing that several attempts were made to disprove it. All of them failed.

Bell's theorem is accepted now. It is referred to by scientists as "the principle of action-at-a-distance." It asserts that once a particle makes contact with a partner, that pair is bonded together forever. They affect each other everywhere and always. While Bell's research was based on the behavior of subatomic phenomena such as photons, later work by other scientists showed that we do *not* exclusively live in a local, here-and-now world. Miles and minutes are mere illusions and convenient measures that we use to calibrate our mechanical world. Love isn't local, it's everywhere.

Physicist Nick Herbert wrote, "No local reality can explain the type of world we live in."[2] He meant that the see-and-touch mechanical world of simple linear cause and effect worked for building bridges and cars. Quantum science, and Bell's theorem of spontaneous immediate change between paired partners no matter where in the universe they may be, showed that beneath the see-and-touch world is a world unbound by our artificially imposed local limits. Therefore, if we love in the tradition of the Great Marriage Myth, we are able to be time travelers, loving faster than light together. We can be instantly linked with each other anywhere at any time.[3] It is this sixth love law—Transcendent, or nonlocal, Love—that offers us the opportunity to learn how to go through the barriers we erect between the natural paired opposites I described in Chapter 9.

Intercourse or Outercourse?

In our everyday see-and-touch world, we interact primarily on a body-to-body basis. We make appointments, meet people, go home, and go to sleep. We feel that we have been very busy, but often we also feel very lonely despite our multiple personal contacts during the day. Even when we make love, sexual intercourse often becomes two persons exchanging bodily favors in order to experience personal release or "self"-fulfillment. We have sex to "get off" rather than to "get in" to one another. Our intercourse becomes an act of particles bumping and grinding with one another, but the particles do not change. We become temporarily entangled but not united. We do not experience an "innercourse" of true merging, because we are too focused on "me doing it to you and you doing it to me" rather than on "us merging together."

I coined the term "outercourse" to refer to going out of ourselves in order to connect with others. Outercourse means developing our sensitivity beyond the self—getting out there to merge with someone else. Outercourse is not "making love"—it is a merging of lovers unlimited by taking turns, doing "it" *to* someone, trying to "come fast enough" or trying to "make *it* last." Outercourse helps make *love* last, because it is free of time constraints, making a partner "come," or trying to be a sexual mechanic or sexpert.

For spouses in Low Monogamy, sex sometimes results in feelings. For spouses in High Monogamy, feelings sometimes result in sex. This difference exists because marriage of the Me Myth is governed by selfish local or physical sexual needs that, when shared with a partner, may elicit the feelings of true merging. Nonlocal loving is a union of two spirits on a deep-feeling level. It sometimes leads to physical expression, but seldom had that as its goal.

"Getting Down" to Our Good Self

It was a beautiful day in early spring. You could smell the sap coming up in the trees, and even though the buds had not yet popped open, you could almost hear them straining to break free and blossom to the warm encouragement of the sun. I was sitting on a bench reading when I noticed one of my most conservative and quiet students dancing to music I couldn't hear. He was gyrating wildly to music that only he could hear on his stereo headset. He swung his coat and tossed it in the air in a gesture of farewell to winter. I stopped reading to watch, and when he saw me, he stopped his spring ritual dance and came to talk to me.

"I was just getting down with my bad self," he said. "I was letting me out for a while."

I wasn't sure what he meant by his "bad self" when his dance had seemed to be such a celebration. "It's just a phrase we use," he explained, wrapping his jacket around his books. "It's a slang phrase that really means your real free and honest self. We probably call it bad because the everyday world doesn't like it when you are your real self. I guess I was getting down to my good real self."

We are each a crowd. All of us are aware that we can communicate all at once with our several inner selves. In the blink of an eye, we can talk to our confident self, our insecure self, our more selfish self, our altruistic self, and our fearful self. All at once, we can check with all the selves we are, and learning this sixth step in this miracle-marriage manual will allow you to bring all of your selves to your marriage whenever you wish and wherever you and your lover are.

The Hidden Lover

If time and space are no obstacle in our communing with our several inner selves, why do we seem far less able to interact instantaneously with the selves of others? Why is it that day-to-day events dominate and limit our sense of reality, while action-at-a-distance and spontaneous occurrences at faster-than-light speed do not seem to be happening to us most of the time? Why is it that the world's greatest gurus so often speak of the miracle of self-enlightenment and the spirit of the self floating free of time and space and uniting with the cosmos, while seldom speaking or teaching of the miracle of a marriage where all of our selves are also free to merge with each other and the cosmos together? I suggest that we have a hidden lover within us that we often keep constrained or lose contact with.

It is our hidden lover who is nonlocal and can travel faster than the speed of light. He or she can pass through any barrier, and cross to the other side of the universe in the flash of a loving feeling. If we only seek the Me Myth of self-enlightenment, we become lonely travelers through the universe but never quite within it. If we seek to make a miracle in keeping with the Great Marriage Myth, we can find a space- and time-traveling companion with whom we can dance through the stars.

An experiment by psychologist Ernest Hilgard illustrates the presence of what he called "the hidden observer,"[4] and what I call the hidden lover. After putting a patient under hypnosis, Hilgard inflicted mild electric shock. He instructed the patient to *not* feel the pain, but he also told the patient's "inside hidden observer" to push a button every time pain was administered. Although the patient himself did not show any signs of reacting to the pain, his hidden observer recorded each administration of electric current. The nonlocal or transcendent self of the patient was feeling the pain, whereas the patient's physical or local self did not.

In a variation of this experiment, Hilgard told his hypnotized patient that he would not be able to hear. Paradoxically, the patient nodded in agreement when Hilgard asked, "You cannot hear me now, can you?" Hilgard then slapped two pieces of wood loudly together next to the patient's ear. While anyone else would have reacted strongly and jerked away as an auditory reflex to the loud noise, the hypnotized patient gave no physical indication that he had heard the loud sound. However, when Hilgard addressed the inner self of his patient and asked softly, "Did you hear that?" the blindfolded patient (still under the hypnotic suggestion of deafness) responded, "No, I did not hear that sound of two pieces of wood you just clapped together." One self—the physical self—was following the hypnotist's instructions by not showing a reaction to the test noise, but the hidden inner self was hearing everything.

This phenomenon of the inner self has been replicated in several experiments with hypnosis. It may explain the statement of this Silver Survivor: "I always wondered how I can hear without listening. I mean that sometimes I will be intensely involved watching a television program, and my wife will say something to me. I didn't really hear exactly what she said, but then later I will answer her in a way that shows that I heard exactly what she said. I guess that proves there are many selves listening at once."

I suggest that, like Hilgard's hidden observer, there is a "hidden lover" within all of us. It is this hidden lover who communicates beyond words, sounds, place, and time and who is capable of outercourse, or coming out to merge with the hidden lover in someone else. If we remain contained by our physical body and the limits of the here-and-now and see-and-touch world, then instantaneous action-at-a-distance with our lover is not possible. If we work to become more aware of our own hidden lover and the hidden lover in our spouse, we become more sensitive to the messages he or she is receiving and sending.

Bringing Your Hidden Lover Out of Hiding

Here is a test to help you be more aware of your hidden lover. The statements from the Silver Survivors that follow each of the ten questions illustrate their own unique discoveries of their nonlocal loving capacity.

THE HIDDEN-LOVER TEST

1. Can you listen to someone other than your lover and still be receiving messages from your lover at exactly the same time? Or must you focus only on one person at a time?

"My wife is so much a part of me that nothing outside ever crowds her image out of me," said one husband. "I can listen intently at a staff meeting at work and still be feeling her with me. I'm not distracted by thoughts of her or messages from her. Nothing is coming *at* me. She's inside me and part of me, and not at a place. Actually, her being a part of me gives me the energy to pay attention more, not less. We're just together on a whole different plane than all of my other relationships."

2. Can you "see" your spouse even when he or she is not with you, instead of feeling it's a case of out of sight, out of mind?

"I have a clear image of my husband with me always," said one wife. "It's not like a picture or visual image. It's more like a thought trace nestled somewhere inside me."

3. Can you sense the presence of your husband or wife even when he or she is not with you, or do you feel alone and deserted without your spouse?

"When my teenage daughter's boyfriend leaves, she goes into a complete funk," said one mother. "When he is gone, he's gone, and she pines like a lost puppy. My husband is with me, and I am with him no matter where we are. I guess that's the difference between puppy love and mature loving."

4. Do you frequently experience "coincidental coupling," such as when your wife calls just when you were thinking of her, or your husband arrives home unexpectedly just when you were thinking about him?

"It's almost eerie how often I will be just thinking about him and my husband will call home from work," said one wife. "Sometimes that will happen several times a day. Call it just chance if you want, but we think that these are very meaningful coincidences of our loving."

5. Do you experience "marital trances" during which, almost involuntarily, you drift inward and start thinking about your husband or wife for several minutes?

"Without warning I will just take off to myself and start thinking about her," said one husband. "No matter where I am, I'll just get into thinking about her or something we did together. It's what we call our LSD flashbacks, or our 'love seeking demand' for our loving that takes us away from the busy here-and-now world."

6. Do you intentionally try to send positive vibrations and energy to your spouse when he or she is not with you?

"When Paul was in the hospital, I never limited my visits to just physically being there," said my wife Celest to one of our friends as she described her support of me during my treatment for cancer. "I would send him messages all the time from home or when I was driving to see him or when I was driving home after visiting him. I gave him as many love transfusions as he ever got blood transfusions, and I didn't have to be there to give them. We were not connected by hospital IVs or intravenous tubes. We were connected by our own IVs or intimacy vibrations."

7. *Can you "feel" the power of your spouse energizing you even when he or she is not physically with you?*

I always knew when my wife was sending the "love transfusions" she mentioned above. I could feel them to such an extent that even some of the nurses seemed to notice. One of my primary-care nurses said, "I could tell even when you were sleeping when Celest was sending her love. I could see you sort of move, and there seemed to be an aura around you." Only by understanding that reality of nonlocal action-at-a-distance can such a phenomenon as my love transfusions be explained.

8. *Can you tell when your spouse is getting sick or "coming down with something" even before the person has any symptoms?*

"We hardly need a thermometer," said one wife. "I can tell when my husband is starting to run a fever sometimes a day or two before he does. He can do the same for me, and we often talk about it together. I think we avoid or minimize a lot of illness by this marital early-warning system."

My wife Celest was often more accurate than the laboratory in predicting how my blood levels would change in reaction to my chemotherapy. Some doctors began to rely as much on Celest's feelings about my condition as they did on the numbers from their own mechanical and physical tests.

9. *Do you feel "sympathy pains" when your husband or wife is hurt or sick—almost as if you are experiencing exactly what they are experiencing?*

"When my wife was giving birth to our son, I felt every pain she had," said one husband. "I have no way of knowing if I felt exactly what she felt, and I'm sure she would say that no man could, but she agrees that we both can feel each other's pain. I've heard of something called couvade, where men in some cultures actually roll on the ground in vicarious contractions of birth, and I sure felt something like that. For me they were my male labor pains."

10. Do you and your spouse feel of One Mind in your day-to-day living, often beginning to speak at exactly the same time, saying things like "I was just going to say that" or "That was just what I was thinking"? Or do you feel out of step, interrupting each other and stumbling over each other's words?

"Many, many times we begin to say exactly the same thing at the same time," said one wife. "I'm sure that when you live together for thirty-two years, that's bound to happen, but it's happened throughout our marriage. We always say we are of one mind, even when we think we are out of our minds or are losing them. As a matter of fact, the more pain and pressure we feel, the more we seem to talk, think, and say the same things at the same time."

The Silver Survivors scored an average of 9.3 on the Hidden-Lover Test, while the control group of unstable relationships had an average score of 2.2.

Caring Couples' Coincidences

One of the best examples of outercourse is the occurrence of the couple coincidence referred in the test above. A coincidence is two events happening together by chance in such a way that some meaning seems inherent in their occurring at the same time.[5] Psychologist Carl Jung suggested that the coincidences of our life (he called them "synchronicities") are not only of great psychological significance, they are also related to the science and laws of physics.[6]

Jung worked with his friend, the well-known quantum physicist Wolfgang Pauli, to prove that coincidences grow out of the nonlocal or the time-and-space-free nature of our existence. Things seem to pop up in the most unusual ways at the most unexpected times, because physics has shown that things can happen all at once everywhere. Jung suggested that these coincidences seem more likely when intense loving is going on. Meaningful coincidences are shared more often by couples who are intensely entwined with one another in a loving bond because the power of that loving seems to invoke the principle of non-locality in their shared daily life.

I suggest that meaningful marital coincidences—a wife discovering she is pregnant just at the time her husband was calling home or a husband feeling very sad for apparently no reason while at work only to discover later that his sadness occurred just when his wife had received bad news—are the evidence of non-locality of the miracle of lasting love, or a profound sense of Oneness between two lovers.

Coincidences of the Whole

Sudden flashes of Oneness—coincidences of the whole that reveal that time and space can be transcended—are commonplace in nature. Consider the following facts:

• A few ants placed in the sand wander aimlessly about, but when a sufficient number of ants is added, they suddenly form a highly organized and hard-working community.[7]
• Pavlov's famous dogs initially required more than three hundred trials to learn a task. After several generations of these dogs were trained, less than ten trials were necessary until—all of a sudden without further training—learning occurred, and each dog "knew" the trick with little or no training.
• A lone macaque monkey named Imo spontaneously discovered how to clean sand from sweet potatoes by dunking them in a stream. A few other monkeys learned to do the same by watching her, until 100 of her monkey friends were performing the same potato trick. Then, "all of a sudden," after the hundredth monkey had learned this behavior, every macaque monkey on islands far away and—as was later verified all over the world—suddenly "knew" how to clean sweet potatoes with the "Imo technique" without being taught. (This is referred to by scientists as the "100th monkey phenomenon" and is a perfect example of Oneness.[8])
• Biologist James Lovelock proposes the Gaea hypothesis, suggesting that planet earth itself exhibits the properties of one living system without barriers. He suggests that when one part

of the planet is poisoned, the entire earth is contaminated instantaneously.[9]

• Studies on the effect of prayer on seeds thousands of miles away from the people praying reveal an instantaneous positive effect on the growth of the prayer target seeds while unprayed-for seeds fail to flourish.[10]

• A cardiologist documents in repeated studies that open-heart surgery patients who are anonymously prayed for by groups hundreds of miles away do much better than those patients not assigned to prayer groups. The effect is shown to take place simultaneously with the praying, no matter how far away the prayers are and without the knowledge of the patients.[11]

The significance of these "coincidences of Oneness" is that they give evidence of the fact of the transcendence of time and space and the possibility of sudden unity. Science knows and miracle lovers experience the fact that local limits are mere illusion.[12] The possibility of nonlocality or action-at-a-distance means that our love can make powerful quantum leaps between us that would seem impossible in a mechanical, linear, see-and-touch world.

As you pass beyond the halfway point in this miracle-marriage manual and as you study the sixth law of Transcendent Loving, remember that the alpha and beta opposites of loving can make a strong whole when we realize we are free of time zones and spatial boundaries. Science has shown us that only the particle person (the Me) is trapped in the here-and-now. By realizing that we are as much energy as stuff, we can go freely to be together anywhere, anytime. What follows are five suggestions that will help you learn to transcend "real" limits and make a quantum leap of love.

HOME LOVE ASSIGNMENTS

1. As you complete your reading of this chapter, try to focus on your image of your spouse. See if you can't actually feel and see your husband or wife, no matter where the other person is right at this moment.

2. Discuss with your spouse those times when you have been

separated for a long period of time. Share what you felt about them then and what images and "vibrations" you felt you received during the absence. One Silver Survivor said, "When we talk about the times we are not physically together, we come up with dozens of examples of coincidences when we were thinking the same thought, feeling the same feeling, or sensing the power of one another just when we needed it."

3. Discuss what the two of you consider to be your biggest "marital coincidence." How did it occur and what symbolism or meaning do the two of you attach to this couple coincidence? Remember to consider creatively the metaphors of the occurrence rather than whether or not the coincidence can be explained by statistical means or probabilities. The lessons that can be learned from the coincidences in your marital life can provide a major source of new ideas about the nonlocal power of your loving and how your loving might be strengthened by using that power.

One Silver Survivor said, "We discussed one of our biggest marital coincidences the other day. We both remember it vividly. I had been offered the chance for a new job in California, but my husband had a good teaching job he had pursued for years here in Michigan. We seemed stuck with two opposite decisions and were talking about what to do when the face of the clock on the wall popped right off. Maybe it was the temperature or humidity, but it popped so loudly and suddenly that it really got our attention. We sat there awhile, and then my husband said, 'I guess it's a sign to give a new face to time and to look at time differently. Maybe it means we should take some time off.' We laughed, but all of a sudden we said almost in unison, 'What about a sabbatical leave from the college?' My husband took a leave and came with me for a year to California. He got a new and better teaching job there, I loved my job, and our marriage and our careers were changed forever. We never take the coincidences in our life for granted, and we learned not to let the demands of daily life make up our marital mind for us. There is always another way to solve a problem together if you think freely together beyond the immediate pressures of here-and-now."

4. Talk about the points in your own relationship when you

felt profoundly together as One. What was it about those times that seemed to unite you? Were these always the good times? Or were times of crisis also times of unity in your marriage? One Silver Survivor said, "The strongest Oneness points in our marriage seem to have three characteristics: They seemed sudden, they all had to do with the meaning and value and limits of our time together, and they were both good and bad happenings and not just the great times. They taught us that our marriage can not only endure but flourish through almost anything."

5. Try a "marital trance" to let your hidden lovers have outercourse together. Sit down in a quiet place, play some of your favorite relaxing music, hold hands, and take a mental trip together wherever your thoughts and fantasies may lead you. You can pick your mental destination together ahead of time or just allow your marriage to go wherever it is drawn. Discuss your journey later and try to identify the common parts of your experience. Even if you went to different imaginary places, try to discover a common theme that seems related to the nature of your marriage.

An example of a marital trance shared by a Silver Survivor couple will serve as summary of the law of transcendent love. "We were stunned when we talked about our marital trance," said the wife. "I was sort of embarrassed because I didn't go anywhere at all. I felt really close to my husband and was totally into where we were instead of going somewhere. I was there sitting on the couch with him feeling like we were free from the demands of daily life, safe together from any danger, and sort of floating on our couch above the earth. My husband began to cry when I told him about my experience and then he said, 'That's exactly what I felt. I was with you in the space shuttle, and we were alone together with no gravity. We were looking down safe and powerful from out in space. You stayed in the living room and I went into orbit, but we traveled exactly the same way together. What a trip we had. What a trip we're having.'"

STEP VII

Chaos, Compassion, and Caring in Sickness and in Health

I will celebrate the chaos of our loving.

Life is a daring adventure or it is nothing at all.
—*Helen Keller*

LOVE LAW SEVEN: THE CREATIVE-CHAOS LAW

The nature of life is not order but chaos. In the short run, everything about the world is a complete mess, but in the long run, there is an attraction toward a mysterious order beyond the see-and-touch world. A love that lasts long enough will discover the rhythm of this mysterious order. A miracle marriage is a way of suffering through chaos together.

Why Is There Sex?

"The idea of working at marriage is in vogue!" So states the prestigious *New York Times*.[1] The Roper Organization in New York polls people on their attitudes toward our major social institutions, and their most recent survey of 2,000 people revealed that success was defined as "being a good wife and mother or husband and father." Four years earlier, the top choice was "being true to yourself." Marriage is in!

Marriage has been one of our most enduring institutions, but why? In terms of evolution, asexual or "solo" reproduction seems to have obvious advantages over struggling to find a procreative partner. Sexual reproduction means that genes from several different individuals are randomly shuffled together in a single descendant, thereby halving the effective gene content passed on by an individual. Asexual procreation, as occurs in some creatures such as bacteria, makes perfect complete copies without halving and randomization. Sexually reproducing females produce less than half the number of offspring of asexual animals.[2] From a purely evolutionary point of view and in keeping with the selfish gene view of sociobiology, why is there sex? Why has the pattern of two getting together to make a new One evolved over solo asexual replication?

Marriage has won over asexual reproduction because marriage makes for "a good mayhem." Sex is nature's way of creating genetic chaos. Because we suffer so in finding someone to pair up with, and because the process can be so chaotic, remarkable genetic variation is introduced into a population. Instead of having mirror-image copies, we end up with a range of "person possibilities," thereby guaranteeing a flexibility and adaptability to change that would be impossible without pairing. Through the deterministic chaos of genetic shuffling caused by paired sex, good mutations are introduced much more rapidly. As a result, our species thrives. The chaotic shuffling of coupling deals our species a strong evolutionary hand.

Chaos theory, one of the most rapidly growing fields in science, asserts that the omnipresent chaos of nature is not mere randomness but a bizarre form of order. Philosopher Immanuel Kant wrote, "God has put a secret art into the forces of Nature so as to enable it to fashion itself out of chaos into a perfect world system."[3] Marriage and merging have won out over selfish asexuality because there is a more wonderful and mysterious order lurking just beneath the upheaval of natural processes and daily living. One purpose of marriage is to create more chaos. Another is to provide a place where the spouses can learn together to find the order beneath the clutter and be creatively chaotic together.

The First Noble Truth of Lasting Love

The first of the Four Noble Truths taught by Buddha is "Life is suffering."[4] The Great Marriage Myth teaches that marriage is first and foremost an ordeal. It is learning to suffer and feel compassion with our beloved and seeing that suffering as a natural consequence of life's necessary chaos. In order to make a miracle marriage, both partners must accept the fact that marriage is not easy, not safe, and not always comfortable, and is typically characterized by one problem after another. Marriage is made by and for chaos, and the best marriages are those in which both partners struggle through the chaos and solve problems together rather than make problems for each other.

Lasting marriages don't ask, "What's your problem?" or complain, "I have a problem." They say, "Let's solve this problem," and "We have a problem." For the miracle marriage, problems and conflicts are not symptoms of marital weakness. They are viewed as the necessary challenges emerging from life's chaos. For Low Monogamists, most problems are aggravations, inconveniences, and obstacles to the development of the individual spouse. For the miracle relationship, the marriage is treated with the same loving care and tolerance as a growing child whose problems are seen as necessary developmental tasks on the way to maturity. Both partners struggle to nurture the marriage through its growing pains.

Marriages based on the Me Myth see problems as hassles, while marriages based on the Great Marriage Myth see problems with the hope of a new way of living and loving. Low Monogamists see problems as spoiling things, while High Monogamists see

problems as sparking the relationship to a stronger type of love—
a form of emotional endurance training that builds the couple's
stress stamina.

Benjamin Franklin said, "Those things that hurt, instruct."
Any marriage worth the loving "hurts" because it is down in the
trenches of chaos trying its best to adjust, learn, and grow
through the problems of living. Psychologist Carl Jung said that
"neurosis is always a substitute for legitimate suffering."[5] Neu-
rotic or "selfish suffering" takes place when we are frustrated in
our attempts to maximize the ego or feel only the pain of ego
damage. Creative suffering occurs as we try to help make the
world a better place through our loving and suffering with someone else.

Like Low Monogamists, High Monogamists also complain and
gripe about their problems. But through the turmoil, there is
always the tacit mutual ageement that "things will work out" and
never the threat that one or the other partner will "bail out" of
the relationship.

If your own marriage is characterized by disruption, conflict,
and turmoil—congratulations! You are experiencing the marital
version of Buddha's first truth. The First Noble Truth of loving
is that lasting love is difficult, painful, and always going through
chaos to a new and higher order. If there is absolutely no suffering at all in your marriage, be on the alert. Life is chaos, and
chaos is life, so your love life might be dead or dying. As you
learned in Chapter 9, life is full of complementary opposites, so
remember in your happiness that you could not experience joy
without the necessary turmoil of crisis that gives joy its meaning.
Low Monogamists struggle within their marriage, but High Monogamists struggle for their marriage, which is a microcosm of
the general chaos of the world.

The Butterfly of Love

The new study of chaos is very complex, but it is essentially
concerned with looking for the mysterious order and patterns
hidden beneath the constant chaos of the world.[6] Scientists who
study the nature of chaos describe the Butterfly Effect, or the
fact that—in theory—a butterfly stirring the air today in Peking
can affect the storm sysems in New York. Chaology is the study

of minute changes as these changes magnify themselves into great turmoil, and turmoil becomes chaos, and chaos results in the long run in a newer and higher order.

While working at his computer, mathematician and founding chaologist Edward Lorenz introduced the smallest of variations into a program designed to predict weather patterns. He discovered that the tiniest modification eventually played itself out in the form of dramatically chaotic weather changes. The smallest quantum differences can result in overwhelming catastrophes or miracles—a phenomenon physicists call "sensitive dependence on initial conditions."[7] Love and suffering operate by these same sensitivities.

Why Little Things Become Big Deals

All serious health problems begin with minute, almost imperceptible changes within a singular cell in the body. Cancer is the end state of a microcosmic alteration inside a cell that eventually stirs up total cellular chaos. Likewise, almost every marital problem I saw in my clinic began as a mild and minor perturbation. As one Silver Survivor put it, "About seven little ouches can result in one major hurt. I can't remember what started it, but whatever it was, it caused everything to fall apart."

Couples who fail to cope constructively with crises interpret chaos and conflict as symptoms of their own or their spouse's failure rather than as a sign of the vitality of lasting love. Almost every major marital storm begins as a small and almost insignificant mistake, dispute, or insensitivity. Making it through marital chaos requires that we pay attention to the little things, because they can eventually result in what seems like sudden upheaval.

Creative or Stochastic Chaos

There are two types of chaos. One creates a new whole and a new order while the other merely stirs things up and leaves them that way. Couples practicing High Monogamy experience "creative chaos," which is a dynamic process evolving from within the marriage and reacting to the world. It involves small changes that result in a beautiful mess, which eventually becomes a higher and more powerful loving relationship.

Couples practicing Low Monogamy experience "stochastic chaos," or a truly random process through which the marriage simply reacts to chance, and both partners guess at how each can best survive as an individual. A different, but not a higher or more meaningful order, is the result of stochastic chaos. Low Monogamy marriages find themselves "in" a mess. High Monogamy marriages go "through" messes together. Step 7 of this miracle-marriage manual requires that you learn to see the difference between the mere mess of external stochastic chaos and the creative chaos experienced by couples on the way to their miracle.

CREATIVE-CHAOS TEST

The Creative-Chaos Test below will help you measure the degree to which the two of you manage to create a loving and mutual problem-solving orientation in your marriage.

1. Does it seem that just when things are peaceful and steady, some crisis always occurs?

"It took us a few years together before we learned that the more messed-up things seem, the better marriage we have," said a Silver Survivor. "We could see trouble coming for our friends' marriages when things seemed so perfect for them. You hardly ever see a marriage end because of problems they are solving together, but they certainly can end because of problems they are blaming each other for. Divorce usually happens after a storm instead of during it because couples who can't stay together don't know how or don't care to try to pick up the pieces and rebuild a stronger love."

2. Have you noticed that your closest times as husband and wife seem to occur at times of chaos and crisis in your marriage?

I have never known such closeness with my wife Celest as when my cancer seemed to be taking me from her. When the life seemed to be leaving my body, and as my wife and I embraced in my hospital room on the bone-marrow-transplant unit, there seemed to be only one of us there. Our marriage had known chaos before. We had endured the tribulations and challenges of raising two impaired children, the sudden death of three of our parents, my near-blindness (due to retinal detachments), two cancers, several serious family illnesses, and numerous other chaotic times. All this, as my wife calls it, "testing turbulence" has resulted in our own form of chaos closeness. I saw this same chaos closeness response in the Silver Survivors encountering other crises such as extramarital affairs, problems with children, the challenge of caring for parents, career setbacks, and the impact of substance abuse.

3. Do you and your spouse seem to have "chaos confidence," feeling even at the worst of times that the strength of your loving will carry you through to the better times?

"Give us a problem, we'll solve it," said one Silver Survivor. "We've certainly had the practice. We could be chaos consultants. Our marital house is not built of straw or wood. It's built brick by brick by the survival of our love through hundreds of crises. No huffing and puffing of any wolf can blow it down."

4. At times of trouble, does it seem that a "chaos coincidence" takes place that provides some direction, symbolism, or metaphor lesson for coping and making decisions?

My wife and I noticed that during the worst times of my chemotherapy and bone-marrow transplant, a series of chaos coincidences seemed to occur. A letter containing good and timely advice would arrive from a doctor friend on just the day I was scheduled for chemotherapy. A song that symbolized something about our love and faith would play on the radio just as I was preparing for a painful treatment or just when we had received more bad news. A television news program sounding the merits and miracles of bone-marrow transplants would come on just hours before my own transplant. The couple's coincidences that I described in Chapter 10 often seem to take place during the chaos of our life. This can happen only if we are willing to give lasting love a chance to make it through the chaos by paying attention and giving meaning to these coincidences and understanding that all chaos is as necessary to a new order as suffering is to joy.

5. *Do you share a common belief system related to the purpose of life and of living and dying? This may include, but may also transcend, formal religious systems and form a shared spiritual belief unique to your own marriage.*

"I'm Catholic and my wife is what she calls a hopeful agnostic," said one Silver Survivor. "But when serious problems happen to us, we seem to share an unspoken belief in what life and death are all about. I don't know if I could put it in words, but each of us seems to know how the other feels about things. Crises seem to bond our beliefs together into one belief about the immortal human spirit."

6. *Is your marriage free of the "poor us" syndrome of feeling that only your relationship receives setbacks and tragedies?*

"It's easy to become marriage martyrs," said one husband. "We have had everything go wrong that could go wrong. We have cried more tears than I thought a person could cry, but we refuse to degrade the sacredness of what we have together by thinking that we are the target or magnet of some evil vibrations. We think that somewhere in all of these problems is where our love and life together is growing. The miracle of our marriage is how much we have come to appreciate the little things, because so many big bad things have happened to us."

7. *Does your marriage have a good reputation among your friends and other relationships as being strong, adaptable, and a source of inspiration and support for others?*

"Our friends call us 'the twin peaks,'" said one wife. "They say we are a mountain of strength, and people seem to know that we can take almost anything. They tend to turn to us for help, support, and ideas. Too bad we don't charge for our services, because we've become the 'marital mess advisers' for dozens of other couples."

8. Does your marriage have the endurance and tolerance to resist quick and easy solutions to problems in favor of reflection, patience, and taking the long, more philosophical view of problem resolution?

"When a problem happens," said a Silver Survivor, "you are tempted to do or say anything to get by it or deny it. The trick is first of all to do nothing at all. The first step in dealing with a life crisis is to stop, look, and listen to your feelings and your spouse. Good marriages can leave things in a mess for quite a long time while they feel their way to a solution. Just as you have to learn to survive in the wild when you are lost, so you have to learn to live with chaos in order to make it through the chaos. When you're lost in the woods, you find your way not by running and running but by sitting down, getting your bearings, and gathering your energy to try a new way out. The same strategy applies to finding your way through marital problems."

9. Can your marriage "think backward" together in a nonblaming manner to track down the original small and apparently insignificant stressors that sometimes result in major catastrophes?

"When you taught us about the Butterfly Effect in our therapy, we began to learn to think backward," said a Silver Survivor. "You tend to see problems in the here-and-now and are unable to think back to the little things that may have led up to your present feeling or the problem you are having at the moment. What you try to understand is not *who* did something wrong. We don't look to blame, just explain and understand. We see whatever happened as happening to both of us and not just one of us as a victim of the other. You have to think back together for whatever little things may have resulted in the big thing you are both confronted with as a couple now. One yell, sexist insult, or hurtful comment today can cause a major marital mess later."

10. Is your marriage free of "maladaptive hyperarousal" to challenges and accepting of the fact that suffering and chaos are necessary and natural parts of loving and living?

"My husband calls it the Holy Defecation reaction," said one Silver Survivor. "Some people go into a complete physical and emotional hyperreaction when something goes wrong. Learning the art of underreaction is one of the most difficult things a marriage can learn, but it is necessary if you are going to prevent marital burnout. The art of staying married is the art of knowing what to overlook. If your marriage never catches fire, it can't burn up or out, so keeping cool really helps."

The Silver Survivors scored an average of 9.3 on the Creative-Chaos Test, while the control group of unstable relationships averaged 1.2. Just as in parenthood, when we deal with the daily emergencies in the life of a developing child, chaos is a pattern of constantly occurring marital emergencies that either strengthen the marriage or tear it apart. Miracle marriages are always stronger for their pain. Crises and chaos are what miracles are made for, and of.

Couple Chaos Control

Imagine that all of life's crises came with a set of instructions. Pretend that, before you attempted to deal with the problems in your marriage, you had a chance to read marital safety warnings that came with every crisis. In place of the usual home love assignments that have concluded each chapter in this miracle-marriage manual, I provide here a set of ten steps in chaos control and marital problem solving. Parenting books became popular years ago to help parents deal with the chaos of the daily development of their children. What follows is a "marenting guide" to help spouses raise their own marriage. I have included some deliberations on divorce, suggestions about the power of negative thinking, and a brief consumers' guide for finding help for your marriage. My Silver Survivors have found these steps helpful. I hope that they help you, too.

TEN STEPS FOR CREATIVE CHAOS CONTROL

Step 1: Panic

Always be sure to allow some panic time for the two of you to share all your feelings of fear and helplessness. Panic is a natural reaction to any serious problem that stresses a marriage. The more severe the problem, the more severe should be your panic. The trick is to realize that the panic phase is always temporary, only natural, and necessary to get the coping chemicals flowing (including adrenaline, endorphins, and various other neuro-transmitters necessary for preparing the body for the stress response). The panic response is nature's way of spurring both partners' physical coping abilities.

Feeling inadequate because you feel panicky is unwarranted, undeserved, and nonproductive and may be a leading cause of premature divorce. Our mammalian evolution made panic one of our most necessary and adaptive abilities. Prolonged panic, however, becomes a crippling emotional, stress-chemical-addicted physical hyperarousal that will prevent your marriage from acting constructively in the face of a challenge. Stress chemicals can call the body to action, but too much of them for too long can result in panic paralysis, helplessness, and burnout.

Step 2: Pause

One or both of you *must* insist on a "panic pause" to settle down, collect your wits, and get back on your feet after the first shock of the reality of the impact of chaos. It is not necessary to *do* or solve anything. Even if you are both still agitated and confused, sit down, shut up, and settle down for a while together. You can adjust the dose of the stress chemical prescription from the brain by pausing to settle your brain, your body, and your marriage down.

One Silver Survivor summarized the pausing steps in chaos control this way. "We call it the SDASU technique. It means Sit Down And Shut Up."

Step 3: Clarify

Write down together *exactly* what has happened. Do *not* write down what might happen or what you are afraid will happen. Work together to record exactly the complete nature of the crisis, challenge, or problem that is impacting on your marriage. Remember, no matter what the problem is (work, health, children, parents, and so on) the impact of the problem is always on the marriage as a unit and on the two of you together. Write down exactly and specifically what has happened *to the marriage*. As one Silver Survivor suggested, "Always mutualize your mess."

Step 4: Get the Facts

The next step is to research, ask, read, consult, check out your friends' gossip, and buy some tabloids containing sensational and distorted claims of "facts." It is helpful to start a "chaos catalogue" to record any facts you can gather about your problem. All facts—even the exaggerated ones from the tabloids—can be helpful by promoting more creative problem solving.

All crises require information, and you can get expert advice in sorting out the junk from the truth later. As Mark Twain pointed out, "First get the facts. Then you can distort them as you need." For now, just get as much information as you can find. When I interviewed families dealing with serious health or developmental problems with their children, their first and foremost need was for information, not necessarily solutions.

Step 5: Get the Implications

Once you have spent some time getting as many facts as you can and entering them in your "chaos log," go over the facts and write down their implications. Remember that implications are mere theory, and nothing in medicine, education, or any science or profession is absolutely certain. Don't be afraid to write down the worst, the best, and the most unrealistic implications you can think of. The more you can anticipate now, the better prepared you will be later. If you can't think of enough implications, consult what I call a "pessimistic professional" who will be able to forecast or give you a verdict rather than a diagnosis about your problems. Professionals privately acknowledge the making of miracles, but in their professional roles they are very good at giving the worst-case scenario. Don't accept these implications as truth—just collect them for recycling later.

Step 6: Develop Your Denial

Denial is very healthy and important to our survival.[8] As psychologist Albert Ellis was fond of saying, we must learn to stop "should-ing on ourselves."[9] The ought-to-dos of our life should not cause us to miss out on another of our natural adaptive skills—enlightened denial. Destructive denial avoids facts, but enlightened denial refuses to ruminate about implications and speculations. Enlightened denial requires that we be strong enough to accept the facts and creative enough to devise strong denial of forecasts that cannot be verified. Discuss as a couple ways in which you will be denying together some of the implications of your problem and help each other maintain the denial when it is challenged by the "must-urbators" who tell you what you must do, feel, and face. I could not deny the fact of my cancer, but I could deny any certainty of the course and outcome of my disease. The illness was fact, but the prognosis was up to me as much as my doctors, my genes, my luck, and God's will. I denied anything they said about the future that did not fit my wife's and my own expectation of a miracle.

Here are three techniques used by the Silver Survivors to achieve enlightened denial:

THE ART OF ENLIGHTENED DENIAL

- Remember the uncertainty principle and the fact that the more certain we think we are about one thing, the less certain we automatically become of another. If anyone around you is certain about negative consequences, he or she is neglecting the equally important certainty of the positive ones. One Silver Survivor said, "When my husband was sick, I didn't let anybody take charge and tell us what we *had* to do. We asked for things to be presented to us in the form of choices and not pronouncements."
- Remember the complementarity principle suggesting that

there is always *another* side to everything and everyone. One view of anything is always incomplete, and "opposites" do not have to be separated from one another by barriers. Remember that being opposite does not mean having to be opposed.

• Remember the remarkable power of participant-observer, which suggests that the observer helps determine what is seen. Your selected point of view *can* help evoke certain potentialities out of any situation. Your view regarding an illness strongly influences your healing powers. You are not a passive observer of chaos and crisis—you are helping to make it what it is. If the Butterfly Effect is valid and the tiniest changes eventually result in chaotic crises, the reverse is also true. The tiniest hopes and actions can make miracles from the chaos.

Step 7: Get Help

Marriages, like people, are never alone. Finding the appropriate type of help for your problem is never easy. Asking friends for suggestions, for their time, for their comfort, and for their help in finding help is vital to dealing with chaos. Marital problems must be brought out of the closet rather than left in the shadows of the shared despair of an isolated husband and wife. All marriages have problems, and the best marriages seem to have more problems because the spouses are able to see them and face them, are not afraid of them, and use them to grow. There is a big difference between privacy and secrecy, and although the exact nature of your problems may be private, the fact that you have problems does not have to be a secret.

Marriages are systems that exist within systems—friends, family, neighbors, and colleagues—so don't try to go it alone or you are more likely to end up alone. There were many times when the couples in my clinic shocked their friends with announcements regarding their impending divorce. "They seemed to be so happy" and "They were the perfect couple" are typical responses when a troubled marriage managed to hide its plight. Even if it seems embarrassing at first to acknowledge your problems, being vulnerable enough to seek help by going not only to professionals but also to friends could help minimize suffering before it needlessly escalates and spreads.

Here are six suggestions for getting appropriate marital help:

A CONSUMER'S GUIDE TO FINDING
HELP FOR YOUR MARRIAGE

1. When seeking a marriage counselor or a therapist, be a consumer first and a patient second. Ask about success rates, the therapist's prior experience with the type of problem you present, anticipated length of treatment, the therapist's criterion for success and definition of a happy marriage, and whether the therapist has any references of past successful cases.

2. *Always* get a second opinion before beginning therapy. There are more than enough (probably too many) psychotherapists to go around, so don't let the urgency of your marital problem cause you to take the first offer of help. Check with another therapist so you have at least one other opinion regarding your marital-problem diagnosis before you get marital surgery.

3. Ask the key consumer question in finding a good marital therapist: "Are you happily married?" If the therapist isn't happily married or if he or she seems uncomfortable with the question, find someone else. As one Silver Survivor warned, "Never go for psychological help to someone who seems more messed up than you are." As categorical and judgmental as this may seem and as angry as I may make some of my colleagues, my nearly thirty years of doing therapy have taught me that therapists can't help a patient achieve what they themselves are not willing to struggle to accomplish. Too many therapists have been trained only in the art of Low Monogamy. Look for one who is willing to take the harder course by showing a reverence for lasting love and being willing to try for a miracle marriage.

4. If you feel you are "going to someone for help" rather than "working with someone trying to grow and learn with you," find someone else to work with. You need a caring, learning professional who doesn't "work on you" or fit you in to his or her therapy theories or orientation. You need someone who sees you and your marriage as a unique entity with a distinctive problem and uncommon coping skills.

5. Try to find someone who can be both healer and a person being healed at the same time along with you. I have found this role to be the most difficult challenge in doing therapy, but the

best teachers are the best learners. Since miracle marriages are always creative loving in progress, a good therapist is constantly learning about the challenges of High Monogamy. You are looking for a fellow "soul student" who is just a little further along in his or her course than you are at the moment and is willing to be in the role of paid tutor. You are *not* looking for a guru who has all the answers and will share them with you one fifty-minute-hour at a time.

6. There is a *big* difference between curing and healing. People suffer and die, marriages fail to survive, and some problems cannot be cured. Healing, on the other hand, is *always* possible because to heal means to become a whole person or to make a whole relationship no matter what problems you have. What follows are some suggestions regarding the issue of divorce as a healing act:

DELIBERATIONS ON DIVORCE

• As you read in Chapter 4, divorce is one of the most devastating events in life. If a therapist speaks of divorce before you do and talks of divorce as a cure or solution to your loving problems, you have the wrong therapist.

• If your therapist speaks often of the flaws in your partner rather than what you can learn about yourself, you have the wrong therapist.

• If your therapist suggests having an affair to "invigorate your marriage," or in any way suggests that he or she might be a good person for you to love or have sex with, you have an unethical, immoral, and dangerous therapist.

• If *you* speak first of divorce and your therapist helps you see that divorce is a drastic and difficult step through the chaos of loving and that it is usually no easier than trying to save a struggling marriage, your therapist can be a helpful healer. When a marriage fails, divorce is never a cure or an end. Divorce is a serious form of chaos, and much learning, healing, and self-examination are required to re-ask the question "Would I want to be married to me?" and add the new question "Would I want to divorce me and why?"

I have pointed out that miracle marriages begin with both spouses asking, "Where am I going and who will go with me?" at the same time and then continuing to ask these questions over and over again throughout their marriage. Being sure of a divorce can be a healing experience and perhaps a step toward a miracle marriage in the future, but it requires the person considering the divorce to ask, "Where have I gone so far and what about me has contributed to this companion choosing to go no further with me?"

A frequent mistake I noticed in my clinic was that spouses who thought of divorce assumed that the thought itself meant that the marriage was doomed. The principle of complementarity teaches that opposites characterize all of life and loving, so your thoughts of divorce can mean a longing for a new loving with your spouse as much as they can signal serious loving trouble. Make sure your therapist helps you think about divorce in terms of its spiritual sense of "splitting" as well as legal sense of ending the marriage and that he or she never assumes that the thought of divorce predicts the final end. Never divorce someone you don't know, and don't divorce unless you are willing to get to know yourself much better than you do. Divorce should always be the last thing considered, never a threat or the first thing.

Step 8: Find Some Good Guilt

Another fallacy of popular psychology is that "guilt is bad." Guilt that leads only to self-blame, surrender, and lowered self-esteem will indeed get you nowhere. Guilt that teaches you what you did wrong can help you learn to do right the next time. No matter how badly you or your spouse may have messed things up, neither of you probably set out intentionally to make a mess of things. Even killers are not sentenced to death unless they *intended* to kill. Don't sentence your marriage to death because of guilt or self-blame. Your guilt should lead and teach you, not cripple and block you from loving.

Step 9: Always Give Up

All of us give up sometimes. Giving up is nature's way of giving us a physical and emotional rest from our constant problem solving, coping, and adjusting. Giving up, however, is not an end. It is a phase of coping with chaos. This is why thoughts of separating or divorcing must not be seen as final. When you do feel like giving up, realize that the feeling is a necessary part of the sequence of the natural chaos of life, not a sign that you have a bad attitude or that you are not trying hard enough to exercise mind over matter. The power of negative thinking is as important as the power of positive thinking if you remember that both are naturally complementary and needed parts of the problem-solving and learning process. Here are three mini-suggestions for more effective negative thinking:

THE POWER OF NEGATIVE THINKING

• Most negative thinking is as unrealistic as positive thinking. The natural chaos of life teaches us that nothing is as good as we thought or as bad as we feared. Our brains were formed during the Ice Age, when pessimism and negativity were absolutely necessary to our survival. These SOBs, or Selfish Old Brains, used a little Pleistocene Pessimism and worry about the reality of storms and floods to help keep our ancestors alive.[10] Protective pessimism has its place and purpose.

• Look for lessons about the positives in your negative thinking by using the complementarity principle. If you think you have been a complete jerk or total fool (I never heard my patients describe themselves as a slight jerk or a partial fool), consider that you are also extremely wise and remarkably brilliant as well.

• Those people you know who tell you how wonderful life is, how tremendous their marriage is, how their attitude is always positive, and that they believe completely in positive thinking and mind over matter are positively out of their mind. No one is always gleeful and optimistic, and all marriages suffer during the terrible times of life. Chaology teaches that life is a glorious mess and mixture of the good, the bad, and the ugly. Don't ask yourself or your marriage to be perfect—just ask of it that it be as complementarily perfect as it is problematic.

Step 10: Believe in Your Power to Make Miracles

Physicist Michael Faraday said, "Nothing is too wonderful to be true." Chaos gives evidence of this fact because no matter how bad things seem, things always change and a new order emerges. Of course, time doesn't heal all wounds and miracles don't just happen. If we go for High Monogamy and the miracle marriage, the seventh law of lasting love—creative chaos—teaches us to stay with the game and learn together when the rules seem to change and everything gets messed up.

Allowing us to make messes for ourselves and presenting us with His own chaotic challenges is God's way of rolling His dice. As chaologist Joseph Ford suggests, God does in fact play dice with the universe, but they are loaded dice. They are loaded in our favor in the long run, but in the short run the dice can seem to roll right over us. The next time the dice are passed to you as a couple, take them in all four of your hands and roll them with the knowledge and faith that—no matter how they fall—the lasting love of a miracle marriage can help you win somewhere, sometime, somehow.

STEP VIII

The Sad Side of Love:

PULLING TOGETHER INSTEAD OF APART

I will share your sorrow and grow with our pain.

And could you keep your heart in wonder at the daily miracles of your life, your pain would not seem less wondrous than your joy.

—*Kahlil Gibran*

LOVE LAW EIGHT: THE LAW OF SHARED SADNESS

In the here-and-now physical world, everything and every
moving toward an end. The universe and everything i
winding down, running out of energy, and falling apart

the way to our physical end, spectacular and beautiful order can emerge spontaneously, and the grief of our passings and losses can become the grit and grace of our merged souls in their struggle to new beginnings. All husbands and wives will experience bereavement and grieve for loving times lost, but they can learn to share in the energy of crises to make their marriage new again.

Eternity Is "Now"

Snowmen melt, statues crumble, and tears dry because of the effect of the Second Law of Thermodynamics. Simply put, this powerful theory says that there is an inexorable tendency in any system that is not totally isolated and completely controlled (such as our universe and our lives) for that system's organization to diminish, for its randomness to increase, and for it to die eventually or burn itself out. All expenditure of energy results in wasted heat, and that heat eventually "wastes" us. The energy of living eventually cooks our goose.

In the macrocosmic world—the world of see, touch, hear, taste, and smell—burning-up-and-ending is *always* the case. In the physical world, the arrow of time points one way—toward an end.[1] There is no going back, and "now" is both the first moment and the last moment of our passing life.

We often think of eternity as a very, very long time or billions of years into the infinite future. Our minds cannot grasp such concepts as "billions" or "infinite," so we tend to dismiss eternity as something without relevance to our day-to-day living. In terms of the Second Law of Thermodynamics, however, eternity means a Now composed of memories or despair of our past and hopes and fears of our future as experienced in the present. Step 8 in learning to make a miracle marriage suggests that since we are all burning up, we can bask together in the warmth of the poignancy of time's passing. We can see the sadness of the end of our physical loving as a necessary complementary opposite to the joy of our sharing of an eternal Now.

Love and Steam Engines

The word "thermodynamics" comes from the Greek words meaning the "power of heat." All of the laws of thermodynamics were discovered in work with steam engines during the Industrial Revolution in Britain in the early nineteenth century. These powerful laws apply to the mechanical here-and-now world. The Second Law of Thermodynamics—that everything is burning up and moving toward an end—is so central to all of life that leading scientist Arthur Eddington said, "If your theory is shown to be against the Second Law of Thermodynamics, I can give you no hope."[2]

The Second Law tells us that, without doubt, everything is moving toward its physical end, but it does *not* say that this process (called "entropy," meaning "movement toward disorder and ending") is synonymous with inexorable collapse into spiritual meaninglessness. Steam engines and human hearts die, but love doesn't have to. The law of Shared Sadness teaches that our loving can be enhanced by our awareness that even in the process of falling apart, we can find love lessons that help us find more meaning to our physical end and hope for our infinite spiritual future. Unlike steam engines, we don't have to waste the heat of life processes. We have a soul, and souls can merge to use the heat generated by physical "burning up" as a source of energy for our growing spirit.

The Sad and Happy News About Thermodynamics

The sad truth is that our time here in earth's soul school is limited. By cosmic time standards, we are the newest (and most rapidly destructive) influence on the planet. If we shrunk earth's entire history into one imaginary year, all that has happened in our human history would have occurred during the last minute of that year.[3] In cosmic terms, we are very low on planetary seniority. Our time here is micromomentary, but our impact has often been cataclysmic.

The Me Myth correctly tells us that we should enjoy every moment of our brief life because the physical duration of the self is very short. The Me Myth teaches that each of us should individually grasp every day as our possible last day. *Carpe diem* is the watchword of Low Monogamy. The happy truth, however, goes far beyond this simplistic orientation to the impact of the Second Law of Thermodynamics. An equally plausible and more optimistic interpretation of the Second Law is at the root of the Great Marriage Myth.

The happy truth is that we ourselves are only inhabiting our body machine for a few years, and the lessons of loving, birthing, developing, celebrating, suffering, and dying are the required curriculum of soul school. The body is a mere parenthesis in the soul's infinite and relative time, and by coming together as One, we can learn to be fascinated with the process of falling apart rather than afraid of it. The good news about the Second Law of Thermodynamics is, as I pointed out in Chapter 9, that we are spirits having a brief human experience. However abbreviated this experience is, our spirit lasts forever.

The Me Myth says that we "are" our body, and when our body ends, so do we. The Great Marriage Myth says that we "have" a body, but it does not have to prevent us from going beyond bones and muscles to find our spirit with someone else. Marriage is a way of discovering our transcendence of physical ending even as we suffer and learn from the entropy or burning up of our physical house. The Second Law may explain how lifeless objects work and what always happens to isolated and contained systems, but it does not block our way to lasting love if we are open and free to love with someone else.

Why Do Things Have to End?

By giving us endings and the reality of transience as predicted by the Second Law, God has given life its poignancy and meaning. Chemist Ilya Prigogine spoke of "self-organization" or the possibility of order emerging from disorder. He saw the process called entropy as a way through which we evolve to a higher state. Marriage can be a process through which two people support each other in being vigilant for the emerging order rather than despairing at impending ends. For the lonely physical self, the process of entropy is a death sentence, but for merged souls, it can be a *very* fascinating learning experience.

Author William Saroyan wrote, "I'm growing old! I'm falling

apart! And it's *very interesting!*" He was expressing his personal
fascination with the complementary side of creating and growing
and what he saw as the wonder of the necessary process of falling
apart. The eighth step in making a miracle marriage involves
using or "eating entropy" by converting the energy generated
by the natural process of deterioration and its related sadness
and grief.

The Poetry of Thermodynamics

The poets understood the great marriage orientation of the Second Law. They were sensitive to the profound power of certain
physical ends to alert the human spirit to the value of the Now.
Poet Robert Graves wrote of "bleeding to death of time in slow
heart beats."[4] Poet Edward FitzGerald wrote, in his translation
of the *Rubáiyát,* "The Moving Finger writes; and, having writ,
Moves on."[5] I have already referred to Shakespeare's words,
"Time will come and take my love away."[6] The pathos of our life
is contained in the fact that time passes, but the joy of loving
makes passing our time together a profound spiritual learning
experience. Miracle marriages are based on the premise that our
sadness is not less wondrous and vital to our love than is our joy.

The Me Myth teaches us only to live for the now and that
"past is past" and "the future is up to us." The Great Marriage
Myth, however, teaches that we can make a meaningful Now
together by revering our past and wondering at our future as
we celebrate these thoughts in the present. Through marriage,
we can constantly remind one another, as Ralph Waldo Emerson
suggested, "to be present to the present." We do not have to be
walled off from our past and future by individual guilt about
what has gone before or a private fear at what might lie ahead.
If we are "in entropy together," we can constantly remind each
other that we make our nows by how we choose to think about
our past, present, and future.

Thoreau urged us "To stand on the meeting of two eternities,
the past and the future.'"[7] Emerson wrote, "These roses under
my window make no reference to former roses or to better ones;
they are for what they are; they exist with God today."[8] There
is something sacred about the fact that we all end, and by helping
one another experience all of the processes of living as we move

toward our dying, we can learn to see the Second Law of our inevitable physical end the way the scientists and poets do—as the manifestation of the joyfully mysterious and intense process of an evolving new order and living "in" the now and not "for" it.

The Evening of Contentment

As I conducted my research for this book, I discovered that almost all so-called marriage manuals are designed for the young. Since so many marriages falter, it appears that we have forgotten the great joy experienced by those spouses who make miracle marriages and live happily together for decades. Every so often, the news media will parade out a couple passing their fiftieth or sixtieth anniversary as a type of cherished old relic, but few researchers have paid much attention to those couples who go far beyond parenting and careers to confront their aging and mortality together.

I studied fifty couples who have been married to one another for more than fifty years. They call themslves the Fantastic Fifties, and I interviewed almost every member of this group and gave them the same tests you are taking in this miracle-marriage manual. Not only were their scores high, but they provided insight into how to make a miracle marriage and the lasting impact of that miracle as two lovers deal with the ultimate entropy of their own mortality and the prospective end of their physical connection.

What follows is a summary of what the Fantastic Fifties members told me. Each statement is taken directly from my taped interviews of the husbands and wives. I hope you find the same wisdom in these loving words about marriage that I did and that these statements help you and your spouse understand the eighth step of making a miracle marriage—the Sharing of Sadness:

- "We are not afraid of death. When we were young, we were consumed with trying to outrun it, avoid it, or we led our life trying to get the most we could before it came. Now that we accept death, it has no effect on us at all."
- "Because each of our 'selfs' died a long time ago and our

marriage replaced them, we can never really die as individuals. We know we will be together somehow forever."

• "We are enjoying life now more than ever before. That's probably because we stopped trying so hard to enjoy ourselves and started to enjoy just being together. I guess we enjoy just being."

• "We still argue and have conflicts, but there is no chance we will end our marriage, because we have accepted that God will do that here on this earth. We're together forever."

• "Our differences as a man and woman have really decreased. We seem like one gender together now. We even look like each other. He has bigger and firmer breasts than I do, but I'm much stronger than he is. He seemed to shrink and I grew. Now I'm taller than he is, but he's cuter than I am."

• "We talk a lot less, but we both seem to say a lot more. Now that we both can't hear so well, we've really learned to listen."

• "We can just sit together and be happy. We don't have to go and do all the time. We don't feel tired, but we feel very peaceful. Even after we argue, we can sit down together and rest happily."

• "My husband is not the young fool he used to be. Now he's an old fool, and so am I. We stopped trying to change one another a long time ago. Now we have a little of both of our good points and bad points in our marriage. We annoy the hell out of each other every day, but we've always done that."

• "When we were first married, we had to work to get each other up to go to work. Now we have to work to get up. But we're still working together."

• "One thing is sure when you've been married sixty-one years. You're old! But our marriage is older and wiser than either of us."

After interviewing one hundred happily and long-married men and women, I sensed that they were in the evening of their contentment. Various illnesses and hospitalizations prevented me from using this large and interesting group as the basis for my research for this book. It was clear, however, that the effects of the Second Law of Thermodynamics had not burned them out but had melted them together into a peaceful, calm couple. They had dined on the disasters of daily life, and were able to digest the entropy of their life and use it to soothe the aches and pains of aging. Like the Silver Survivors, they provided evidence of the power of the miracle of lasting love.

Love Epochs

Physicist and theologian Gerald Schroeder asserts that the "entropy" of the Second Law was described in the Bible. He writes, "Biblically, we also see a flow from chaos to cosmos."[9] He suggests that the "evening" and "morning" sequences in the first chapter of Genesis are actually God's "epochs" marked by significant periods of flow from disorder toward increasing order. When the Revised Standard Bible says "And there was evening and there was morning," Schroeder suggests, it refers to the root meaning of the Hebrew words for "evening" representing disorder and "morning" representing a higher order.

Because every Now is a simultaneous beginning and ending, our marriages also go through "morning times" and "evening times," and the eighth law of lasting love tells us to try to use the evening epochs not as nightmares of helplessness but as times through which we gather the resulting entropic energy to nourish our growth together toward the morning or beginning of our fondest dreams. We can learn to see the worst of times in our loving as the transitional and necessary love epochs from which we can recycle what thermodynamics calls the "wasted heat energy" of life and use it as fuel in our voyage to find a patience for the present, hope for our future, and fondness for our past.

My own near-death from cancer drove home the reality of mortality and the eventual physical end to my loving with my wife Celest. During this night epoch of our marriage, we learned together that the reality of our ending made our Nows together even more valuable, what had gone before more meaningful, and what lay ahead of us even more challenging. When I would cry in despair and hopelessness about my prognosis and what was happening to Me, my wife would protest against my self-imposed "entropic isolation" and my wasting of our love energy.

During my worst times of despair of life's end, my wife would say, "Don't talk to me about 'you.' Talk to me about Us. Don't let this cancer rob our Nows by letting it trap you in a future I can't be part of. Hold me *now*, cry with me, be here with me *now* as intensely as you can be. Let me feel all of this with you *now*.

We can't miss a single *now*." I am sure that a part of my cure was the power of our marriage to help make a miracle by using the entropic energy of two developing souls against millions of malignant cells. Our marriage overwhelmed them!

Open Marriages

In completely enclosed and isolated systems, entropy always occurs. Leave plants and flowers in a completely sealed container free of the challenge of storms, wind, and rain, and after some time you will return to find total destruction. If we neglect our marriage by seeking only to enhance our ego rather than to form a new Us, we close the loving system, and the marriage deteriorates into nothing and consumes us in the process. Marriages have been burning out because they have been closed, isolated systems constituted by two "selfs" rather than open systems interacting with the world.

Low Monogamy is based on a closed and contained system of two hot and burning lovers seeking a love object to meet their selfish needs. There is much wasted energy in the Me marriage, because two selves are seeking their own ways with no system available through which two people use crises and endings to grow. For the Me marriage, every crisis is a source of friction between two people trying to be self-fulfilled.

High Monogamy is a form of open marriage in which both partners confront crises as a system or growing unit that uses the heat of its problems to grow. The Fantastic Fifty group saw crises as expected and as a necessary component of sharing daily living with someone else. When illness strikes one partner, both become "ill," because they share a single marital body and a common understanding of the meaning of their mortality. Mediocre marriages bemoan their crises, but miracle marriages need their crises to live. One Silver Survivor said, "I'll bet if you added it all up, we had at least as many bad times as good times. It seems like we're always going into or coming out of really good times. Some of our friends talk as if their husband or wife is in or out of some midlife personal crisis, but for us it's our marriage that is growing up. We have an open marriage that is always changing, and we need our problems as much as we need our joy, because they're both so much a part of how we're married.

We know we won't end our marriage, but we will physically have to leave it someday. That's what makes us cherish it all the more."

So-called open marriages described and practiced in the 1960s and 1970s allowed sexual intercourse with partners outside marriage. Paradoxically, these open marriages were the most closed marriages of all. They were based on hot, romantic love designed to satisfy the hungry ego rather than to generate a lasting union made to deal with life crises. As the eighth law of lasting love would predict, these marriages seldom continued their practice of consensual extramarital sex.[10] The entropy or negative energy and the friction between two egos rubbing together for self-pleasure eventually burned out everyone concerned.[11]

Ego Obstacles or Growing Pains

Psychologist Mihaly Csikszentmihalyi identifies a central component of the Great Marriage Myth when he writes about "negentropic life themes" or the "transference of attention from personal [ego] problems to the problems of others [the beloved *and* the world in general]."[12] By "negentropic," Csikszentmihalyi refers to making entropy "positive" or "negating" its wasteful burning nature by turning one's attention inward to the relationship rather than focusing on protecting the physical self. "I" am mortal, but "we" are forever.

Psychologist William James wrote, "Those who survive great illness or great loss are twice born—they have drunk too deeply of the cup of bitterness ever to forget the taste—and their redemption is into a universe two stories deep."[13] Our marriages can also be reborn through the birthing pain of entropy or the falling-apart times in our loving by asking, "What's happening to *us*, why, and what can *we* do about it?" rather than "What's happening to *me*, why *me*, and what can *I* do?".

It's OK if You're Not OK

The history of our world has been written by those who managed to direct their individually experienced pain toward more loving, creating, and growth for other people rather than their "self."

Thomas Edison was a sickly child who was told he was inferior and worthless through much of his young life. He turned his pain (entropy or burning up) into a creative energy for improving the life of everyone in the world. Eleanor Roosevelt was continually repressed and guilt-ridden throughout her childhood, but she turned her suffering into an energy to support humane causes, to love and assist her husband, and to give her unique intelligence to the nation. Albert Einstein's childhood was full of fears for his life and humiliation, but the entropy of his living was turned to an as-yet-unequaled intellectual capacity aimed at helping us see a new way to understand nothing less than "everything."

Our SOB, or Selfish Old Brain, sees pain, suffering, and endings in terms of its own discomfort and as a threat to its life-support system. Our brain wants us to get "more selfish" when we hurt, but our minds can tell our brains to be quiet. Our minds know that there is something about suffering that calls on us to merge with others rather than separate from them. Our brain needs our body, but our mind needs our love.

All our greatest minds have not only experienced the intensity of entropy; they have managed to eat it up and to spit out the most remarkable new order for us to learn from and grow with. They all speak well and lovingly of their parents, even though there were bitter and terrible times in their childhoods. A recent study of 300 successful men and women revealed little correlation between terrible conditions of childhood and ultimate adult accomplishments.[14] Author William Sloane Coffin wrote, "I'm not OK . . . you're not OK . . . and that's OK." We need to be messed up to grow up.

Author Phillip Sandbloom examined the role of suffering, illness, and life predicaments in creative people across the spectrum of the arts.[15] He describes how Albert Einstein suffered throughout his most productive times with severe stomach problems and illness but refused to follow his doctor's advice toward a cure. "At least the gods seem well intentioned toward me when they squeeze the gallbladder," he said. "I work much more successfully when I have an attack." Sigmund Freud said, "I have to be somewhat miserable to write well." The people who shaped our world were fueled to some extent by the negative energy of their life, and they changed personal challenge to interpersonal love. If the First Noble Truth of Buddhism is that "life is suffering," a central truth of the miracle marriage is that suffering is the stuff that lasting love is made of.

Taking Pride in and from Your Parents

Throughout the history of psychology and psychotherapy, parents have been blamed for making their children dependent and for helping to cause their depression, guilt, anxiety, shame, substance abuse, and other serious problems. Parents are accused of creating a dysfunctional inner child who seeks love and someone to live life with instead of showing a strong independence. I suggest that our problems in daily living are *not* problems that are caused by our failures to be an independent person. They are problems that stem from our inability to silence the self by learning to love and be *inter*dependent with someone else.

Instead of looking back with anger or resentment, our inner child can learn to love, forgive, and thank our parents for leaving us incomplete. The most important thing a parent can do to produce a miracle maker is to be sure to instill in their child a personal awareness and comfort with his or her halfness. The child should be assured that he or she has a worthy half to give and is worthy of receiving another person's half.

Most parents, after all, did their best. Even when the terrible crises of child abuse or parental drug abuse occurs, actual parental *intent* to harm is rare. The Fifth Commandment says that we should *honor* our parents, and it is not necessary to love all that they did in order to honor the persons they will always symbolize in our life. Our parents were incomplete people, too. If our parents helped to make us feel incomplete, they only helped point us toward one of the most rewarding experiences of a lifetime—needing and merging with someone else with whom to try to solve life's problems.

If our parents made you feel that you need the love, approval, support, and caring of someone else to take on the natural entropy or crises of life, they were only practicing very good science related to the eighth law of lasting love. Some popular psychologists suggest that we write a letter to our parents scribbled with our nondominant hand so that we can get in touch with and purge our dependent, negative, childish feelings about them. I suggest, instead, that you write your parents a long, loving, thank-you letter. Write it with your dominant hand so they can read it easily and clearly. We should be busy looking for the hidden inner lover I mentioned in Chapter 10 rather than trying to rediscover our inner selfish child who wants to go out to play alone.

Healthy Falling Apart

San Diego psychiatrist and chaologist Arnold Mandell suggests that human systems—like quantum and cosmic systems—naturally undergo their own form of flow through disorder to a new and more complex order.[16] He states that when a person is in total equilibrium, he or she is actually not as healthy or growing and developing as when going through change, entropy, or chaos. Pathological arrhythmias of the heart, changes in the cell associated with cancer, and alterations in blood chemistry are not only mechanical pathologies but also examples of disorder and entropy that can lead to physiological readjustments and, if not a curing or fixing, at the least a healing or new level of wholeness.

Some physicians have begun to theorize that entropy and falling apart—"dis-ease"—is actually a form of health or a way of evolving to a new state of being. Sickness gets our attention and is the evening epoch of a new morning in our spiritual development. Instead of seeing illness, depression, anxiety, and despair as something going wrong, scientists suggest that these processes are as necessary as they are painful and that they are the entropy of an open and dynamic living. They are the complementary counterparts of feeling good and of being happy and hopeful.[17]

I have never before known the pain I felt when cancer ate away my hips. As I suffered that agony, I seemed to be more alive than ever before. I was aware of parts of my body—growing bone and flowing blood—that I had never felt before. Now that I am cured, every moment of freedom from pain is a blessing I will never again take for granted. We become used to complaining when we hurt, but we too seldom celebrate those times when we don't. Pain is a terrible but necessary reminder of the glorious sensations of a healthy body.

Machines don't get sick, feel depression, grieve over the loss of their parts, or cry when a fellow machine breaks down. Machines comply with the Second Law by functioning, breaking, and being thrown away. Machines that are burning up can send mechanical signals to their operators, give off smoke and fumes, and send numbers to computers regarding their ending, but they cannot truly experience and share their suffering with their operators or other machines. The eighth law of lasting love reminds us that we have been given the gift of sharing our suffering and the capacity not only to be affected by the entropy of the Second Law but the gift of experiencing, thinking about, and sharing the progression toward physical end. When we merge with someone else in a miracle marriage, we combine our individual consciousnesses to reflect together about the meaning of illness, loss, sadness, crises, and inevitable endings. The marriage vow "in sickness and in health" might read "through sickness we will find new health."

Just as physical "death throes" signal the changing of one form of physical here-and-now energy to a new and infinite energy and order, lasting love goes through its own form of "love throes." These "soul spasms" are signals that love is not dying but is in the process of becoming much more than a mechanical, see-and-touch love. As you will read in the next chapter, while we are falling apart on one level of reality, we may be falling together in another.

The Agony of Ecstasy

A natural consequence of our awareness of life's entropy is the experience of depression I described earlier. One reason we become depressed is that we often feel helpless and alone in the face of the Second Law—that everything and everyone ends. Depression is the complementary price we pay for the elation we feel at life's exciting beginnings. It has been called the "common cold of psychological disorders."[18] In its most serious forms, depression is much more like life-threatening pneumonia than a cold. Psychiatrists consider depression to be a "mood" disorder, either in the form of unipolar depression (in which the individual is depressed almost constantly) or bipolar depression (in which there are episodes of both mania or excessive elation and deep depression). Depression is also viewed either as exogenous (related to outside factors) or endogenous (associated with biochemical imbalance and other internal factors).

Some studies have suggested that proneness to depression, particularly the bipolar type, may be carried as a dominant gene on the X chromosome.[19] In Chapter 3, I mentioned that there are differences between men and women in the frequency of serious depression, and there may be a feminine predisposition to endogenous, bipolar depression. However, exogenous factors no doubt interact to influence who gets depressed when, how deeply, and how the depression is shown to others. The beta Adams or Eves I described in Chapter 9 are more prone to pessimism and rumination.[20]

Alpha Depression and Beta Blues

"My husband is an alpha," said one Silver Survivor. "He never seems to be sad, but when he gets down, he really crashes. He gets totally depressed. I'm a beta, so I'm used to the blues. I'm in a constant state of sadness with spurts of joy, so I never really bottom out." This description illustrates how alpha and beta lovers differ in how they deal with the feelings of sadness that are a natural part of daily living.

In Chapter 9, I described complementary alpha and beta thinking and loving styles. In coping with the depression associated with entropy or the endings and crises in our lives, failure to see alpha and beta differences can result in frustration, feelings of ineffectiveness, and a worsening of depression. Instead of maximizing the marriage's strengths in dealing with the impact of the Second Law and developing a marital sense of "couple competence" and adaptability, conflicts in styles of control and power in a marriage can result in what researchers call "learned helplessness."[21]

Psychologist Paula Johnson reviewed the complementarity of power or the way in which people influence one another.[22] One exogenous source of the differences in frequency of depression, as I suggested in Chapter 3, is how the genders choose to show that they are sad. If the couple combines different and complementary styles of handling depression and in exerting personal power to cope with sadness and the problems that cause it, couple competence is increased. If differences in power style are not recognized, or are ignored or exaggerated, a conflicted marriage results.

I have pointed out that alpha Adams and Eves—oriented to do rather than be—try to distract themselves when they are depressed by trying to work or play "it" out. The alpha approach is to try to get "my mind off my problems." Beta Adams and Eves—oriented to being and reflection—tend to recycle or ruminate negativity in their minds. Betas keep their minds "on" their problems. One Silver Survivor husband who is a musician said, "Alphas do the blues, and betas be the blues." A marriage based on the Me Myth tends to experience conflict and ineffectiveness as alpha and beta styles of sadness clash rather than combine. A miracle marriage combines both orientations into a balance of reflection and, when possible, corrective or remedial action— being and doing the blues together.

Beta persons (usually women) tend to attempt power or control over adversity in the following ways:

    Indirect power: manipulation, crying, nagging, and ingratiating, ruminating

    Personal power: threatening not to meet other people's individual needs for approval, loving, or sex

    Helplessness power: expression, sometimes through stereotypical behaviors associated with weakness, such as demonstrating or exaggerating a lack of ability or skill to meet life's demands

Alpha persons (usually men) tend to attempt power in the ways below, which are complementary to the beta power system:

    Direct power: demanding, commanding, assertive

    Concrete power: influence attempts backed up by money, status, or knowledge

    Competency power: strength, force, and demonstrations of mastery

This wife's report illustrates the marital "learned helplessness" that results from failure to resolve alpha and beta coping or power style differences in marriages:

"We fell into this pattern of me whining and nagging to get the attention and loving I wanted. When things went wrong, like they are bound to do sometimes, I thought I would appeal to his sense of decency or that he would feel my sadness. Instead, when something happened that was sad, he just got more demanding of his own way, his own time, his own space, and started ordering me around even more. When I wanted to sit and talk about what had happened, he wanted to 'go and do something about it' or 'get it out of our mind.' Usually, while I cried, he just went to his study and read. He's a college English instructor, and even when he does talk, he uses words as weapons. There isn't any real feeling—just an oral dissertation, and then it's over. Just talking about our troubles over and over seems to help me, but he hates it. The more we tried to resolve things, the more sad and helpless I felt all day and most of the night. The more helpless I was, the more effective he tried to be. As a result, we became effectively helpless together."

The marriage referred to above had failed to use a combination of alpha and beta complementary styles in confronting their sadness. They had not learned that eighth law of Shared Sadness. As the alpha withdrew to reading alone and the beta wept alone, their marriage succumbed to the Second Law by burning out and ending in divorce court. The following Silver Survivor husband's statement illustrates the power of the complementarity of shared sadness:

"I'm the crier, talker, and sitter in the marriage. My wife is talk a little, come up with a plan, and solve the problem. If the problem can't be solved—something terrible like a death in the family—we combine both of our styles. I'm the beta one, so we do my crying together and my wife tries my talk-and-talk style for a while with me. She's the alpha, so she makes a plan to do something about the problem or to get our mind off the problem. We have a 'mind-on-mind-off' and what we call our 'do-be-do-be-do' alternating rhythm to our marriage. It works well for us during our worst times."

Conducting a Marital Autopsy

"How do you think I felt?" asked the husband during the therapy session I call the marital autopsy. In my clinic, I asked couples to conduct autopsies on the death of their relationship. This technique seemed to help couples learn from their failures even

262 ◆ THE SAD SIDE OF LOVE

after a divorce, so they could see within their ending love another beginning for learning more about lasting love. "I felt like I couldn't get her to see things the way they were for me. She thought she was always the weak and damaged one, but what about me? She always said that I was so smart, so happy, and always got my way, but I really felt more helpless than she did."

Some couples *fight* the battles of alpha and beta power differences throughout their marriage. They implode into an enduring hate relationship of contrasting ineffectual alpha/beta power styles and fail to learn a joint unit power of both alpha and beta powers to deal with entropy. Many of the couples I worked with seemed to be in a battle to prove who was the sadder instead of joining in an effort to discover the source of and ways to solve their mutual pain.

If you have been divorced or separated, or your marriage is troubled, I suggest you consider the "deliberations on divorce" section in Chapter 11. Then, check to see if your marriage is or was characterized primarily by one of the following three styles:

Fighting: Instead of forgiving the limits of and seeing the potential in the natural alpha- or beta-oriented differences in dealing with sadness and crises, each spouse in the *fighting* couple sees the other's styles as a source of weakness, irritation, or inadequacy. Marital time is spent defending one's own style and attacking or demeaning the partner's style rather than trying to find a way to use both styles effectively together.

Fleeing: Both partners in the *fleeing* marriage accept the other partner's alpha or beta style but fail to use it personally in trying to develop a joint marital coping style. One or both partners take a "that's just how he or she is" attitude, and as a result, the marriage does not fully benefit from either coping style.

Flowing: Both partners in the *flowing* marriage alternate back and forth between each partner's alpha or beta style and use a blend of both to make a stronger and more adaptable union.

The Silver Survivors learned to *flow* together and make a new omega marriage by intentionally trying to include both alpha and beta styles of dealing with their sadness. Their purpose was to take on every problem using *both* partners' "ways" to make a "marriage way" of coping with the natural endings, losses, and pressures of life.

The fighting and fleeing marital styles burden the court systems, fill the therapists' offices, endlessly seek new ways to be "self"-sufficient and deal with "their own problems." They contribute to the entropy that eats away at the fabric of a stale society. The flowing miracle marriages are able to, as psychologist Mihaly Csikszentmihalyi writes about his research subjects who learned to flow together, "extract energy out of entropy—to recycle waste into structured order."[23]

THE TEST OF THERMODYNAMIC LOVE

The following test items will help you assess the status of your own relationship in terms of its capacity to share sadness and survive through entropy to a stronger marriage.

1. Are you and your spouse able to see conflict, sadness, and stress in your relationship as a sign of your closeness? Or do you interpret it as a symptom of mutual helplessness?

"Don't think we go looking for problems," said one wife. "But we do see our problems as necessary to being as much in love as we are."

2. Do the two of you seem able to turn the bleakest situations into challenges for two instead of attempting to look for the guilty party?

"When our marriage was young, we were like kids," said one husband. "When we had problems, our first instinct was to point and blame. Now, a problem means we have to get together to solve it. We don't point at each other, we hold each other."

3. Do you give the gift of self by clearly and specifically saying what makes you happy and what makes you sad instead of hoping that your partner will guess?

One Silver Survivor wife said, "I was taught as a young girl that if a man really loved you, he could tell what you wanted and needed without you having to say a word. Now

I know that the best gift I can give him is letting him know what I need and want. I want him to give me that same gift by letting me know what he wants."

4. *Are you and your spouse centered on the marriage instead of fighting about and worrying about external factors most of the time?*

"It is all too easy to forget you are married," said one husband. "Much of our society doesn't really care, and there are so many other things demanding our time and attention that, if you're not careful, the only time you really know you're married is when the two of you have to fill out a joint tax return."

5. *Do you feel that you both can exercise influence in your relationship in your own alpha or beta style and still keep the relationship growing?*

"Now I think we've got it," said the husband. "I'm an alpha, so I often deal with our problems by trying to distract myself and us from the problem. My wife is a beta, so she wants to go over and over and over the problem. Now we do both. We talk and we distract ourselves. By making what you called an omega or whole out of our alphaness and betaness, we have many more ways to solve our problems."

6. *Can you both completely stop your defenses in a marital conflict because you both are unconditionally committed to making your love grow?*

"I was taught always to keep my guard up," said the husband. "That may work in boxing, but not in a marriage. We assume that neither one of us ever intends to hurt the other, so we just open up and go after the problem. We are defensive of our marriage but not of our egos."

7. *Are the times when things seem to be falling apart seen as challenging times instead of more evidence that the marriage is in trouble?*

"We seemed always to be looking for proof that the marriage wasn't going to last," said one wife during a marital autopsy. "Every conflict between us seemed to be another nail in the coffin, and we finally nailed it shut. We were never looking for signs of life and love—only for weaknesses and an excuse to prove our marriage wouldn't work."

8. *Are the two of you often depressed together or do you feel sad alone?*

"It's a strange thing about being sad," said the wife. "Lonely sadness seems so helpless, but shared sadness seems to have a hope and comfort to it."

9. *Even when you are physically and emotionally exhausted by re-peated problems or conflicts, does it seem that the more problems you have, the more psychological and spiritual energy the marriage seems to find?*

"We have found that the more problems we have, the more energy we get," said the wife. "Just when we are at rock bottom, we seem to find energy we never knew we had. I guess it just makes sense, doesn't it? It doesn't take much love or energy to be happy, so God gives you more of both for the problem times."

10. *Do you see your marriage as a resource for dealing not only with your problems and your partner's problems but also with the problems of the world? Or do you see it as a refuge or place to hide from the reality of the natural constant chaos of living and loving?*

"We have a kind of cockiness about our marriage," said the Silver Survivor. "It can solve any problem either of us ever had and still have plenty left over to help others. Nothing seems to make our marriage stronger than when we are trying to make the world stronger."

The more "yes" answers you have to the above items, the more your marriage is a flowing relationship characterized by accom-modating both alpha and beta styles of dealing with life's entropy. The Silver Survivors averaged a score of 9.5 on this test, while the control group of failing marriages average score was 1.0.

In the fourteenth century, philosopher Meister Eckhart wrote: "There is no stopping-off place in this world, no, nor was there ever one for any man, no matter how far along his path he'd come."[24] He was writing about the Second Law of Thermody-namics and the eighth law of lasting love—that life is constant change, challenge, and movement toward physical end. Eckhart sums up the eighth step in making a miracle marriage when he writes, "This above all then, be always ready for the gifts of God and always for new ones. And always remember, God is a thousand times more ready to give than you are to receive."

HOME LOVE ASSIGNMENTS

In chapter 1, I pointed out that lasting love is more a way of thinking than it is a way of feeling. For this eighth step in our miracle-marriage manual, I have provided home love assignments in the form of a sadness survivor's handbook based on the application of the basic principles of cognitive psychology to loving relationships.[25] These are the ABCDEs of dealing with the entropy of love.

A SADNESS SURVIVOR'S HANDBOOK

A. Identify marital *Adversity* as a starting point, not as an ending point. Clearly identify your problems by writing them over and over until both of you agree on the Adversity definition. After several hours of reworking their Adversity statement and blaming each other, one husband and wife wrote this brief statement about one of their problems. "Our aunt keeps interfering in our marriage by calling and coming over unannounced."

Failing couples seldom agree on what their problem is, and they see Adversity as the end or as the sign of the end of their relationship. Miracle-making Silver Survivors saw the identification of Adversity as a first step to dealing with their problems, and with mutual and patient hard work, could finally agree on exactly what was wrong or threatening their marriage.

B. Discuss your marital *Beliefs* about Adversity. Adversity has no meaning until we give it meaning. Without using blame, discuss what the two of you think about your problems, once you have identified them one by one. I am referring here to what you "think" and not what you feel and to the effort to come up with a joint and shared belief and a "couple way" of thinking about your problems.

The couple above wrote, "We think our aunt is trying to interfere in our marriage and tell us what to do because we're young and newly married. She's trying to take advantage of us."

C. What are the *C*onsequences of your Beliefs? For example, if an Adversity was seen as an unreasonable and troublesome interference by a relative and the Belief was that people other than the spouse should not have any effect on marital decisions, what is the Consequence of that Belief (a feeling of anger, sulking, revenge).

Couples should recognize that Consequences are feelings while Beliefs are thoughts. Feelings and actions result from what and how we think about a given problem and not directly from Adversity itself. Spend time in your marital discussions differentiating between the "fact" of an Adversity, the Beliefs and thoughts about it, and the actual feelings and behaviors that have resulted from the chosen point of view regarding the stressful event.

The couple in my example wrote, "Because it's our theory that our aunt is trying to interfere in and control our marriage, we feel angry and helpless because of how we see this thing. We think she is our 'agony aunty.'"

D. *D*ispute the Belief by considering alternative views and Beliefs about the problem. Draw on the unique strengths of the complementary alpha or beta styles within your marriage. Use the alpha and beta strengths of each spouse to find another way to think about the Adversity. (Perhaps the interfering relative feels alone and needs people to relate with and try to have some influence over. Perhaps she's not trying to interfere but to find someone to care about her.) Constructive marital disputes (sometimes called "forced positivization") focus on questioning nonproductive and pessimistic beliefs regarding adversity rather than on quarreling and selfish feelings.

Here is a disputation session conducted by the couple with Agony Aunty. "We're angry because we don't know how to deal with our aunt. Because she's interfering, we think she wants to hurt us, but that's just how we think about it. She may not be doing that at all. She really doesn't 'make' us feel anything. Our feelings are our reactions to how we are thinking about what she's doing. Maybe she hangs around us so much because she is terribly lonely and afraid in her old age. Maybe it's because we have such a great marriage with so much extra love that she turns to us instead of to other relatives. If our marriage is strong, nothing outside it can ruin it unless we let it. Giving her our time might even strengthen our love and make us feel good about our marriage."

E. *Energize* your relationship by remembering that the process of conflict, while tiring and time-consuming, is actually generating a new source of growth energy for your marriage. The ABCDE method is an entropy-eating system that converts negative energy to growth energy.

Here is a part of the energizing session in the Agony Aunty case. "Dealing with our Agony Aunty while we are so young has helped us see problems we would never have seen. We'll get old, too, and we'll need love. Dealing with this whole problem has made us stronger together, because we aren't arguing about our aunt anymore. We're discussing our marriage and its strengths."

Remember the ABCDE approach to marital entropy when your life or your marriage seems sad. Add an F to the ABCDE equation by promising each other that through your struggles and even though your physical contact must eventually be broken, your love is *F*orever.

13

STEP IX

The Ways of Love:

PLAYING TOGETHER—
STAYING TOGETHER

Our love will be limitless.

The greatest discovery of the seventeenth century was that one way of explaining things would explain everything in the universe. The greatest discovery of the twentieth century is that it won't.
—Lawrence LeShan

LOVE LAW NINE: THE LAW OF LOVING REALITIES

Just as true genius and creativity break free of the limits of one domain, or set of rules, so lasting love is a love of Shared Multiple Realities.

Lovers' Quarrels

"You just don't get it, do you?" said the angry wife. "It's as plain as the nose on your face, but you just can't see how wrong you are about my mother. She's been a saint to us, and you make her out to be a demon. Can't you see reality? You're the one causing all of the problems and fights with her."

"How can you say that?" answered the husband. "Anybody in their right mind or with an ounce of intelligence could see what a bitch your mother is. Get real!"

This argument illustrates one of the most important decisions that must be made if we are to take the ninth step in making a miracle marriage. We can choose to spend our marriage struggling to determine what is "real," or we can begin with the premise that there are many realities. Science has discovered that the second choice is more valid and helpful in understanding our world, and miracle marriages have proved that the choice of many realities is the way of lasting love.

Monogamy Maps to Reality

Low Monogamy is dedicated to the pursuit of reality. Each spouse is convinced that he or she knows fact from fiction on the basis of his or her own mental set. Husband and wife have separate cognitive maps, and any turn or twist that departs from the "right" way is dismissed as misdirected or wrongheaded. To be "realistic"—in one's own sense of reality—is viewed as the high mark of intellect and determines what will be accepted or rejected as "real."

The reality of the Me Myth is self-verifying and circular. It involves cognitive confirmation or the strengthening of one's own brand of reality by looking for what "logically" fits and the dismissal of what doesn't. The Low Monogamist is convinced that he or she knows what is real and proceeds to select for acceptance or rejection those thoughts, points of view, and feelings expressed by his or her spouse that match that self-reality. This wife's statement illustrates the Low Monogamist's map of reality: "I know what is real. My husband is out of touch with reality. Sometimes he says something that makes sense, but usually he's really off the wall and just plain wrong. He doesn't know what is really real from what is really dumb."

High Monogamists know that their cognitive map is only one-half of the way to the treasure of lasting love. They learn to accept one of the most remarkable discoveries in the history of science—that there are other worlds and parallel universes all around us! Physicist Paul Davies writes, "The world of our experience—the universe that we actually perceive—is not the only universe."[1] According to the most recent discoveries of quantum science, "reality is not a property of the external world on its own but is intimately bound up with our perceptions of the world."[2]

While the general public and some scientists have yet to come to grips with the lessons of quantum science, miracle marriages have. They know that reality is *not* objective and "out there." They integrate into their daily life the lessons of quantum realities that science has exposed in the laboratory. High Monogamists are constantly challenging themselves to redraw their evolving mutual cognitive couple's map to lasting love.

Finding "The" Way or "Many Ways"

Recent experiments have shown that what scientists thought were real things are not. Atoms and subatomic particles do not have well-defined, demarcated boundaries. Their "identity" is a matter of many realities depending on where the observer is, how he or she is observing, how fast the quantum stuff is moving, and where it temporarily is.[3] The quantum world isn't real, it's potential realities.

The fascinating finding that there are many and parallel realities in which we can choose to participate can be applied to making many loving realities. The following two statements illustrate the difference between the one "reality" and the multiple "realities" approach to marriage.

"I know what's real and what's not," said the Low Monogamist. "I know fact from fiction. I know what I need, and I know how to get it." A Silver Survivor said, "What seems so real at one time seems much less real at another, depending on what is going on for my husband and me in my marriage. My needs always change along with the different needs of my husband, and I need him to help me understand my needs and how to meet them." As these statements indicate, Low Monogamy seeks "the way," but High Monogamy looks for "its ways."

The Invention of Mother

The couple described at the beginning of this chapter who were arguing over the "real" nature and personality of the wife's mother learned to break free of their one-reality trap. Their recent discussion of the mother illustrates how the ninth law of loving *realities* helps couples to solve their problems.

"My mother is a loving, caring pain in the neck," said the wife. "When she's in the domain of mothering, she is unbelievably patient, gentle, and tolerant. But when she is in the domain of mother-in-lawing, my husband has shown me that she has no patience at all, is overcontrolling, and can be a real bitch."

The husband said, "My wife has shown me a side to her mother I never saw. All I saw was a bitchy mother-in-law, but seeing things through my wife's eyes has helped me see the mothering and caring ways of her mother, too. We see now that her mother is our own invention and our own way of looking at and creating our own reality. Now we've coinvented our marital version of her mother."

The husband and wife in this example knew and experienced realities about the mother that neither of them could have known as an individual. By understanding and being willing to see the partner's reality, they learned from one another not only new realities about the mother but also new ways of thinking. By accepting plural realities, they have opened up new domains of loving for their miracle-making marriage.

Are We Real?

If you have recently won a marital battle by proving that you were right, your marriage actually lost the war, because it destroyed its options to see other and perhaps better solutions based on other realities. The more domains you and your spouse can discover, the more options for loving and solving problems you will have.

Scientists call the view of the existence of many realities domain theory. This theory suggests that our experience of the universe is divided into many realms, or domains, each with its own unique laws.[4] Prior to the early 1900s, scientists believed that their task was to discover more and more about the "real" or correct nature of life. As they searched for more information about the one domain of reality, their discoveries seemed to make human consciousness and emotion almost irrelevant. Reality was becoming more and more "out there" instead of "in us."

Copernicus robbed us of our heavenly haughtiness when he contradicted our "reality" that we and our earth were the center of the universe. Charles Darwin removed our biological arrogance by showing our direct ties with everything that lives and that, even though we gloat over so-called lower animals, these same animals are our biological cousins. Edwin Hubble's discovery that the Milky Way is only one of billions of galaxies exploding out through space took away our pompous illusion that we are all there is in the universe. Each of these discoveries and most other major scientific breakthroughs seemed to expose humans as less and less significant.

The quantum and cosmic scientific revolution of the early 1900s, on the other hand, put humans back on center stage. Quantum physics proved that how we see the world, who we are, how we feel, and our cognition and consciousness actually help create realities. Low Monogamy is governed by old science that says that humans are artifacts of a great cosmic scheme who must defer to the real world outside and beyond them. High Monogamy is based on new science and teaches that we have a choice as to what realities we will see and help create. Low Monogamists cohabit in the world trying to figure out what is real and what is not. High Monogamists cocreate their world and try to figure out what new realities they can discover together. The Great Marriage Myth teaches not only that we are real, but that reality is us!

Cognitive Caring Styles

Every generation of artists has depicted its own view of reality. Artists often precede scientists in understanding the universe, so it is not surprising that scientists only recently are catching up with the idea that there are many realities to choose from and an infinite number of ways they are expressed.

Currently, scientists are examining at least four unique domains, or realms.[5] Each of those four domains has its own laws, rules, predictions, purposes, and promises regarding life and living. I suggest that we can apply these domains as a starting point for learning the ninth law of lasting love—the law of loving realities. I propose that these domains offer doors to different parallel worlds for us to think and love in.

During my decades of work with couples, I found that most psychological theories offered little in the way of understanding High Monogamy's combination of thinking and loving styles. Behaviorism, with its emphasis on here-and-now rewards and punishments, seemed to work well for Low Monogamy. It failed, however, to explain why so many Silver Survivors struggled and stayed through terrible times in their relationships to make their miracles. Psychoanalysis seemed to focus on narcissistic concerns about self-fulfillment and understanding. It offered much about the "I" but little about the "Us." Gestalt therapy, family therapy, transpersonal therapy, and many other movements offered clues for how Low Monogamists discover "reality" and happiness, but another approach seemed necessary to understand how High Monogamists created their lasting love and multiple realities together.

Borrowing from cognitive psychology, or the study of how we think about the world, I developed my own theory that miracle marriages thrive because they are able to combine what I call "cognitive caring styles." As I searched for these cognitive caring styles, I saw traces of the alpha and beta brain patterns I described earlier. I wondered how the Silver Survivors thought and loved and why they seemed so able to make lemonade of the lemons of their life. I spent hours asking the Silver Survivors how they thought, imagined, dreamed, and cared. I discovered through my interviews that I could classify cognitive caring styles using four domains identified by scientists.

By combining a scientific domain with a style of consciousness, we can propose four lover's cognitive caring styles that result in either conflict or creativity within a relationship. High Monogamy draws from the strengths of all these styles. Consider the following descriptions and examples from my interviews with the Silver Survivors as these styles may apply to you, your spouse, and your marriage:

THE LOVER'S DOMAINS: COGNITIVE CARING STYLES

1. The Sensory Domain

This is the realm of here-and-now, see-and-touch, local daily living. In this domain of reality, absolute time is kept by mechanical clocks, only objects are real, and the philosophy is "If I can see it and touch it, then I will believe it."

I call the thinking and loving style of the person functioning in this domain the "concretist" style. It is an alpha style of intellectualization over emotionality. The alpha man or woman seems asleep when it comes to intangible things. He or she tends to be cynical, distrusting, suspicious, highly rational, and constricted in his or her thinking patterns.

People relating to the concretist find him or her logical and reasonable but are often put off by his or her tendency to be overly critical and to mock or demean another person's view of reality. "My husband is a complete alpha concretist," said one wife. "He has all the characteristics of the doing and single-minded alpha, and he is so concrete in his thinking that his dreams are even dull."

2. The Quantum Domain

This is the realm of tiny things going very fast. It is the world of quantum waves and particles. Here identities and lifestyles are determined by the power of the observer. Time is irrelevant, nothing "is" until we look for it, and uncertainty, paradox, and mystery are the way of life. In this domain, the philosophy is "If I believe it, I will see it."

I call this cognitive and caring style the "romanticist." It is a beta style of images and feelings over action and objects. The beta man or woman is a dreamer who is completely trusting, open, creative, gullible, and imaginative. This type of thinker is so ingenious and inventive that others often find him or her to be strange or unusual. "My wife is a beta space cadet," said the concretist husband of the wife I quoted above. "She has such a vivid imagination that we don't have to go to the theater anymore. She creates her own theater of the absurd every day. Her dreams are complete dramas."

3. The Cosmic Domain

This is the realm of huge things moving in units of measurement that cannot be measured by our direct mechanical instruments. Time and space are the same, and both are relative to who, how, and where we are. Everything takes place on a huge and almost incomprehensible scale. The philosophy of this realm is "Things are too infinite to see."

I call this style of thinking "cosmotist." This style is a combination of the alpha's concern with control and the beta's proneness to fantasy. This person is "hypnotized" and sometimes intellectually paralyzed by the huge possibilities of life, and he or she thinks on such a grand scale that others often find him or her unrealistic or impractical. The thinking patter of cosmotists is one of grandiosity, distractibility, optimism, confidence, and idealism. "I know I'm a cosmotist," said one of my patients. "I have such big dreams and schemes and such huge expectations of everything that I'm bound to be disappointed most of the time. I'm even disappointed with most of my dreams. They aren't wild enough."

4. The Consciousness Domain

This is the realm of human thought and awareness. It is a world in which we talk to ourselves, wish, pray, love, hurt, and worry. Unless we learn to make a miracle marriage, this becomes a domain of the private individual alone with his or her thoughts. The philosophy of this domain is "I see with my mind and not my eyes."

This style is the pattern I call the "contemplatist." This person is a creator, and his or her cognitive and caring style is one of reflection, contemplation, meditation, introspection, and self-analysis. It is a blend of alpha effort and beta insight—what one Silver Survivor called "hard-hat thinking." When encountering this style, some people (particularly the concretist) find it to be frustrating, slow, aggravating, and self-effacing.

"I fit your contemplatist category very well," said one of the Silver Survivors. "Just say a word and I can think about it for hours. I'm always thinking about the meaning of life, and my dreams are hard work because I make them into puzzles and mysteries for me to solve."

All of the cognitive and caring domain styles overlap and all of us hop from one to another on the basis of the joys and sorrows of our daily life. Remember that loving is a way of thinking and not just of feeling. One cognitive caring style is not better than the other, but miracle marriages depend on the ability to function much of the time in the realm of the contemplatist. When problems happen, the contemplatist takes the time to reflect on how to think together with someone else—to use someone else's cognitive caring style—to explore several domains of reality and is not limited by mechanical, quantum, or cosmic rules.

The Language of Love

One of the major contributions to psychology comes from the new cognitive psychology, which asserts that we can "talk with our selves to change ourselves."[6] This is the psychology upon which Lawrence Kohlberg based his theories of moral thought described in Chapter 4. Instead of focusing on behavior or the ego, cognitive psychology studies the nature of our self-talk— thought processes as they affect our behavior and emotions. The contemplatist engages in almost constant self-talk, reflecting over and over again on the key questions "Where am I going?" and "Who will go with me?" In the journey to discover reality, the contemplatist seems best able to draw from the strengths of the styles of the concretist, romanticist, and cosmotist to travel through new realities.

How do you talk to yourself about your spouse, love, sex, caring, conflict, hope, and joy? What is your inner language of love?

• Do you talk in the cynicism of the concretist, as this patient did: "You meet someone by chance, you marry them, you work, raise kids, and die. You do your best. What else do you want?"
• Do you talk in the mysticism of the romanticist, as this patient did: "Love is so remarkable that it transcends all time and space. It's a wonderful magic that explodes within you like an atomic bomb, and everything but your love loses its meaning."
• Do you talk in the hyperbole of the cosmotist, as this patient did: "Love is infinitely larger than the universe. You can't begin to measure it. It is deeper than the deepest ocean and higher than the highest mountain."
• Do you talk in the reflectiveness of the contemplatist, as this patient did: "When I think of love, I think of cleaning up the damn crumbs he leaves on the couch, the little tears I feel when I see him sleeping, and the thrill of sharing mysteries I can't yet imagine with him. Most of all I think he is becoming how I think and not just who I think of."

The contemplatist's statement reveals an integration of all four cognitive caring styles. Our language of love always betrays us. Listen to what you say, what your spouse says, and how your marriage tends to talk together, and you will learn what reality your marriage is in. What you say is where you are.

Marriage and Mirth

In reseaching how couples deal with reality, I discovered that cognitive caring styles and the related language of love are only part of the explanation of why some couples live in High Monogamy. I learned that couples who play together stay together.

The most effective way to realm-hop or discover the many realities of life and love is to play. Psychologist Edward Whitmont writes that play is "enjoyment of one's own and of others' possibilities."[7] To play is to admit *any* possibility and to dance back and forth between realities, and couples who learn to play together learn to stay together.

Play is a ritual within the Great Marital Myth and is a way of freeing ourselves from the day-to-day Newtonian world and to "kick up a little chaos" in our life so that some new order may emerge. Play is a way of framing the events of life in our chosen realm of reality. Through play, we achieve a lighthearted open-ness to all realities, and we come to expect what is unexpected in the see-and-touch sensory realm of reality.[8] When we play, we can hopscotch from reality to reality.

Jesus said, "And if you would understand what I am, know this: all that I have said I have uttered playfully, and I was by no means ashamed thereby. I danced."[9] By using our imagination to free ourselves to pretend and play, we can experience make-believe chaos. Without the actual disruption of true life turmoil, we can practice our chaos control. Through mutual play, we can try on all the realms of reality together and see what seems to fit our marriage the best. The key to mental health is not to ask if we are well adjusted but to ask what we have become adjusted to. Remember that being normal can be dangerous to your health and that laughter and play are passports to the paranormal of many realities.

Can Men and Women Play with Each Other?

In Chapter 9, I discussed the complementarity of alpha and beta lovers. Men, who are more likely to be alpha lovers, and their beta women counterparts, tend not to learn to play with each other.[10] Alphas and betas not only have different cognitive caring styles and love languages, they have different playing styles. Boys play in groups with other boys while girls play with one close friend at a time. Boys compete and conflict while girls share and care.[11] These gender differences tend to remain throughout life, continuing into marriage, and husbands and wives seldom play together as a couple. As a result, boys and girls and men and women do not learn together to suspend sensory reality for other realities, tending to do so only with their own gender. Step 9 toward a miracle marriage involves learning to play together as husband and wife and to pretend together, dance together, and share an imaginary lovers' journey together.

Harvard psychologist Carol Gilligan points out that men and women differ in their moral development not only regarding their sense of justice but also in terms of caring.[12] When facing a moral dilemma, boys attempt to resolve it by taking action, while girls try to talk things out, compromise, and smooth things over.[13] The miracle marriage is able to incorporate these complementary styles into playing together for life.

"I saw early in our marriage that my husband never played with me," said one Silver Survivor. "We loved each other, and we made love, but he would go out to play with his friends instead of with me. When we learned to play together, including children's games, dancing, running, teasing, laughing, pretending, joking, and freeing ourselves from being so stodgy and adult all the time, we fought less and loved a lot more. He's still awfully alpha in most of his play, and he tries to do it right and win, but I'm pretty beta in that I just enjoy the game with him, and we are learning to play together." We live in a culture that encourages us to play to win. The miracle marriage wins by playing.

THE LOVER'S DOMAIN TEST

The following ten questions will give you insight into the degree to which you and your spouse can realm-hop together and combine your cognitive caring styles.

1. Do you and your spouse go out to play together, or does each of you go out to play with your same-gender friend or friends?

"We now schedule what we call relationship recess," said one Silver Survivor wife. "At least once a week, we play together. We play cards, a board game, and we have even played jacks and skipped rope. It takes us away from reality for a while."

2. Can you and your spouse play together without competing with each other?

One husband said, "I used to feel like I was playing to her as my audience. I was trying to impress her or defeat her any time we played at something. I finally learned that I don't have to prove I'm a man by getting my wife's applause. We just play as two people, not as a man and a woman."

3. Can the two of you play together without other couples being present?

"It started very early in our marriage," said a wife. "Whenever we went out, we went with other couples. We never seemed to just go out alone together. We do now, and it means a lot to us to be just with each other. We giggle and are free just to be our own marriage instead of an image."

4. Do you and your wife or husband suggest and accept each other's suggestions about different ways to see and understand things?

"She's my eye-opener," said one husband. "She sees what I could never see and hears what I could never hear. I do the same for her. We make a marital point of view between the two of us that is totally different from that of either one of us."

5. When you make love, do you play, laugh, and fantasize together?

"When we were dating, we would play and laugh right up to when we started to make love," said one wife. "Then, everything got sort of urgent and serious. Sometimes we still get that way, but other times we laugh and play and share fantasies out loud. We have to watch it when we stay at a hotel for fear we will entertain the people in the next room."

6. Do you tell each other about your night's dreams and help each other understand their many meanings and not just their "real" meaning?

"We love to talk about our dreams," said one husband. "You might not believe it, but we can intentionally choose to become a part of one another's dreams at night and send our dreams back and forth between one another."

7. Do you laugh together very hard and very often?

"There is nothing better than a laugh-gasm," said the wife. "We have laughed so hard together for so long sometimes that our sides ache. We even forget what we're laughing about, but we just laugh and laugh. It takes us a long time to get back to reality."

8. Do you enjoy sharing memories together, with each of you bringing up unique and different aspects of your memories?

"We like to rehash our significant times together," said a wife. "Some couples go over and over their problems, but we try to relive the key times that built our marriage. The more we do it, the more new things we each bring to the marital memories."

9. Can you pretend together?

"It was very, very embarrassing at first," said one Silver Survivor husband. "I hadn't pretended since I was a little boy, but sometimes we just play a role for a day and try on another personality for a while. I was Tom Selleck for a whole day, and she was Julia Roberts. It's a very private thing just between us."

10. Do you sometimes cry very hard together instead of trying to hide your tears from your spouse?

"There is no closeness like the closeness of crying together," said one wife. "When we hold each other and cry together, we seem to enter a whole private reality that is just our own. Shared sadness is the best kind of sadness. Whenever we feel like crying, we call our crying partner in to join us."

The Silver Survivors averaged 9.0 on this test, while the control group of unstable relationships averaged 1.1. A true miracle marriage of merged partners in lasting love provides the safety of a traveling companion who is discovering along with you who he or she is, even while discovering where the two of you may want to go together.

HOME LOVE ASSIGNMENTS

What follows are five suggestions for marital games. In each case, the idea is to broaden your marriage's perception of what is "normal" and "well-adjusted" so that you become constructively crazy together.

Doing Dream Dialogues

1. Decide to engage in a marital dream dialogue. In the sensory realm, communicating through dreams is not possible. In the quantum and cognitive realms, however, practice and patience may result in an actual dream merging. Before going to sleep, discuss a dream you would like to share and agree to try to dream it. It may take a while, but many couples report being able to accomplish a dream dialogue together.

Reality Hopscotch

2. Try activities that force you to function outside the domain of the here-and-now. Buy a new toy and play with it together. Tell each other three outrageous lies. More than a century ago, Oliver Wendell Holmes suggested that we could increase our brain power by thinking ten impossible things before breakfast. Make a list of ten things that would seem impossible for two people to do together. Try anything from a video game to a pogo stick, but play and try to think as children to escape the limits of the mechanical, sensory realm of reality.

Tear Letting

3. We are conditioned to cry only in reaction to "real" tragedy or loss. Every so often, make some time to cry together. Watch a sad movie or review an old personal loss that one of you has experienced or some other deep feeling of sadness and cry it out. Tears contain the remnants of stress chemicals, so cry your toxins out.

Intestinal Jogging

4. When confronted with a potentially fatal illness, author Norman Cousins laughed himself to health. He described laughter as "jogging for the intestines."[14] Laughing does

shake the intestines, improve circulation, and decrease stress chemicals. Mutual laughter is often the most hearty laughter, so rent a funny audiotape or videotape and laugh long and hard together. Don't wait for something funny to happen—make it happen. One couple recorded their laughter together and played it back when they felt they needed a good "love laugh." There is something about hearing your own joint laughter that is guaranteed to cause you to laugh hard and long.

Modeling Reality

5. Make something new together. Buy some clay or paints and do a joint artwork. Using finger paints, do a large marital mural, or simply buy some crayons and draw pictures of each other. Remember, the more "unrealistic" this marital artwork is, the better for helping the two of you go where no marriage has gone before.

Many marriages have become focused on coping, surviving, and getting by day by day. It is time we learned how to get away from it all before we lose it all. Playing together in order to cross realms of reality together is one of the most energizing things you can do, and the following chapter explores further the magical energy generated by the playful miracle marriage that enjoys so many Loving Realities.

14

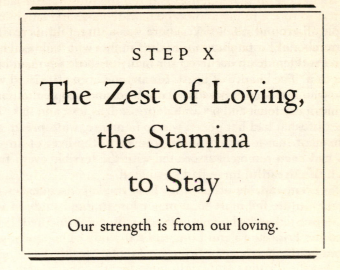

STEP X

The Zest of Loving, the Stamina to Stay

Our strength is from our loving.

Love is as love does.

—*M. Scott Peck*

LOVE LAW TEN: THE ENERGIZING-LOVE LAW

There is a powerful healing energy that emanates from loving, but when loving goes wrong, this same energy turns poisonous and can cripple or even kill us. Lasting love is made of and gives off this loving, or L, energy, and we can learn to sense it, send it, and make it grow. We are energized by love if we put our energy into loving.

The Most Powerful Force in the Universe

People all around it fell sick. There was a threefold increase in the number of hospitalizations in the families who had been near it, and sudden death occurred for many of those who had been close to it. The chance of death for anyone even associated with those who had been exposed to it doubled, and people thousands of miles away felt it and became depressed, listless, and sick. The power of what had happened was so immense, widespread, and permanent that it caused havoc forever in the lives of anyone who had been remotely associated with the terrible event from which this dreadful force had emanated.

The event capable of causing these tragic consequences was divorce. In the fall of 1985, a major longitudinal study of who gets depressed and who fails in grade school was initiated. It was called the Princeton-Penn Longitudinal Study.[1] This study, supported by the National Institute for Mental Health, has already revealed the startling and frightening fact that the *primary* cause of pessimism, depression, and failure in our children is turmoil between parents in their marriage and the impact of separation and divorce.[2] Thus the tenth and final step in this miracle-marriage manual is to recognize the enormous positive or negative power of love energy, or L energy, on everyone in its path.

The Misery of Mis-Marriage

In Chapter 2 of this book, I described the true story of a husband and wife fighting in court in front of their children over which parent would *have* to take responsibility for their twin daughters. The failure of our marriages is resulting in an epidemic of unhappy young people disabled by the destructive "energy" given off by the misery of their parents.

In Chapter 3, I described the devastating effect on adult men and women when love fails, but the innocent bystanders to the tragedy of love gone wrong suffer, too. Consider the following data elicited so far from the couples and their children I studied at Sinai Hospital of Detroit and from those in the Princeton-Penn study:

- Children of divorce are much more depressed than children from intact families.
- Three years after a divorce or separation, the children remain much more depressed than children from intact families.
- Children of divorce get in more trouble in school and do much worse in their studies.
- Children of divorce and separation have less physical and emotional energy.
- Children of divorce have lower self-esteem than other children.
- Children of divorce worry much more than children from intact families.
- Children of divorce or separation have more bodily complaints and symptoms of physical illness than other children.

These findings are based on statistical averages. While certainly some children of divorce are not doomed to depression and academic failure, the trend is alarming and clear nonetheless. Love crises result in the emission of a poisonous energy that spreads out like an invisible cloud of radiation to contaminate everyone.[3]

Will I Get My Way or Our Way?

Staying married but miserable also can have devastating effects on the children of these marriages. The Princeton-Penn study showed that children whose parents did *not* divorce but fought constantly also showed many of the same problems as those listed above for the children of divorce.[4] My data and the findings of the Princeton-Penn study are not sufficient to tell us if fleeing the marriage or fighting in the marriage is the only cause of the poisoned L energy, but I believe we have enough research now to make the following three statements about marriage and its powerful effects on the world:

1. A miracle marriage is one of lasting love that is designed primarily for giving rather than taking, for everybody rather than for the ego. It is a permanent union of two unselfish people, and as such it is a miraculous and valuable gift to the lovers themselves, to those who love them, and to those they love.

2.   It is almost always better to forgo separation and divorce whenever possible and learn how to make a miracle instead of a mess of your marriage.

3.   Whether you choose High or Low Monogamy, learn to stop putting your energy into fighting and start putting it into loving and teaching your children how to love.

Poisonous Love-Leak Emissions

When love fails and two "selfs" collide in conflict, L energy is spoiled. Negative energy is given off that sweeps over not only the children but family, friends, and the world in general as well. According to my data and that of one of the researchers in the Princeton-Penn study, here are some of the aftershocks that happen to children of divorce and separation:

• The mother usually is absent more, because she starts a new job.

• Classmates are less friendly to children from homes in "love distress."

• One parent joins a new church or changes religious beliefs, causing children to be confused in their moral development.

• A parent is hospitalized.

• A parent remarries.

• For the first time, a child fails a course in school.

• Children report hearing their parents argue and perhaps threaten each other.

• Fathers leave or go on more business trips or go out more often with their friends.

• A parent loses a job.

• A brother or sister is hospitalized (this is three and a half times more likely to happen to children of divorce than to siblings in intact homes).

• The child's own chance of being hospitalized is increased three and one half times (my data showed four times as many hospitalizations).

• The chance that a grandparent or close friend will die is twice as great for children of divorce.

Certainly, all of the above crises can happen to any child, but the significantly higher chance of bad things happening to the children of divorce is alarming evidence of the spread of poisoned L energy resulting from the corruption of caring. My advice, based on all we know about marriage and divorce, is—if at all possible—stay married!

Stop Fighting and Grow Up!

While shopping the other day, I heard two young children arguing. They appeared to be about four or five years old, and they were face to face in heated debate. "I'm smarter and better than you are," said the little girl shaking her finger in her brother's face. "Oh yeah?" responded her brother, grabbing his sister's finger and twisting it. "I'm smarter and better than you are." The boy twisted harder and said, "I don't want you to be my sister anymore." The little girl answered, "OK. We're divorced."

The mother hid her smile as she took each of her children by the hand and turned them toward her. "Both of you stop fighting and grow up!" she said sternly. "You're upsetting the whole shopping center." I thought how relevant this mother's words were to some Low Monogamy marriages and how she was revealing the negative power of L energy to spread out from these couples in conflict.

As you have read, a miracle marriage can cure, heal, and help solve any problem. The energy from a lasting love is infinitely powerful, but like nuclear energy, the abuse of L energy can be as cataclysmic as its appropriate use can be spectacular. The greatest gift you can give your children is your happy, lasting, loving marriage. Like the dangers of passive inhalation of cigarette smoke, being too close to troubled love can result in a serious risk to one's health.

Combat or Caring?

Upon close examination, the ultimate source of the bad energy that comes from loving gone wrong seems related to the conflicts that arise when two egos collide. When we try to fit our two natural halves—our alpha and beta natures—together, the fit is not always perfect or easy. Over the years of watching husbands and wives work very hard to destroy each other, I often wanted to disregard all my training and psychological theories and tell these spouses to grow up and use their energy for learning how to couple instead of combat. I wanted to tell these spouses to stop spatting like two selfish children and to warn them that there would be drastic negative effects from how they were behaving. I wanted to admonish them that the negative energy of couple conflict is nonlocal and can immediately desolate an entire family and anyone near it.

For the sake of these suffering couples, their children, and the world, the six words that repeated in my brain during stormy marriage-therapy sessions were similar to the mother disciplining her children. I wanted to shout, "Grow up, stop fighting, start loving." This book represents my attempt to emphasize this message now. Everything considered, it is better for spouses, children, and the world to learn how to love than to learn how to be divorced. Don't try to win *in* your marriage, win *for* your marriage instead.

Stuff and Energy

If you are in marital distress, I hope this book will help you decide to face and solve your problems rather than to run from them. I hope this book will help you make a miracle of your marriage by learning how to use your love to tap into the most powerful energy source in the world. The energy of the third thing of lasting love—L energy—is not based on myth, occult science, or New Age jargon. This energy is real and necessary for the survival of the human spirit.

Scientists throughout the world are beginning to study L energy. They usually call it the fifth or X energy, and some call it E energy or the energy of empathy. The other four forms of energy known to science are gravity, electromagnetic energy, and strong and weak nuclear energy.[5] It is possible to study and learn about L energy without reverting to a simplistic psychology about "good and bad vibes." As author John White warns, we must be able to keep "an open mind without having a hole in our head."

Every quantum scientist now acknowledges that matter is an expression of energy.[6] A rock is a stack of potential energy and energy is extremely diffuse matter in process. You have read that energy and matter are dual expressions of the same universal substance, and this substance is the primal energy of which we all are made.

Bad Energy and Horrible Habits

In 1981, a major scientific debate began. A revolutionary new theory about life's energy was proposed by respected biologist Rupert Sheldrake.[7] Sheldrake hypothesized and subsequent research is documenting that there are energy fields that are the templates of our life. This energy resonates nonlocally through time and space to determine who and how we are. He referred to this energy as "a morphic resonance, a connection across time and space, based on similarity."[8]

When we connect with one another, we become similar to varying degrees and we fall into habits together. These may be habits of toleration, caring, and silencing the self for the good of the relationship or habits of impatience, selfishness, and enhancement of the ego. Sheldrake suggests that these habits continue to evolve not as genetic codes or patterns of DNA but as energy fields passed on forever. He writes, "I think that habit is not just an important principle in the evolution of life, but that it may be at the very root of the evolution of nature as a whole."[9]

I suggest that Sheldrake's theory can be applied to loving. Lovers' habits are passed on through the family, out to the world, and throughout time. Sheldrake feels that our evolution is more the development of the energy of our habitual styles of living and loving than survival of the fittest, the inheritance of acquired characteristics, or competition between selfish genes.[10] According to this view, our brains are not storehouses of memories or amazing computers capable of filing millions of bits of information. Our brains are more like radios that can tune in to the energy from the past and present. When we get into the mental habit of tuning our brain to loving, that is the energy we receive.

The love styles or cognitive caring styles I discussed in Chapter 13 may be seen as our mental habits or the way in which we attend to the energy available to us. These habits are in the form of a resonating timeless energy that shapes our loving and the loving of those around us and descended from us. If we engage in the horrible habit of fighting for the self instead of the higher habits of fighting together for the welfare of everyone, we send out a negative L energy as powerful as any of the other four energies known to traditional science. Miracle marriages are made when we learn to broadcast and receive love.

Measuring the Energy of Love

Several studies have confirmed the existence of morphogenic energy fields, or what I call L energy. At Harvard University, generations of rats were trained to run mazes while other rats were left untrained to find their own way through. As I related earlier, over ten years the descendants of the trained rats became "smarter" and were able to learn to run new mazes much quicker than had their predecessors. It was initially thought that the rats had somehow inherited "a mazing mentality" from their parents, but it was discovered that rats *all over the world* who were not related to the Harvard rats also were becoming mazewise. They had been influenced by the energy of the habits of their animal ancestors.[11]

At the University of California at Berkeley, strains of "bright and dull" rats (good and not-so-good maze runners) were bred. As expected, over several generations the descendants of bright parents got brighter. However, the dull descendants got brighter too! They did not become as bright as the descendants of the smart parents, but the dull descendants continued to get brighter and brighter. Regardless of their breeding, they had picked up the "bright rat energy" and been influenced by rat resonance.

Complex studies of humans done at Yale University have shown that human learning is also affected by morphogenic fields or the passing on and timeless communication of the energy of our habits. The details of these studies are too complex and elaborate to describe here, but psychologist Gary Schwartz, who conducted the studies on learning of forms of ancient Hebrew words, summarized his findings by concluding that the subjects attempting to learn these words somehow resonated with the energy of the millions of Jews and Hebrew scholars over the centuries who had seen, used, and read these words. The students picked up some of the energy of ancient habits. Perhaps this is why Mark Twain suggested, "The ancients have stolen all of our best ideas."

These studies and hundreds of others suggest the existence of an energy beyond most of our current measuring instruments. I propose that this energy is the L energy that comes from our loving habits. Low Monogamy reverberates with selfish energy and is less likely to cause us to glow with the bright and vital vibrations of the lasting love of a miracle marriage.

The Vitality of L Energy

We all know that there is a life force that seems to leave when someone dies, and we all sense negative and positive energy that we cannot measure with traditional scientific instruments. The power of love energy is as glorious as the power of the sun and the stars. It is an animating life force—an energy field that permeates everything.[12]

The word "energy" in its original meaning referred to vitalization or the ability to move or quicken inert matter. When we merge in love, we magnify this "L" energy. This is why we feel vitalized by loving, and the vitality of that energy explodes outward and everywhere. When we are having a bad day at work and feel like we are deenergized, just hearing the voice of our lover can charge us up again. One of the Silver Survivors said, "My husband energizes me. He's like the Energizer Bunny in that commercial who just keeps our love going and going and going."

Electrical engineer Lawrence Beynam of Ankara, Turkey, described L energy as one of the most pervasive and powerful forces in the world.[13] Doctors and nurses speak of the energy of healing, and few people would deny that some people seem to radiate an energy that makes us stronger.

Love Pollution and the Threat to the Family Ecology

In March 1989, Exxon's huge oil tanker *Valdez* collided with Bligh Reef in Prince William Sound, Alaska, and spilled 24,000 barrels of oil all over Alaska's coast. Thus precious energy intended for fuel became the negative energy of an ecological crisis that will be felt on our planet forever. Plants, animals, and people were irreversibly damaged by the toxic goo that altered the landscape, changed the food chain, and may threaten the survival of entire species. Similarly, when two meet and merge into a loving union, the result is a radiation of L energy that can fuel our life. If the collision is serious, there is an L spill.

If lovers silence their selfs to make a new One, they can use this L energy to grow together and to heal each other and others. They can also spread this energy to help heal the world by keeping families intact. However, if their selfs spill out in conflict and egoistic struggle for dominance and freedom, a negative L energy contaminates those who loved or have been loved by the spouses. Like the fish, birds, sea otters, and countless other life forms maimed or killed by the *Valdez* oil spill, they are drowned by a spoiled love.

Psychologist Martin Seligman, one of the chief researchers in the Princeton-Penn study, is puzzled by his own findings on the widespread impact of the negative energy of divorce on children and those near the ending of a love. He wrote, "We cannot imagine how the death of a good friend of the child's or a grandparent dying could be a consequence of divorce or how it could be a contributing cause. Yet the statistics are there."[14] I suggest that it is the leakage of a poisoned L energy that causes these remarkable negative and poisoning effects on the ecology of the family and those around it.

What Are We Fighting For?

Since the data is insufficient to tell us for sure if it is the fighting or the divorce that is polluting the family ecology, the authors of the Princeton-Penn study suggest, as I do, that if both the separation and the fighting do turn out to be co-causes of the pollution of L energy, we will have to take more seriously the saving of our marriages and learn to refrain from destructive fighting.

Unfortunately, the compassion of lasting love requires that we suffer together, and in our suffering we will naturally go through periods of conflict and struggle. My work with the Silver Survivors has indicated that these couples experienced conflicts regularly and in many cases as often as the control group of failing couples, but there was one key difference. Unlike Low Monogamists, miracle marriages know how to *resolve* their conflicts. Their fighting works.[15]

When you are confronting anger and conflict in your marriage, the key question in preventing L pollution is "What are we fighting *for*?" Have the two of you fallen into the mutual habit of battling selfs, or are you fighting for the loving life of your marriage?

Fighting for Your Love

I have ended most of the ten chapters in the miracle-marriage manual with five home love assignments. For this chapter, I offer "five fair fighting rules," based on my experience with the Silver Survivors and my reviews of their video- and audiotaped fights, that these relationships of lasting love seemed to use.

FIVE RULES OF FAIR FIGHTS: MASTERING THE MARITAL MARTIAL ARTS

1. Avoiding the Hot Spots: During their entire fight, each spouse was aware of the particular weak points of the other and intentionally avoided hitting these hot spots even as the fight raged on. Vulnerable points such as body image or weight, feelings about parents, or prior failures are examples of such hot spots. By contrast, couples failing at lasting love often aimed directly for and took advantage of these hot spots.

"When we fight, we never forget where we can hurt each other and where we might devastate one another," said one Silver Survivor. "As angry and upset as we get, we never go too far. We engage in noncontact marital martial arts."

2. Faith in Resolution: Both partners assumed that the fight would result in a resolution of the problem, never in separation, divorce, or walking out. Phrases such as "Then I guess divorce

is the only way to solve this" and "If that's how you feel, why don't you get a divorce" are surrender and not solving statements. Couples engaging in destructive quarrels tended to question the viability of their relationship easily and openly and often threatened to end it.

"When we're really going at it, we can heat up the place," said one husband. "But never—and I mean *never*—do we think or say anything about the marriage ending. What is the purpose of fighting if you're not fighting to save your relationship?"

3. Chosen Conflict: Silver Survivors were careful to pick the times when they fought and chose issues to fight about that were related to enhancing life in the marriage and family rather than to working toward self-enhancement. Verbal battles over future plans, joint ways of handling money, and plans for the children were more frequent than fights over one or the other partner feeling indignant about not getting enough personal respect or not having enough say in the marriage. Failing couples fought over almost anything at any time, and the theme of most of their fights was self-enhancement rather than marriage protection.

One wife said, "When we listen to our neighbors fight, they sound like children. They argue over their rights, who is bossing whom around, and who is the smartest or dumbest. When my husband and I fight, it's almost always about what we're doing, planning, or experiencing together."

4. Clear Conclusions: The Silver Survivors resolved their fights clearly, specifically, and measurably. While fights might go on for days, each mini-battle had a conclusion with such statements as "OK for now, but we're going to go at this again" or "I feel really terrible, but we'll try again later." When the fight was over, it was over at least for then. There was little sulking and lingering feelings of wounded ego, because they were fighting *for* their marriage and not *with* each other. As I pointed out in Chapter 6, the Silver Survivors could tolerate uncertainty in their loving, so they did not always expect things to be definitive and clear. They were motivated by the need to love and not the need to win.

Sometimes the Silver Survivors gave up together to the uncertainty, as illustrated by this wife's statement: "We fought about a month's worth of wars. We fight like boxers without coming to blows. Instead of rounds, we have 'marriage-go-rounds,' and at the end of each round, we get back to living and being married. At the last fight, we declared it no contest. We decided our marriage was more important than the issue, so we both lost and the marriage won." The couples failing at loving sulked; they used sarcasm, slander, and shaming techniques; and they seldom seemed to resolve their conflicts, despite much time spent fighting. Whatever the issue at hand, it sometimes continued into the divorce courtroom and even after the divorce.

5. Cheek Turning: One of the most important things couples should keep in mind is that fighting is a human choice and not a human right. Contrary to popular psychology, we do not have to "let it all hang out" and "get it all off our chest." People who feel the need to vent themselves are usually letting out the hot air they are full of. The results of swallowing our anger are not nearly as negative as popular psychology suggests, and only the selfish ego suffers from the taste. The effects of destructive fighting are, however, always negative and widespread, and the loving relationship and everyone it touches are hurt by it. Couples who did not try to make a miracle of their marriage were quick to take up the slightest challenge or provocation and considered fighting their personal right rather than a responsible choice. They were ready to defend their selves whenever they felt their egos threatened. They fought for self-entitlement rather than marital enrichment.

Before you respond to a provocation from your spouse or try to provoke a fight in your marriage, step back and ask yourself two questions: "What am I fighting for?" and "Do I *choose* to fight about this?" Remember, it is your child's, family's, and eventually the entire world's well-being and not just your own that is at stake. If not for the miracle of Us, perhaps we should at least try harder not to fight or fight more fairly for the sake of our children.

THE MARITAL-ZEST TEST

I end this chapter with the last test of this manual. It is a test for your L energy level. Each item and the sample illustrative statement by a Silver Survivor is intended to help you reflect on the stamina and zest of your loving relationship.

1. Is your marriage relatively free of BS—blaming and shaming?

"We can hear neighbors fighting two or three times a week," said one wife. "We can hear the BS over and over. He blames her, and she tries to shame him. We have a firm rule in our marriage. We never blame or try to cause shame during our fights. We assume that when one of us speaks, he or she is representing a part of our marriage and not just their own individual point of view. We don't try to blame or shame one another for not doing something or for doing something wrong."

2. Can both of you "energize" each other rather than leach energy from each other?

"My best friend says that her husband is an energy leech," said one wife. "Just by being next to him, I can feel him drain my energy, too. My husband and I give each other energy instead of taking energy from each other. I feel stronger just by being around him. We make sure we let each other know what we each do that energizes us."

3. Are both of you always "looking out for number two" by keeping in mind the point of being married rather than trying to make points for yourself in your marriage?

"The old saying was to 'look out for number one,' but we've learned to look out for number two," said a husband. "If you fight for yourself, only you can win. When you fight for your marriage, your love wins. You have to look out for your partner and your marriage as well as yourself—you have to look out for the two of you."

4. Do you both have a high DQ, or docility quotient, being willing and ready to learn from each other?

"I used to think that being docile was a bad trait," said one husband. "Now we've learned that being docile really means to be willing to learn from someone else and benefit from his or her view of reality."

5. Do your marital conflicts end clearly at the end of a fight, or do they linger on, causing you to suffer from the reality rumination—in which one or both partners are unable to or refuse to look for other realities and solutions?

"Early in our marriage, our fights were just the beginning of days of trouble," said one husband. "We'd fight and not even remember what we fought about. Now, we always try to resolve the fight at the end or at least agree to disagree and then leave it at that until we decide to fight again. If a fight starts something, it's one of our bad fights, but if it ends something if only for a little while, it's a good one. We've finally gotten by that ruinous rumination."

6. After a conflict, do you feel energized rather than tired out?

One wife said, "I used to feel zonked out after our fights. It was like he had mopped up the floor with me. Now, since we try to avoid fights as often as possible, we use up much less energy and have more energy left for a good fight. Our former therapist told us never to hold anything in, but when you told us to try to hold a lot of our anger in and turn the other cheek, we found a lot more energy to fight a lot less. I guess when you turn the other cheek, you can see the other side."

7. Do the two of you look as though you glow with health or do you look drained and done-in, like the stoic couple in Grant Wood's famous painting American Gothic?

"It's frightening to look at pictures of ourselves years ago," said one wife. "We look like two bank robbers in a mug shot, and I guess back then we were robbing ourselves of our love. Now our pictures show us much more alive and vibrant. You can see the energy in us. We take a picture every year in the same place just to keep a check on how we look together."

8. Does your marriage seem to radiate a healing energy that others can feel?

"I think that we get invited over to people's houses in order to bring in some fresh energy," said one husband. "I notice that when our friends are feeling down, they ask us over to bring them up. We both know couples who bring some really bad vibrations with them, and you can feel it even after they leave."

9. Do you feel that your marriage has more than enough energy or barely enough energy to get by?

"The phrase 'boundless energy' seems to apply to us most of the time," said one Silver Survivor. "We never seem to be running near empty."

10. Is your marriage happy?

"When you first asked us that question, it seemed strange," said one wife. "I thought you were asking if I was happily married, but then I understood that you were not referring to how I felt about my marriage but about how my husband and I felt about it together. That's a completely different question, and thank God and thank us, our marriage is very happy and getting happier."

The average score on this marital-zest test for the Silver Survivors was 9.5. The control group of failing marriages scored lower on this test than on all of the other tests presented in this book, averaging a score of .6. The toxicity of destructive fighting and the toll it takes on loving is reflected in this low marital-zest score.

The Miracle Spouse

Now that you have determined the zestfulness of your marriage and gone through all ten steps of the miracle-marriage manual, you can see that there is one central characteristic of the spouse who is capable of High Monogamy and lasting love. I call this characteristic domestic docility, or the willingness to learn from others and particularly from and with one's spouse.

A recent article by Nobel Prize laureate Herbert Simon suggested that altruism is rooted in the trait of docility.[16]. Altruism is at the base of the Great Marriage Myth, because it implies a primary regard for the welfare of others and the willingness to modify or silence the interests of the self for the good of another. Dr. Simon suggests that business, psychology, and medicine make a major mistake in assuming that selfishness is the ultimate human motive. He feels that we are genetically determined to be altruistic and writes, "Mother nature has made sure nice people still win in the end." He points out that survival of the fittest really means that the caring people who love for life and are able to give up the self for the good of merging with another are the fittest of all. It is this same docility and altruism that can protect the love energy of our children and others from the ravages of constant conflict and of trying to get "my" way, helping us instead to find "the way" with our beloved.

15

Two Ways to Love:

VOWS FOR A MIRACLE MARRIAGE

The soul attracts what it secretly harbors.

—*Sondra Ray*

You have read about two ways to marital love. First, there is the more traveled path of Low Monogamy. This is the way of passion, the avoidance of suffering, the enhancement of the self, and the using of marriage for safety, comfort, and survival of the stress of daily living. The second way is much less traveled, and it is the way to a miracle marriage. It is the way of the silenced self and compassion, and it involves the continued creation of the marriage as a place that brings more joy and peace to the world.

You have seen that the easier path of Low Monogamy is one that is charted to go around the disappointments and hassles of life so that the self can enjoy its brief stay on earth. Should you choose the more difficult way, you must be willing to accept disappointment, because High Monogamy first acknowledges, then forgives, and finally proceeds to combine our natural inadequacies, incompleteness, and halfness so that One love can grow. The more difficult way to love is charted right through the chaos of life toward the destination of a loving that transcends space and time.

Because miracle marriages based on Us have a higher purpose

than marriages of the Me, you have read about ten laws of lasting love based on the thinking of our most creative scientific minds. Here is a brief summary and review of each of these laws:

The Two-Time Law

1. Don't deceive yourself with the promise that you will put in quality time with your spouse. Make your effort now to put in the majority of the *quantity* of your time in your loving relationship.

The Confident Uncertainty Law

2. Don't be so certain of yourself or your spouse. Realize that you will never know all there is to know about your beloved and that the more you think you know, the less you are trying to learn.

The One-Love Law

3. The miracle of marriage is based on silencing the self and quieting the ego to combine one and one to make a powerful, infinite One.

The Love-Look Law

4. You see your marriage and your beloved less as they are and more as a reflection of how *you* are. Instead of going out *looking* for the right partner, try to *be* the right partner.

The Complementary-Love Law

5. You and your lover are not alike. Each of you tends either toward an alpha or toward a beta orientation to life. Paradoxically, the more different you are, the more potential there is for making a creative new whole.

The Transcendent-Love Law

6. There is a hidden lover within both of you who feels beyond the physical senses and can love beyond time. Don't be distracted by the here-and-now and lose your forever in the process.

The Creative-Chaos Law

7. The more chaotic your relationship, the more potential there is for miracles. It is natural for your marriage to be part of the inherent turmoil of the universe, and lasting love will help you find an ever-changing and evolving order beneath the chaos.

The Law of Shared Sadness

8. Love is always sad and full of disappointments because lovers sense the profound limitations of the physical world that is not capable of housing the full range of the potential of their loving. Lovers always go through depression and despair, but they can learn to convert the negative energy of pain and sadness into the joy of enduring love.

The Law of Loving Realities

9. By silencing the self and the ego, we can travel to realms of reality far beyond the see-and-touch world. We don't have to be "real." We can explore together our different cognitive caring styles in order to discover together all the realities of the human spirit.

The Energizing-Love Law

10. To feel and be nurtured by the energy of love, we must become more docile or teachable and decide to give up the self's lonely quest for fulfillment. We can learn *with* someone else the answer to where *we* are going and why.

Ceremonies of Connection

Ceremonies and rituals are ways of reconnecting with the great cultural myths of the past and bringing the energy of these myths to the present. Similar and repeated patterns are our attempts to tune in to and resonate with the energy, habits, and ways of our past. Scientist Rupert Sheldrake describes several such "connection ceremonies," including the feast of the Passover, recalling the first Passover in Egypt, the Christian Eucharist, re-creating the Last Supper of Jesus, and November's Thanksgiving dinners as re-creations of the first Thanksgiving in New England. The connection ceremony of the Great Marriage Myth is one of our most common and cherished rituals, so I offer as a conclusion to this course in a miracle marriage ten vows for a lasting love.

These are the vows of High Monogamy. They are ritualistic promises of a developing love. They are designed to help you and your beloved connect with the tradition of the Great Marriage Myth of total merging. To help you remember each of science's guides to lasting love, I have included the abbreviated description of each love law after each vow. I hope you will take these vows with someone with whom you choose to love forever.

Unlike the traditionally separate and alternating vows made in a marriage ceremony, the vows of a miracle marriage are to be taken and pronounced by you and your partner in unison as One. This symbolizes the spiritual merging of the two people who choose to make their shared life a miracle for each other and for the world.

Vows of a Miracle Marriage

We promise
to cherish our sacred time together,
and to put our marital moments before all others.
(Taking Time for Two)

We promise
to learn about and with each other forever.
(Tolerating Confident Uncertainty)

We promise
to be as and for our One
(Loving as One)

We promise
to look at each other for and with love
(Looking with Love)

We promise
to accept our differences to make us stronger together
(Complementing Our Lover)

We promise
never to let time or space separate us
(Loving Everywhere Anytime)

We promise
to accept, tolerate, and grow with the chaos of our life
(Caring Through the Chaos)

We promise
to see our sadness as symbolic of the intensity of our loving
(Sharing Our Disappointments)

We promise
to explore realities of our spirit far beyond
what we can see and touch
(Creating Our Own Realities of Love)

And we promise
to create a growing loving energy between us and for the world
(Energizing and Being Energized by Our Love)

I hope you will now pronounce yourselves man and wife in a
miracle marriage and live together forever in each other's hearts.

NOTES

Chapter 1: Total Marriage: Two Ways to Wed

1. Author George Leonard defined High Monogamy as "a long-term relationship in which both members are voluntarily committed to erotic exclusivity, not because of legal, moral, or religious scruples, not because of timidity or inertia, but because they seek challenge and an adventure." See G. Leonard, "The End of Sex," in *The Fireside Treasury of Light,* edited by M. O. Kelly (New York: Simon & Schuster, 1990), p. 168.

2. M. Scott Peck's classic book *The Road Less Traveled* speaks of accepting the challenge of individual growth by acknowledging the fact that suffering is necessary not only for personal growth but for the good of the world. High Monogamy is traveling down the "road less traveled" hand in hand and two by two. See M. Scott Peck, *The Road Less Traveled* (New York: Simon & Schuster, 1978). Suffering for love means quieting selfishness in favor of confronting life's natural pain as a couple.

3. Mythologist Joseph Campbell writes about "finding and following our bliss," making choices, and pursuing with vigor the life we choose and dream about. See Joseph Campbell and B. Moyers, *The Power of Myth* (New York: Doubleday, 1988).

Chapter 2: Marriage or Me?: The Challenge of Becoming One

1. S. L. Hofferth, "Social and Economic Consequences of Teenage Childbearing," in S. L. Hofferth and C. D. Hayes, eds., *Risking the Future: Adolescent Sexuality, Pregnancy, and Childbearing: Working Papers* (Washington, D.C.: National Academy Press, 1987).

2. G. Leonard, "The End of Sex," in M. O. Kelley, ed., *The Fireside Treasury of Light* (New York: Simon & Schuster, 1990), pp. 168–71.

3. Joseph Campbell and B. Moyers, *The Power of Myth* (New York: Doubleday, 1988), p. 6.

4. Quoted in M. Hunt, *The Natural History of Love* (New York: Minerva Press, 1967), pp. 143–44.

5. B. Murstein, *Love, Sex, and Marriage Through the Ages* (New York: Springer, 1974).

6. See R. G. Walters, *Primers for Prudery: Sexual Advice to Victorian America* (Englewood Cliffs, NJ: Prentice-Hall, 1974). Physician John Kellogg invented Kellogg Cornflakes as a replacement for the bland taste of the graham cracker that would still prevent what he called the "overexcited and convulsed heart" that led to selfish lust.

7. J. L. Flandrin, "Repression and Change in the Sexual Life of Young People in Medieval and Early Modern Times," *The Journal of Family History* 2 (1977): 196–210.

8. Lawrence LeShan, *The Dilemma of Psychology* (New York: Dutton, 1990), p. xiii.

Chapter 3: Falling Apart at the Dreams: How We Fail Our Marriage

1. E. Bersheid, "Emotion," in H. H. Kelley, ed., *Close Relationships* (New York: W. H. Freeman, 1983), pp. 110–68. See also T. C. Martin and L. L. Bumpass, "Recent Trends in Marital Disruption," *Demography* 26 (1989): 37–51.

2. M. E. Hetherington, "Coping with Family Transitions: Winners, Losers, and Survivors," *Child Development* 60 (1989): 1–14.

3. P. C. Glick and A. J. Norton, "Marrying, Divorcing, and Living Together in the United States Today," *Population Bulletin of the United States,* 1977.

4. W. Goode, *Women in Divorce* (New York: Free Press, 1956).

5. R. S. Weiss, "The Emotional Impact of Marital Separation," *Journal of Social Issues* 32 (1976): 135–45.

6. B. L. Bloom, S. J. Asher, and S. W. White, "Marital Disruption as a Stressor: A Review and Analysis," *Psychological Bulletin* 85 (1978): 867–94.

7. I describe and document the details of the emotional impact of separation and divorce on the immune system in my book *Super Immunity: Master Your Emotions and Improve Your Health* (New York: McGraw-Hill, 1987).

8. P. M. Lewinshohn, W. Mischel, and R. Barton, "Social Competence and Depression: The Role of Illusory Self-Perceptions," *Journal of Abnormal Psychology* 89 (1980): 203–12.

9. T. Smith, "Adult Sexual Behavior in 1989: Number of Partners, Frequency, and Risk," paper presented at the American Association for the Advancement of Science, February 1989.

10. E. Hetherington, M. Cox, and D. Cox, "Divorced Fathers," *Family Coordination* 25 (1977): 417–28. See also these authors' work in "The Aftermath of Divorce," in J. Stevens, Jr., and M. Mathews, eds., *Mother/Child, Father/Child Relationships* (Washington, D.C.: NAEYC Publishers, 1978).

11. B. L. Bloom and S. W. White, "Factors Relating to the Adjustment of Divorcing Men," *Family Relations* 30 (1981): 349–60.

12. R. Ornstein and L. Carstensen, *Psychology: The Study of Human Experience* (San Diego and New York: Harcourt Brace Jovanovich, 1991), p. 82.

13. Bloom and White, "Factors Related," pp. 349–60.

14. R. A. Brandwein, A. Brown, and S. M. Fox, "Women and Children Last:

The Social Situation of Divorced Mothers and Their Families," *Journal of Marriage and the Family* 36 (1974): 495–514.

15. C. K. Reissman and N. Gerstel, "Marital Dissolution and Health: Do Males or Females Have Greater Risk?" *Social Science and Medicine* 20 (1985): 617–36.

16. K. A. Clarke-Stuart and B. L. Bailey, "Adjusting to Divorce: Why Do Men Have It Easier?" *Journal of Divorce* 13 (1989): 75–94.

17. L. Weitzman, *The Divorce Revolution* (New York: Free Press, 1989).

18. D. Bernard, *The Future of Marriage* (New York: Bantam Books, 1972).

19. L. B. Rubin, *Worlds of Pain* (New York: Basic Books, 1976).

20. G. Sheehy, *Passages: Predictable Crises in Adult Life* (New York: Dutton, 1976).

21. Ibid.

22. J. Lynch, *The Broken Heart: The Medical Consequence of Loneliness* (New York: Basic Books, 1977).

23. W. R. Gove, "Sex Roles, Marital Roles, Mental Illness," *Social Forces* 51 (1972): 34–44.

24. P. W. Blumstein and P. Schwartz, "Intimate Relationships and the Creation of Sexuality," in B. J. Risman and P. Schwartz, eds., *Gender and Intimate Relationships* (Belmont, CA: Wadsworth Publishing Company, 1989), pp. 120–29. See also the earlier findings of A. C. Kinsey, W. Pomeroy, and C. Martin, *Sexual Behavior in the Human Male* (Philadelphia: Saunders, 1948), and these same authors in *Sexual Behavior in the Human Female* (Philadelphia: Saunders, 1953).

25. E. Frank, C. Anderson, and D. Rubenstein, "Frequency of Sexual Dysfunction in 'Normal' Couples," *The New England Journal of Medicine* 299 (1978): 111–15.

26. B. Thorton, "Toward a Linear Prediction Model of Marital Happiness," *Personality and Social Psychology Bulletin* 3 (1977): 497. See also J. W. Howard and R. M. Dawes, "Linear Prediction of Marital Happiness," *Personality and Social Psychology Bulletin* 2 (1976): 478–80.

27. J. S. Wallerstein and J. B. Kelly, *Surviving the Breakup: How Children and Parents Cope with Divorce* (New York: Basic Books, 1980).

Chapter 4: Love Logic and the Marriage of Minds: Learning to Think for "Us"

1. R. Ornstein, *The Evolution of Consciousness—of Darwin, Freud, and Cranial Fire* (New York: Prentice Hall Press, 1991), p. 105.

2. A. Moir and D. Jessel, *Brain Sex: The Real Difference Between Men and Women* (New York: Carol Publishing Company, 1991).

3. E. H. Hess, *Imprinting* (New York: Von Nostrand Reinhold, 1973).

4. K. Z. Lorenz, "Die Angeborenen Formen Möglicher Erfahrung," *Zeitschrift für Tierpsychologie* 5 (1953): 276.

5. Ibid.

6. D. Dutton and A. Aron, "Some Evidence for Heightened Sexual Attraction Under Conditions of High Anxiety," *Journal of Personality and Social Psychology* 30 (1974): 510–17.

7. I. Stone, *The Greek Treasure* (New York: Doubleday & Company, 1975).

8. L. and G. Poole, *One Passion, Two Loves: The Story of Heinrich and Sophia Schliemann, Discovers of Troy* (New York: University Press, 1966).

9. W. M. Calder III and D. A. Traill, eds., *Myth, Scandal, and History: The Heinrich Schliemann Controversy* (Detroit: Wayne State University Press, 1986).

10. Ibid., p. 9.

11. J. A. Lee, "Love Styles," in R. J. Sternberg and M. L. Barnes, eds., *The*

Psychology of Love (New Haven, CT, and London: Yale University Press, 1988).

12. Ibid.

13. D. Tennov, *Love and Limerence* (New York: Stein & Day, 1979).

14. K. S. Pope, "Defining and Studying Romantic Love," in K. S. Pope, ed., *On Love and Loving* (San Francisco: Jossey-Bass, 1980), pp. 1–26.

15. S. Peele and A. Brodsky, *Love and Addiction* (New York: New American Library, 1976), p. 70.

16. M. R. Liebowitz, *The Chemistry of Love* (Boston: Little, Brown Publishers, 1983).

17. Ibid.

18. A. Moir and D. Jessel, *Brain Sex*.

19. L. Kohlberg, "Stage and Sequence: The Cognitive Developmental Approach to Socialization," in D. A. Goslin, ed., *Handbook of Socialization Theory and Research* (Chicago: Rand McNally, 1969).

20. Lee, "Love Styles."

Chapter 5: Step I: Two-Timing

1. M. Eliade, "Time and Eternity in Indian Thought," in *Man and Time*, Joseph Campbell, ed. Bollingen Series 30:3 (Princeton, NJ: Princeton University Press, 1957), p. 196.

2. A. Eddington, *The Nature of the Physical World* (Cambridge: Cambridge University Press, 1928), p. 68.

3. For an excellent scientific discussion that merges the new-physics view of directionless time with our human experience of flowing time, see P. Coveney and Roger Highfield's *The Arrow of Time* (New York: Fawcett Columbine, 1991).

4. K. Wilbur, *No Boundaries* (Boston and London: New Science Library, 1985), p. 69.

5. Ibid., p. 64.

6. The use of the word "conspiracy" to refer to a positive collusion and "breathing together" is found in M. Ferguson, *The Aquarian Conspiracy* (Los Angeles: Tarcher, 1980), p. 19.

7. M. Eliade, "Time and Eternity," p. 196.

8. I first proposed the concept of MIMs, or marital investment minutes, in my book *Super Marital Sex: Loving for Life* (New York: Doubleday, 1989). Sexual problems are almost always intimacy timing problems, and this book focused on ways to take control of the marriage's sex time to be free of "coming too soon or too late" and to learn how to make the time to make love.

9. F. Perls, *Gestalt Therapy Verbatim* (New York: Bantam, 1969).

10. A. Bloom, *The Closing of the American Mind* (New York and London: Simon & Schuster, 1987). See also C. Lasch, *The Culture of Narcissism* (New York: Warner Books, 1979).

11. S. M. Johnson, *Humanizing the Narcissistic Style* (New York and London: W. W. Norton & Company, 1987).

12. Quoted in D. Zohar, *The Quantum Self: Human Nature and Consciousness Defined by the New Physics* (New York: William Morrow & Company, Inc., 1990), p. 157. This outstanding book is a clear discussion of new physics and basic human nature, relationships, and love.

13. A. Bloom, *Closing*, p. 125.

14. A. Maslow, *The Farther Reaches of Human Nature*, 2nd ed. (New York: Viking Press, 1971).

Chapter 6: Step II. The Power of Uncertainty: Maintaining Marital Mysteries

1. I. Prigogine, *From Being to Becoming* (San Francisco: W. H. Freeman, 1980), p. 51.

2. P. Pearsall, *Making Miracles: Finding Meaning in Life's Chaos* (New York: Prentice-Hall, 1991).

3. Heisenberg's example of the weather house is described in E. Regis, *Who Got Einstein's Office?* (Reading, MA: Addison-Wesley, 1987), p. 30.

4. The impact of the "death difference" is described by coauthor Laura Carstensen of Stanford University in R. Ornstein and L. Carstensen, *Psychology: The Study of Human Experience* (San Diego and New York: Harcourt Brace Jovanovich, 1991), p. 705.

5. D. Symons, "Précis of the Evolution of Human Sexuality," *Behavioral and Brain Science* 3 (1980): 131–44.

6. K. Wilbur, "Sex, Gender, and Transcendence," *The Quest* 4 (Summer 1991): 46.

7. M. Wilson, "Marital Conflict and Homicide in Evolutionary Perspective," in R. W. Bell and N. J. Bell, eds., *Sociobiology and the Social Sciences* (Lubbock, TX: Texas Tech University Press, 1980).

8. M. F. Small, "Sperm Wars," *Discover* 12 (July 1991): 48–53. See also R. L. Travis, *Social Evolution.*

9. Travis, *Social Evolution,* p. 49.

10. M. M. Weisman and C. L. Kiessman, "Sex Differences in the Epidemiology of Depression," *Archives of General Psychiatry* 34 (1977): 98–111.

11. S. Nolen-Hoeksema, "Sex Differences in Unipolar Depression: Evidence and Theory," *Psychological Bulletin* 101 (1987): 259–82.

12. For a review of the in-utero impact of testosterone (20 times less for girls than boys) on brain development and subsequent differences in behavior and thought, see A. Moir and D. Jessel, *Brain Sex: The Real Difference Between Men and Women* (New York: Lyle Stuart, 1991).

13. Ibid.

14. For a complete review of the literature on depression and its relationship to objectivity, optimism, and pessimism, see Martin E. P. Seligman, *Learned Optimism* (New York: Alfred A. Knopf, 1991).

15. Ibid.

16. P. M. Lewinshohn, W. Mischel, and R. Barton, "Social Competence and Depression: The Role of Illusory Self-Perceptions," *Journal of Abnormal Psychology* 89 (1980): 203–12.

17. E. Friedl, "Society and Sex Roles," *Human Nature* 1 (1978): 68–75.

18. W. Leutenegger, "Scaling of Sexual Dimorphism in Body Size and Breeding System in Primates," *Nature* 272 (1977): 610–11.

19. Friedl, "Society and Sex Roles."

20. M. Wilson, "Marital Conflict."

21. A. Hall, *Nonverbal Sex Differences: Communicational Accuracy and Expressive Style* (Baltimore: Johns Hopkins University Press, 1984). See also N. Henley, "Status and Sex: Some Touching Observations," *Bulletin of the Psychosomatic Society* 2 (1973): 91–93.

22. D. E. Bugenthal, L. R. Love, and R. M. Gianetto, "Perfidious Feminine Faces," *Journal of Personality and Social Psychology* 17 (1971): 314–18.

Chapter 7: Step III. Beyond Boundaries: How One Plus One Equals One

1. H. F. Harlow, *Learning to Love* (New York: Aronson, 1974). Harlow researched the impact not only of touch and contact comfort between baby and mother monkeys, but also the importance of adult-adult "affectional ties" to general survival.

2. C. Moss, *Portraits in the Wild* (Chicago: University of Chicago Press, 1976). Fifteen thousand observations of elephants by Iain Douglas-Hamilton showed that no two elephants are alike and that they often try to heal one another and even check out the dead bodies of their herd in the form of an "animal autopsy," smelling, moving, tasting, and examining various body parts.

3. For a carefully thought out discussion of the biological/analytical basis of affectional ties, see Reuben Fine, *The Meaning of Love in Human Experience* (New York: John Wiley and Sons, 1985).

4. K. Wilbur, *No Boundary* (Boston and London: New Science Library, 1985), p. 15.

5. Ibid., pp. 16–17.

6. P. Coveney and R. Highfield, *The Arrow of Time* (New York: Fawcett Columbine, 1991), p. 116.

7. Ibid., p. 115.

8. A. Einstein, "M. Besso Correspondence 1903–1955," as quoted in A. Pais, *Subtle Is the Lord: The Science and Life of Albert Einstein* (Oxford and New York: Oxford University Press, 1982), p. 382.

9. H. Margenau, *Open Vistas: Philosophical Perspective of Modern Science* (New Haven, Conn.: Yale University Press, 1961). Dr. Margenau suggested the use of the word *onta,* borrowed from the Greek, to refer to electrons and other quantum "entities" that are neither particles nor waves. They are a "oneness" of particle, wave, electrical points charges, vortices, and almost anything all at once! There is nothing in what we have come to know in the see-and-touch world that compares to onta or these beings.

10. N. Bohr, quoted in P. Schilpp, ed., *Albert Einstein: Philosopher-Scientist* (New York: Tudor Press, 1949).

11. H. Margenau, *The Miracle of Existence* (Woodbridge, CT: Ox Bow Press, 1984).

12. Ibid., p. 107.

13. Fine, *The Meaning of Love,* p. 317. Psychoanalyst Reuben Fine clearly describes what he calls "regression in the service of the spouse" as reenacting prior child-parent conflicts in marriage.

14. I describe the Carthage Complex in my book *The Power of the Family: Strength, Comfort, and Healing* (New York: Doubleday, 1990).

15. Psychologist Robert Zajonc at the University of Michigan reported positive findings in his study of increasing facial resemblance in spouses living together for several years. He did not find such resemblance in the newly married or couples together only a few years. Reported in R. Flaste, ed., *The New York Times Book of Science Literacy* (New York: Random House Times Books, 1991), pp. 115–16.

Chapter 8: Step IV. Creating Your Beloved: Looking with Love

1. As quoted in J. Borysenko, *Guilt Is the Teacher, Love Is the Lesson* (New York: Warner Books, 1990), p. 193.

2. N. Bohr, quoted in P. Schilpp, ed., *Albert Einstein: Philosopher-Scientist* (New York: Tudor Press, 1949).

3. An experiment by Baidyanath Misra and B. George Sudarshan at the University of Texas at Austin documented this remarkable fact. See "The Zeno Paradox in Quantum Theory," *Journal of Mathematical Physics* (1977). (The Zeno Paradox is named after Zeno the Eleatic, an ancient Greek philosopher, who designed many time paradoxes.)

4. See K. Floyd, "Of Time and Mind," in J. White, ed., *Frontiers of Consciousness* (New York: Julian Press, 1974), and C. T. Tart, *Altered States of Consciousness* (New York: Wiley, 1969).

5. This exercise was first described by Itzhak Bentov, pp. 60–61.

6. The concept of participatory universe is introduced by J. A. Wheeler in "Beyond the Black Hole," in H. Woolf, ed., *Some Strangeness in the Proportion* (Reading, MA: Addison-Wesley, 1980). Physicist David Bohm also uses this term in "A New Theory of the Relationship of Mind and Matter," *The Journal of the American Society of Psychical Research* 87 (1958).

7. I. Prigogine and I. Stengers, *Order Out of Chaos* (New York and London: Bantam, 1984), p. 299.

8. L. E. Cahoone, *The Dilemma of Modernity* (Albany, NY: State University of New York Press, 1988), pp. 233–44.

9. J. D. Barrow and F. J. Tipler, *The Anthropic Cosmological Principle* (New York: Oxford University Press, 1986).

10. D. Zohar, *The Quantum Self* (New York: William Morrow Company, 1990), p. 199.

11. C. G. Jung, *The Meaning of Psychology for Modern Man,* vol. 10 in Sir Herbert Read, ed., *C. G. Jung: The Collected Works* (London: Routledge & Kegan Paul Publishers, 1964), p. 23.

Chapter 9: Step V. Complements of Love: Marry Quite Contrary

1. As quoted in K. Wilbur, *No Boundary* (Boston and London: New Science Library, 1985), p. 23.

2. For a thorough discussion of sexual dimorphism and inductor theory in the differentiation of female into male, see R. R. Francoeur, *Becoming a Sexual Person,* 2nd ed. (New York: Macmillan Publishing Company, 1991).

3. I describe Alan Alda's "testosterone poisoning" and the issue of maleness and femaleness and its impact on love maps or loving styles in my book *Super Marital Sex: Loving for Life* (New York: Doubleday, 1989).

4. For a much more thorough and technically accurate discussion of the concept of love maps, see J. Money, *Lovemaps* (New York: Irvington Publishers, 1986).

5. R. C. Pillard and J. D. Weinrich, "The Periodic Table Model of the Gender Transpositions: Part I: A Theory Based on Masculinization and Defemination of the Brain," *Journal of Sex Research* 23: 425–54.

6. S. F. Wittelson, "Sex and the Single Hemisphere: Specialization of the Right Hemisphere for Spatial Processing," *Science* 193 (1976): 425–27.

7. A. Buffrey and J. Gray, "Sex Differences in the Development of Spatial and Linguistic Skills," in C. Ounsted and D. Taylor, eds., *Gender Differences: Their Ontogeny and Significance* (New York: Churchill Livingstone, 1972).

8. M. P. Bryden, "Auditory-Visual and Sequential-Spatial Matching in Relation to Reading Ability," *Child Development* 43 (1973): 824–32.

9. The best summary of male and female brain bias is in A. Moir and D. Jessel, *Brain Sex: The Real Difference Between Men and Women* (New York: Crown Publisher, 1991).

10. J. McGlone, "Sex Differences in Human Brain Asymmetry: A Critical Survey," *Behavioral and Brain Sciences* 3 (1980): 215–63.

11. Quoted in J. Achenbach, "Why Aren't People with Surgically Severed Hemispheres of the Brain Considered to Be Two Separate Human Beings?," *Detroit Free Press Magazine,* March 31, 1991, p. 11.

12. P. Weintraub, "The Brain: His and Hers," *Discover* 2 (1981): 15–20. See also S. P. Springer and G. Deutsch, *Left Brain, Right Brain* (San Francisco: W. H. Freeman, 1981).

13. I am exaggerating biological and neonatal developmental research findings to make my point about complementarity, but some authors feel that men are modified versions of the more natural female form. See M. J. Sherfey, *The Nature and Evolution of Female Sexuality* (New York: Vintage Press, 1973).

14. Aristotle, *Basic Works,* edited by R. McKeon (New York: Random House, 1941).

15. As quoted by J. Borysenko in *Guilt Is the Teacher, Love Is the Lesson* (New York: Warner Books, 1990), p. viii.

16. K. Wilbur, "Sex, Gender, and Transcendence," *The Quest,* Summer 1991, p. 47.

Chapter 10: Step VI. The Quantum Leap of Love: Coming Together Anywhere

1. J. S. Bell, *Speakable and Unspeakable in Quantum Mechanics* (Cambridge: Cambridge University Press, 1987).

2. N. Herbert, *Quantum Reality* (New York: Anchor Books, 1987), p. 245.

3. Ibid., p. 249.

4. E. Hilgard, "Hypnosis and Consciousness," *Human Nature* 1 (1978): 42–49.

5. B. Singer, "To Believe or Not to Believe," in G. O. Abell and B. Singer, eds., *Science and the Paranormal* (New York: Charles Scribner's Sons, 1983), pp. 7–23.

6. A. Combs and M. Holland, *Synchronicity: Science, Myth, and the Trickster* (New York: Paragon House, 1990).

7. Ibid., p. 43.

8. L. Watson, *Lifetide: The Biology of Consciousness* (New York: Simon & Schuster, 1980).

9. Ibid., p. xxix.

10. I review the research documenting the effects of prayer in my book *Making Miracles* (New York: Prentice Hall Press, 1991).

11. R. C. Byrd, "Positive Therapeutic Effects of Intercessory Prayer in a Coronary Care Unit Population," *Southern Medical Journal* 81: 826–29.

12. I. Progoff, *Jung, Synchronicity, and Human Destiny: Acausal Dimensions of Human Experience* (New York: Dell, 1973).

Chapter 11: Step VII. Chaos, Compassion, and Caring in Sickness and in Health

1. T. Hall, "Breaking Up Is Becoming Harder to Do," *New York Times,* March 17, 1991, p. C 1.

2. J. Maynard Smith, *The Evolution of Sex* (Cambridge: Cambridge University Press, 1978).

3. I. Kant, *Universal Natural History and Theory of the Heavens,* translated by S. Jake (Edinburgh: Scottish Academic Press, 1981), p. 87.

4. Psychiatrist M. Scott Peck's inspirational book *The Road Less Traveled* (New York: Simon & Schuster, 1978) describes the natural chaos or suffering of life

by saying, "It is a great truth because once we truly see this truth, we transcend it," p. 15.

5. C. G. Jung, *Collected Works of C. G. Jung*, Bollinger Series, No. 20, 2d ed., translated by R. F. C. Hull (Princeton, NJ: Princeton University Press, 1973), p. 75.

6. J. Gleick, *Chaos: Making a New Science* (New York: Penguin Books, 1987). This outstanding work describes the evolution of the field of chaology and gives several colorful examples of the nature of chaos.

7. Ibid., p. 8.

8. For a clear discussion of the healthy nature of constructive denial, see D. Goleman, "Denial and Hope," *American Health* 3 (1984): 54–61. See also Goleman's book *Vital Lies: Simple Truths* (New York: Simon & Schuster, 1985).

9. A. Ellis, *Reason and Emotion in Psychotherapy* (New York: Stuart, 1962).

10. Martin Seligman, *Learned Optimism* (New York: Alfred A. Knopf, 1991).

Chapter 12: Step VIII. The Sad Side of Love: Pulling Together Instead of Apart

1. For a brilliant discussion of the nature of time as related to the Second Law of Thermodynamics, see P. Coveney and R. Highfield, *The Arrow of Time* (New York: Fawcett Columbine, 1991).

2. A. Eddington, *The Nature of the Physical World* (Cambridge: Cambridge University Press, 1928), p. 74.

3. For an interesting review of the 25-million-year evolution of humans, see R. Ornstein and L. Carstenson, *Psychology: The Study of Human Experience* (New York: Harcourt Brace Jovanovich, 1991), p. 141.

4. R. Graves, "Counting the Beats," in *The Oxford Book of Twentieth Century English Verse* (Oxford: Oxford University Press, 1973), p. 298.

5. E. FitzGerald, *The Rubaiyat of Omar Khayyam*, 5th ed. (London and Glasgow: Collins Publishers, 1953).

6. W. Shakespeare, *The Sonnets of William Shakespare* (London: Shepheard-Walwyn, 1975).

7. As quoted in D. R. Changler, "Thoreau: The Making of an American Yogi," *The Quest*, Summer 1991, p. 87.

8. As quoted in K. Wilbur, *No Boundaries* (Boston and London: New Science Library, 1985), p. 65.

9. G. L. Schroeder, *Genesis and the Big Bang* (New York: Bantam Books, 1990), p. 156.

10. Consensual extramarital sex is described in N. O'Neill and G. O'Neill, *Open Marriage* (New York: Avon, 1972). See also R. H. Rimmer, *The Harrad Experiment* (Los Angeles: Sherbourne Press, 1966).

11. R. J. Jenks, "Swinging: A Replication and Test of a Theory," *The Journal of Sex Research* 21 (1985): 199–205.

12. M. Csikszentmihalyi, *Flow: The Psychology of Optimal Experience* (New York: Harper Collins, 1990), p. 279–80.

13. W. James, *The Varieties of Religious Experience* (New York: Longmans Green, 1980).

14. V. Goertzel and M. G. Goertzel, *Cradles of Eminence* (Boston: Little Brown Publishers, 1962).

15. P. Sandbloom, *Creativity and Disease: How Illness Affects Literature, Art, and Music* (Philadelphia: George F. Stickley Company, 1985).

16. A. J. Mandell, "From Molecular Biological Simplification to More Realistic Central Nervous System Dynamics: An Opinion," in J. O. Cavenar, ed., *Psy-*

chiatry: Psychobiological Foundations of Clinical Psychiatry 3 (New York: Lippincott, 1985).

17. F. A. Wolf, *The Body Quantum: The New Physics of Body, Mind, and Health* (New York: Macmillan, 1986).

18. D. L. Rosenhan and M. Seligman, *Abnormal Psychology* (New York: Norton, 1985).

19. R. J. Cadoret, G. Winokur, and P. Clayton, "Family History Studies: Part 6: Depressive Disease Types," *Comprehensive Psychiatry* 12 (1977): 148–55.

20. See M. Seligman, *Learned Optimism* (New York: Alfred A. Knopf, 1991). He denies that the reason for female proneness to depression is that women report it more, go to therapy more, are hormonally predisposed to be depressed, or are trapped in depression by their sex role. Instead, he suggests that women (I suggest beta Eves and Adams) ruminate pessimistically more often than men (I suggest alpha Eves and Adams), pp. 83–85.

21. M. E. P. Seligman, *Helplessness: On Depression, Development, and Death* (San Francisco: W. H. Freeman, 1975).

22. P. Johnson, "Women and Power: Toward a Theory of Effectiveness," *The Journal of Social Issues* 32 (1976): 99–110.

23. Csikszentmihalyi, *Flow*, p. 201.

24. As quoted in L. LeShan, *The Dilemma of Psychology* (New York: Dutton, 1990), p. 21.

25. The concepts here are based on the work of A. Ellis, *Reason and Emotion in Psychotherapy* (New York: Stuart, 1962), and A. Beck, *Cognitive Therapy of Depression: A Treatment Manual* (New York: Guilford, 1979). See also M. E. P. Seligman, *Helplessness*.

Chapter 13: Step IX. The Ways of Love: Playing Together—Staying Together

1. P. Davies, "Other Worlds," in M. O. Kelley, ed., *The Fireside Treasury of Light* (New York: Fireside, 1990), p. 200.

2. Ibid., p. 201–2.

3. The concept of parallel universes and multiple realities is described in detailed scientific terms by F. A. Wolf, *Parallel Universes* (New York: Simon & Schuster, 1988).

4. Domain theory is discussed in detail in L. LeShan and H. Margenau, *Einstein's Space and Van Gogh's Sky* (New York: Macmillan, 1981).

5. These domains are described in L. LeShan, *The Mechanic and the Gardener* (New York: Holt, Rinehart, & Winston, 1982), p. 81.

6. For a clear discussion of cognitive psychology and the possibility of self-direction, self-talk, and cognitions changing behavior, see A. T. Beck, *Cognitive Therapy and the Emotional Disorders* (New York: New American Library, 1976).

7. E. C. Whitmont, *The Return of the Goddess* (New York: Crossland, 1982), p. 231.

8. For a wonderful discussion of the relationship between playing in setting the stage for synchronicities and meaningful coincidences, see A. Combs and M. Holland, *Synchronicity: Science, Myth, and the Trickster* (New York: Paragon House, 1990), pp. 133–39.

9. *New Testament. Apocrypha II*. English Translation. London, 1963, p. 88.

10. J. M. Gottman, "The World of Coordinated Play: Same- and Cross-Sex Friendships in Young Children," in J. M. Gottman and J. C. Parker, eds., *Conversations of Friends: Speculations on Affective Development* (Cambridge: Cambridge University Press, 1986).

11. For differences in gender regarding play, see E. E. Maccoby, "Gender and Relationships," *American Psychologist* 45 (1990): 513–20.
12. C. Gilligan, *In a Different Voice: Psychological Theory and Women's Development* (Cambridge, MA: Harvard University Press, 1980).
13. Psychologist Carol Gilligan illustrates male and female differences in resolving moral conflicts (one example is the Heinze Dilemma, in which a man must make a decision concerning his sick wife and a life-saving drug that is unfairly priced to cost more money than he has). For a description of this moral dilemma, see L. Kohlberg, "Stage and Sequence: The Cognitive-Developmental Approach to Socialization," in D. A. Goslin, ed., *Handbook of Socialization Theory and Research* (Chicago: Rand McNally, 1969).
14. N. Cousins, *Anatomy of an Illness* (Toronto and New York: Bantam Books, 1981).

Chapter 14: Step X. The Zest of Loving, the Stamina to Stay

1. This study is described in detail in Martin Seligman, *Learned Optimism* (New York: Alfred A. Knopf, 1991), pp. 143–45. A longitudinal study is designed to learn about people over several years, so findings will continue to come in, but so far the number-one predictor of poor classroom performance is pessimism, and this pessimism and associated depression is related to parental strife at home and the impact of divorce. For a representative article based on this important study, see S. Nolen-Hoeksema, J. Girgus, and M. Seligman, "Learned Helplessness in Children: A Longitudinal Study of Depression, Achievement, and Explanatory Study," *Journal of Personality and Social Psychology* 51 (1986): 434–42.
2. The data on the deleterious effect of divorce, separation, and parental conflict with one another beginning to accumulate in an alarmingly predictive pattern to show that it is the primary etiological factor in our children's suffering. See J. Wallerstein and S. Blakeslee, *Second Chances: Men, Women, and Children: A Decade After Divorce* (New York: Ticknor & Fields, 1989). See also E. M. Hetherington, M. Cox, and C. Roger, "Effects of Divorce on Parents and Children," in M. E. Lamb, ed., *Non-Traditional Families* (Hillsdale, NJ: Erlbaum, 1982). And see E. M. Cummings, D. Bogel, J. S. Cummings, and M. El-Sheikh, "Children's Responses to Different Forms of Expression of Anger Between Adults," *Child Development* 60 (1989): 1392–1404.
3. All of the findings reported here are from the 1,000 couples studied in my clinic and the Princeton-Penn study quoted above.
4. Seligman, *Learned Optimism*, p. 147.
5. It is beyond the scope of this book to review the research on X energy. See J. White, "On Mind and the Physics of Paranormal Phenomena," in *The Meeting of Science and Spirit* (New York: Paragon House, 1990), pp. 7–86.
6. For a fascinating and carefully documented review of the role of energy in healing, see R. Gerber, *Vibrational Medicine* (Santa Fe, NM: Bear Publishing Company, 1988).
7. R. Sheldrake, *A New Science of Life* (Los Angeles: Tarcher, 1981).
8. R. Sheldrake, "The Past Is Present," in M. Toms, ed., *At the Leading Edge* (New York: Larson Publications, 1991), p. 211.
9. Ibid., p. 199–200.
10. Ibid., p. 203–4.
11. This and other remarkable studies documenting the existence of morphogenic energy fields are summarized in R. Sheldrake, "The Past Is Present."
12. For a scientific description of L energy and what scientists are calling X

or the "fifth energy," see I. Sanderson, "Editorial: A Fifth Force," *Pursuit* 5 (October 1972).

13. Ibid.

14. Martin Seligman, *Learned Optimism,* p. 146.

15. For experiments on resolution of fights, see E. M. Cummings, "Children's Responses to Different Forms of Expression of Anger," referred to in C. Tavris, *Anger: The Misunderstood Emotion* (New York: Simon & Schuster, 1982). For a step-by-step guide to conflict resolution, see H. Weisinger, *Dr. Weisinger's Anger Work-Out Book* (New York: Quil, 1985).

16. As reviewed in T. Adler, "In Terms of Evolution, Altruism Makes Sense," *The American Psychological Association Monitor* 22 (April 1991): 11.

BIBLIOGRAPHY

Achenbach, J. "Why Aren't People with Surgically Severed Hemispheres of the Brain Considered to Be Two Separate Human Beings?" *Detroit Free Press Magazine*, March 31, 1991, p. 11.

Adler, T. "In Terms of Evolution, Altruism Makes Sense." *The American Psychological Association Monitor* 22 (April 1991).

Argyle, M., and M. Henderson. *The Anatomy of Relationships*. New York: Penguin Books, 1985.

Aristotle. *Basic Works*. Edited by R. McKeon. New York: Random House, 1941.

Barrow, J. D., and F. J. Tippler. *The Anthropic Cosmological Principle*. Oxford and New York: Oxford University Press, 1988.

Beck, A. "Cognitive Therapy: A 30-Year Retrospective." *American Psychologist*, 46 (1991).

———. *Depression*. New York: Hoeber, 1967.

———. *Cognitive Therapy and the Emotional Disorders*. New York: New American Library, 1976.

———. *Cognitive Therapy of Depression: A Treatment Manual*. New York: Guilford, 1979.

Bell, J. S. *Speakable and Unspeakable in Quantum Mechanics*. Cambridge: Cambridge University Press, 1987.

Bem, S. L. "Gender Schema Theory: A Cognitive Account of Sex Typing." *Psychological Review* 88 (1981).

Bernard, D. *The Future of Marriage*. New York: Bantam Books, 1972.

Bersheid, E. "Emotion." In H. H. Kelley, ed., *Close Relationships*. New York: W. H. Freeman, 1983.

Bloom, A. *The Closing of the American Mind*. New York: Simon & Schuster, 1987.

Bloom, B. L., S. J. Asher, and S. W. White. "Marital Disruption as a Stressor: A Review and Analysis." *Psychological Bulletin* 85 (1978).

Bloom, A., and S. W. White. "Factors Related to the Adjustment of Divorcing Men." *Family Relations* 30 (1981).

Blumstein, P. W., and P. Schwartz. "Intimate Relationships and the Creation of Sexuality." In B. J. Risman and P. Schwartz, eds., *Gender in Intimate Relationships.* Belmont, CA: Wadsworth Publishing Company, 1989.

Bohm, D. "A New Theory of the Relationships of Mind and Matter." *The Journal of the American Society for Psychical Research* 80 (1958).

Bohr, N. "On Atoms and Human Knowledge." *Daedalus* 87 (1958).

Borysenko, J. *Guilt Is the Teacher, Love Is the Lesson.* New York: Warner Books, 1990.

Bradshaw, J. *Healing the Shame That Binds You.* Deerfield Beach, FL: Health Communications, 1988.

Branden, N. *Honoring the Self.* Los Angeles: Tarcher, 1983.

Brandwein, R. A., A. Brown, and S. M. Fox. "Women and Children Last: The Social Situation of Divorced Mothers and Their Families." *Journal of Marriage and the Family* 36 (1974).

Bryden, M. P. "Auditory-Visual and Sequential-Spatial Matching in Relation to Reading Ability." *Child Development* 43 (1973).

Buber, M. *I and Thou.* Edinburgh: T. & T. Clark, 1937.

Buffrey, A., and J. Gray. "Sex Differences in the Development of Spatial and Linguistic Skills." In C. Ounsted and D. Taylor, eds., *Gender Differences: Their Ontogeny and Significance.* New York: Churchill Livingstone, 1972.

Bugenthal, D. E., L. R. Love, and R. M. Gianetto. "Perfidious Feminine Faces." *Journal of Personality and Social Psychology* 17 (1971).

Burr, H. S. *The Fields of Life.* New York: Ballantine Books, 1972.

Byrd, R. C. "Positive Therapeutic Effects of Intercessory Prayer in a Coronary Care Unit Population." *Southern Medical Journal* 81.

Cadoret, R. J., G. Winokur, and P. Clayton. "Family History Studies: Part 6: Depressive Disease Types." *Comprehensive Psychiatry* 12 (1977).

Cahoone, L. E. *The Dilemma of Modernity.* Albany, NY: State University of New York Press, 1988.

Calder, W. M., III, and D. A. Traill, eds. *Myth, Scandal, and History: The Heinrich Schliemann Controversy.* Detroit: Wayne State University Press, 1986.

Campbell, J. *The Inner Reaches of Outer Space.* New York: Viking, 1959.

———, and B. Moyers. *The Power of Myth.* New York: Doubleday, 1988.

Capra, F. *The Turning Point.* New York: Wilwood House, 1982.

Casti, J. L. *Searching for Certainty.* New York: William Morrow & Company, 1990.

Changler, D. R. "Thoreau: The Making of an American Yogi." *The Quest,* Summer 1991.

Clark, R. W. *Einstein: The Life and Times.* New York and Cleveland: World Publishers, 1971.

Clarke-Stuart, K. A., and B. L. Bailey. "Adjusting to Divorce: Why Do Men Have It Easier?" *Journal of Divorce* 13 (1989).

Cleek, M. G., and T. A Pearson. "Perceived Causes of Divorce: An Analysis of Interrelationships." *Journal of Marriage and the Family* 47 (1985).

Combs, A., and M. Holland. *Synchronicity: Science, Myth, and the Trickster.* New York: Paragon House, 1990.

Cousins, N. *Anatomy of an Illness.* Toronto and New York: Bantam Books, 1981.

Coveney, P., and R. Highfield. *The Arrow of Time.* New York: Fawcett Columbine, 1991.

Csikszentmihalyi, M. *Flow: The Psychology of Optimal Experience.* New York: Harper Collins, 1990.

Cummings, E. M., D. Bogel, J. S. Cummings, and M. El-Sheikh. "Children's Responses to Different Forms of Expression of Anger Between Adults." *Child Development* 60 (1989).

Curtin, M. E., ed. *Symposium on Love*. New York: Behavioral Publications, 1973.

Davies, P. *God and the New Physics*. New York: Simon & Schuster, 1983.

———. "Other Worlds." In M. O. Kelley, ed., *The Fireside Treasury of Light*. New York: Fireside, 1990.

Descartes, R. *Philosophical Letters*. Edited and translated by Anthony Kenny. New York: Oxford University Press, 1981.

Dossey, L. *Recovering the Soul*. New York: Bantam Books, 1989.

Dukas, J., and B. Hoffman, eds. *Albert Einstein: the Human Side. New Glimpses from His Archives*. Princeton, NJ: Princeton University Press, 1979.

Dutton, D., and A. Aron. "Some Evidence for Heightened Sexual Attraction Under Conditions of High Anxiety." *Journal of Personality and Social Psychology* 30 (1974).

Eliade, M. *The Sacred and the Profane*. New York: Harcourt, Brace & World, 1959.

———. "Time and Eternity in Indian Thought." In J. Campbell, ed., *Man and Time*. Bollingen Series XXX, no. 3. Princeton, NJ: Princeton University Press, 1957.

Eysenck, H., ed. *A Model for Personality*. Berlin: Springer-Verlag, 1981.

Ellis, A. *Reason and Emotion in Psychotherapy*. New York: Stuart, 1962.

Ferguson, M. *The Aquarian Conspiracy*. Los Angeles: Tarcher, 1980.

Fine, R. *The Meaning of Love in Human Experience*. New York: John Wiley & Sons, 1985.

FitzGerald, E. *The Rubaiyat of Omar Kyayyam*. 5th ed. London and Glasgow: Collins Publishers, 1953.

Flandrin, J. L. "Repression and Change in the Sexual Life of Young People in Medieval and Early Modern Times." *The Journal of Family History* 2 (1977).

Flaste, R., ed. *The New York Times Book of Science Literacy*. New York: Random House Times Books, 1991.

Francoeur, R. R. *Becoming a Sexual Person*. 2d ed. New York: Macmillan, 1989.

Frank, E., C. Anderson, and D. Rubenstein. "Frequency of Sexual Dysfunction in 'Normal' Couples." *New England Journal of Medicine* 299 (1978).

Friedl, E. "Society and Sex Roles." *Human Nature* 1 (1978).

Gerber, R. *Vibrational Medicine*. Santa Fe, NM: Bear Publishing Company, 1988.

Gilligan, C. *In a Different Voice: Psychological Theory and Women's Development*. Cambridge, MA: Harvard University Press, 1980.

Gleick, J. *Chaos: Making a New Science*. New York: Penguin Books, 1987.

Glick, P. C., and A. J. Norton. "Marrying, Divorcing, and Living Together in the United States Today." *Population Bulletin of the United States*, 1977.

Goertzel, V., and M. G. Goertzel. *Cradles of Eminence*. Boston: Little, Brown, 1962.

Goleman, D. "Denial and Hope." *Amerian Health* 3 (1984).

———. *Vital Lies, Simple Truths*. New York: Simon & Schuster, 1985.

Goode, W. *Women in Divorce*. New York: Free Press, 1956.

Gottman, J. M. "The World of Coordinated Play: Same- and Cross-Sex Friendships in Young Children." In J. M. Gottman and J. C. Parker, eds., *Conversations of Friends: Speculations on Affective Development*. Cambridge: Cambridge University Press, 1986.

Gove, W. R. "Sex Roles, Marital Roles, Mental Illness." *Social Forces* 51 (1972).

Graves, R. "Counting the Beats." In *The Oxford Book of Twentieth Century English Verse*. Oxford: Oxford University Press, 1973.

Hall, A. *Nonverbal Sex Differences: Communicational Accuracy and Expressive Style.* Baltimore: Johns Hopkins University Press, 1984.

Hall, T. "Breaking Up Is Becoming Harder to Do," *New York Times,* March 17, 1991.

Harlow, H. F. *Learning to Love.* New York: Aronson, 1974.

Haywood, J. W. *Perceiving Ordinary Magic.* Boulder, CO, and London: Shambhala Press, 1984.

Hazo, R. G. *The Idea of Love.* New York: Praeger, 1967.

Hegel, G. *Philosopher of Right.* Translated by T. M. Knox. Oxford: Clarendon Press, 1942.

Henley, N. "Status and Sex: Some Touching Observations." *Bulletin of the Psychosomatic Society* 2 (1973).

Herbert, N. *Quantum Reality: Beyond the New Physics.* New York: Doubleday/Anchor, 1985.

Hess, E. H. *Imprinting.* New York: Van Nostrand Reinhold, 1973.

Hetherington, M. E. "Coping with Family Transitions: Winners, Losers, and Survivors." *Child Development* 60 (1989).

———, M. Cox, and D. Cox. "Divorced Fathers." *Family Coordination* 25 (1977).

———, M. Cox, and D. Cox. "The Aftermath of Divorce." In J. Stevens, Jr., and M. Mathews, eds., *Mother/Child, Father/Child Relationships.* Washington, D.C.: NAEYC Publishers, 1978.

Hetherington, M. E., M. Cox, and C. Roger. "Effects of Divorce on Parents and Children." In M. E. Lamb, ed., *Non-Traditional Families.* Hillsdale, NJ: Erlbaum, 1982.

Hilgard, E. "Hypnosis and Consciousness." *Human Nature* 1 (1978).

Hofferth, S. L. "Social and Economic Consequences of Teenage Childbearing." In S. L. Hofferth and C. D. Hayes, eds., *Risking the Future: Adolescent Sexuality, Pregnancy, and Childbearing: Working Papers.* Washington, D.C.: National Academy Press, 1987.

Hofstadter, D. R. "Analogies and Metaphors to Explain Godel's Theorem." *College Mathematics Journal* 13 (1982).

———. *Gödel, Escher, Bach: An Eternal Golden Braid.* New York: Vintage Books, 1980.

Hollon, S. D., and P. C. Kendall. "Specificity of Depressotypic Cognitions in Clinical Depression." *Journal of Abnormal Psychology* 95 (1986).

Howard, J. W., and R. M. Dawes. "Linear Prediction of Marital Happiness." *Personality and Social Psychology Bulletin* 2 (1976).

Hunt, M. *The Natural History of Love.* New York: Minerva Press, 1967.

Jahn, R. G., and B. J. Dunne. *Margins of Reality.* New York: Harcourt Brace Jovanovich, 1987.

James, W. *The Varieties of Religious Experience.* New York: Longmans Green, 1980.

Jantsch, E. *The Self-Organizing Universe.* New York: Pergamon, 1980.

Jenks, R. J. "Swinging: A Replication and Test of a Theory." *The Journal of Sex Research* 21 (1985).

Johnson, P. "Women and Power: Toward a Theory of Effectiveness." *The Journal of Social Issues* 32 (1976).

Johnson, S. M. *Humanizing the Narcissistic Style.* New York and London: W. W. Norton & Company, 1987.

Jung, C. *Collected Works.* Edited by M. Read Fordham and G. Adler. Bollingen Series. New York: Pantheon Books, 1953.

———. *The Meaning of Psychology for Modern Man.* Vol. 10 of *C. G. Jung: The*

Collected Works. Edited by Sir Herbert Read. London: Routledge & Kegan Paul Publishers, 1964.

Kephart, W. M. "Some Correlates of Romantic Love." *Journal of Marriage and the Family* 29 (1967).

Kinsey, A. C., W. Pomeroy, and C. Martin. *Sexual Behavior in the Human Male.* Philadelphia: Saunders, 1948.

Kinsey, A. C., W. Pomeroy, and C. Martin. *Sexual Behavior in the Human Female.* Philadelphia: Saunders, 1953.

Klerman, G. "The Age of Melancholy?" *Psychology Today,* April 1979.

Kohlberg, L. "Stage and Sequence: The Cognitive Developmental Approach to Socialization." In D. A. Goslin, ed., *Handbook of Socialization Theory and Research.* Chicago: Rand McNally, 1969.

Kuhl, J. "Motivational and Functional Helplessness: The Moderating Effects of State Versus Action-Orientation." *Journal of Personality and Social Psychology* 40 (1981).

Lasch, C. *The Culture of Narcissism.* New York: Warner Books, 1979.

Lee, J. A. "Love Styles." In R. J. Sternberg and M. L. Barnes, eds., *The Psychology of Love.* New Haven, CT, and London: Yale University Press, 1988.

Leonard, G. "The End of Sex." In M. O. Kelley, ed., *The Fireside Treasury of Light.* New York: Simon & Schuster, 1978.

LeShan, L. *The Dilemma of Psychology.* New York: Dutton, 1990.

———. *The Mechanic and the Gardener.* New York: Holt, Rinehart & Winston, 1982.

Leshan, L., and L. Margenau. *Einstein's Space and Van Gogh's Sky: Physical Reality and Beyond.* New York: Macmillan, 1982.

Leutenegger, W. "Scaling of Sexual Dimorphism in Body Size and Breeding System In Primates." *Nature* 272 (1977).

Lewinshohn, P. M., W. Mischel, and R. Barton. "Social Competence and Depression: The Role of Illusory Self-Perceptions." *Journal of Abnormal Psychology* 89 (1980).

Liebowitz, M. R. *The Chemistry of Love.* Boston: Little, Brown, 1983.

Lorenz, K. Z. "Die Angeborenen Formen Möglicher Erfahrung." *Zeitschrift für Tierpsychologie* 5 (1953).

Lynch, J. *The Broken Heart: The Medical Consequences of Loneliness.* New York: Basic Books, 1977.

Maccoby, E. E. "Gender and Relationships." *American Psychologist* 45 (1990).

Mandell, A. J. "From Molecular Biological Simplification to More Realistic Central Nervous System Dynamics. An Opinion." In J. O. Cavenar, ed., *Psychiatry: Psychobiological Foundations of Clinical Psychiatry,* vol. 3, no. 2. New York: Lippincott, 1965.

Margenau, H. *The Miracle of Existence.* Woodbridge, CT: Ox Bow Press, 1984.

———. *Open Vistas: Philosophical Perspective of Modern Science.* New Haven, CT: Yale University Press, 1978.

Martin, T. C., and L. L. Bumpass. "Recent Trends in Marital Disruption." *Demography* 26 (1989).

Maslow, A. *Motivation and Personality.* New York: Harper & Row, 1954.

———. *The Farther Reaches of Human Nature,* 2d ed. New York: Viking Press, 1971.

———. "The Taboo of Tenderness and the Disease of Valuelessness." Unpublished lecture. History of American Psychology Archives. Akron, Ohio, University of Akron, March 1965.

Masters, W., V. Johnson, and R. Kolodny. *Human Sexuality.* Boston and Toronto: Little, Brown, 1982.

May, R. "Historical and Philosophical Presuppositions for Understanding Therapy." In O. H. Mowrer, ed., *Psychotherapy, Theory, and Research*. New York: Ronald Press, 1953.

McGlone, J. "Sex Differences in Human Brain Asymmetry: A Critical Survey." *Behavioral and Brain Sciences* 3 (1980).

Mermin, N. D. "Is the Moon There When Nobody Looks? Reality and the Quantum Theory." *Physics Today*, April 1985.

Moir, A. and D. Jessel. *Brain Sex: The Real Difference Between Men and Women*. New York: Carol Publishing Company, 1991.

Money, J. *Lovemaps*. New York: Irvington Publishers, 1986.

Morowitz, H. J. *Cosmic Joy and Local Pain*. New York: Charles Scribner's Sons, 1987.

Moss, C. *Portraits in the Wild*. Chicago: University of Chicago Press, 1976.

Msu, F. L. K. *American and Chinese: Passage to Difference*, 3d ed. Honolulu: University of Hawaii Press, 1981.

Murstein, B. *Love, Sex, and Marriage Through the Ages*. New York: Springer, 1974.

New Testament. Apocrypha II. English Translation. London: 1963.

Nigren, A. *Agape and Eros*. Chicago: University of Chicago Press, 1982.

Nolen-Hoeksema, S. "Sex Differences in Unipolar Depression: Evidence and Theory." *Psychological Bulletin* 101 (1987).

———, J. Girgus, and M.E.P. Seligman. "Learned Helplessness in Children: A Longitudinal Study of Depression, Achievement, and Explanatory Style." *Journal of Personality and Social Psychology* 51 (1986).

Norton, A. J., and J. E. Moorman. "Current Trends in Marriage and Divorce Among American Women." *Journal of Marriage and the Family* 49 (1987).

Ochs, C. *Behind the Sex of God: Toward a New Consciousness: Transcending Matriarchy and Patriarchy*. Boston: Beacon Press, 1977.

O'Neill, N., and G. O'Neill. *Open Marriage*. New York: Avon, 1972.

Ornstein, R. *The Evolution of Consciousness—of Darwin, Freud, and Cranial Fire*. New York: Prentice Hall Press, 1991.

———, and L. Carstensen. *Psychology: The Study of Human Experience*. San Diego and New York: Harcourt Brace Jovanovich, 1991.

Ornstein, R., and D. Sobel. *Healthy Pleasures*. Reading, MA: Addison-Wesley, 1990.

Pais, A. *Subtle Is the Lord: The Science and the Life of Albert Einstein*. Oxford and New York: Oxford University Press, 1982.

Pearsall, P. *Making Miracles: Finding Meaning in Life's Chaos*. New York: Prentice Hall Press, 1991.

———. *The Power of the Family: Strength, Comfort, and Healing*. New York: Doubleday, 1990.

———. *Super Immunity: Master Your Emotions and Improve Your Health*. New York: McGraw-Hill, 1987.

———. *Super Marital Sex: Loving for Life*. New York: Doubleday, 1988.

Peck, M. Scott. *The Road Less Traveled*. New York: Simon & Schuster, 1978.

Peele, S., and A. Brodsky. *Love and Addiction*. New York: New American Library, 1976.

Perls, F. *Gestalt Therapy Verbatim*. New York: Bantam, 1969.

Pfleegor, R. L., and L. Mandel. "Interference of Independent Photon Beams." *Physical Review* 159:5 (July 1967).

Piaget, J. *The Origins of Intelligence in Children*. New York: International Universities Press, 1952.

Pillard, R. C., and J. D. Weinrich. "The Periodic Table Model of the Gender

Transpositions. Part I. A Theory Based on Masculinization and Defeminization of the Brain." *Journal of Sex Research* 23.

Plato. *The Collected Dialogues.* Bollingen Series LXXI. E. Hamilton and H. Cairns, eds. New York: Pantheon Books, 1961.

———. *The Works of Plato.* Edited by I. Edman. New York: Simon & Schuster Modern Library, 1927.

Poole, L., and G. Poole. *One Passion, Two Loves: The Story of Heinrich and Sophia Schliemann, Discoverers of Troy.* New York: University Press, 1966.

Pope, K. S. "Defining and Studying Romantic Love." In K. S. Pope, ed., *On Love and Loving.* San Francisco: Jossey-Bass, 1980.

Prigogine, I., and I. Stengers. *Order Out of Chaos.* New York and London: Bantam, 1984.

Progrof, I. *Jung, Synchronicity, and Human Destiny: Acausal Dimensions of Human Experience.* New York: Dell, 1973.

Regis, E. *Who Got Einstein's Office?* Reading, MA: Addison-Wesley, 1987.

———. *Great Mambo Chicken and the Transhuman Condition.* Reading, MA: Addison-Wesley, 1990.

Reissman, C. K., and N. Gerstel. "Marital Dissolution and Health: Do Males or Females Have Greater Risk?" *Social Sciences and Medicine* 20 (1985).

Ricci, J. "Inner Child Won't Get with the Program." *Detroit Free Press,* April 4, 1991.

Rimmer, R. H. *The Harrad Experiment.* Los Angeles: Sherbourne Press, 1966.

Robins, L., M. Helzer, H. Weissman, E. Orvaschel, E. Gruenberg, J. Burke, and D. Reigier. "Lifetime Prevalence of Specific Psychiatric Disorders in Three Sites." *Archives of General Psychiatry* 41 (1984).

Rosenhan, D. L., and M. Seligman. *Abnormal Psychology.* New York: Norton, 1985.

Rubin, L. B. *Worlds of Pain.* New York: Basic Books, 1976.

Sandbloom, P. *Creativity and Disease: How Illness Affects Literature, Art, and Music.* Philadelphia: George F. Stickley Company, 1985.

Sanderson, I. "Editorial: A Fifth Force." *Pursuit* 5 (1972).

Scantoni, L., and J. Scantoni. *Men, Women, and Change: A Sociology of Marriage and Family.* New York: McGraw-Hill, 1976.

Schilpp, P. A. *Albert Einstein: Philosopher-Scientist.* 2 vols. LaSalle, IL: Open Court Publishers, 1982.

Schrodinger, E. *What Is Life?* Cambridge: Cambridge University Press, 1947.

Schroeder, G. *Genesis and the Big Bang.* New York: Bantam Books, 1990.

Seligman, M.E.P. *Helplessness: On Depression, Development, and Death.* San Francisco: W. H. Freeman, 1975.

———. *Learned Optimism.* New York: Alfred A. Knopf, 1991.

Shakespeare, W. *The Sonnets of William Shakespeare.* London: Shepheard-Walwyn, 1975.

Shapiro, L. "Guns and Dolls." *Newsweek,* 1990.

Sheehy, G. *Passages: Predictable Crises in Adult Life.* New York: Dutton, 1976.

Sheldrake, R. *A New Science of Life.* Los Angeles: Tarcher, 1981.

———. "The Past Is Present." In M. Toms, ed., *At the Leading Edge.* New York: Larson Publications, 1991.

Sherfey, M. J. *The Nature and Evolution of Female Sexuality.* New York: Vintage Press, 1973.

Shimony, A. "The Reality of the Quantum World." *Scientific American* 258, (1988).

Shortridge, K. "Poverty Is a Woman's Problem." In J. Freeman, ed., *Women: A Feminist Perspective,* 3rd ed. Palo Alto, CA: Naxfield, 1984.

Shucman, H., and W. Therford. *A Course in Miracles.* Tiburon, CA: Foundation for Inner Peace, 1985.

Siegel, L. *Sacred and Profane Dimensions of Love in Indian Traditions.* New York: Oxford University Press, 1978.

Silny, A. J. "Sexuality and Aging." In B. Wolman, ed., *Handbook of Human Sexuality.* Englewood Cliffs, NJ: Prentice-Hall, 1980.

Singer, B. "To Believe or Not to Believe." In G. O. Abell and B. Singer, eds., *Science and the Paranormal.* New York: Charles Scribner's Sons, 1983.

Small, M. F. "Sperm Wars." *Discover* 12 (1991).

Smith, T. "Adult Sexual Behavior in 1989: Number of Partners, Frequency, and Risk." Paper presented at the American Association for the Advancement of Science, February 1989.

Stone, I. *The Greek Treasure.* New York: Doubleday, 1975.

Symons, D. "Précis of the Evolution of Human Sexuality." *Behavioral and Brain Science* 3 (1980).

Tavris, C. *Anger: The Misunderstood Emotion.* New York: Simon & Schuster, 1982.

Teilhard de Chardin, Pierre. *The Phenomenon of Man.* New York: Harper & Row, 1959.

Tennov, D. *Love and Limerence.* New York: Stein & Day, 1979.

Thompson, W. I. *The Time Falling Bodies Take to Light.* New York: St. Martin's Press, 1981.

Thorton, B. "Toward a Linear Prediction Model of Marital Happiness." *Personality and Social Psychology Bulletin* 2 (1977).

Tillich, P. *A History of Christian Thought.* New York: Simon & Schuster, 1968.

Vissell, B., and J. Vissell. *The Sacred Heart.* Aptos, CA: Ramira Press, 1984.

Wallerstein, J., and Sandra Blakeslee. *Second Chances: Men, Women, and Children A Decade After Divorce.* New York: Ticknor & Fields, 1989.

Wallerstein, J. S., and J. B. Kelly. *Surviving the Breakup: How Children and Parents Cope with Divorce.* New York: Basic Books, 1980.

Watson, L. *Lifetide: The Biology of Consciousness.* New York: Simon & Schuster, 1980.

Weinrich, J. D. *Sexual Landscapes.* New York: Charles Scribner & Sons, 1987.

Weintraub, P. "The Brain: His and Hers." *Discover* 2 (1981).

Weisinger, H. *Dr. Weisinger's Anger Work-Out Book.* New York: Quil, 1985.

Weisman, M. M., and C. L. Liessman. "Sex Differences in the Epidemiology of Depression." *Archives of General Psychiatry* 34 (1977).

Weiss, R. S. "The Emotional Impact of Marital Separation." *Journal of Social Issues* 32 (1976).

Weitzman, L. *The Divorce Revolution.* New York: Free Press, 1989.

Wheeler, J. A. "Beyond the Black Hole." In H. Woolf, ed. *Some Strangeness in the Proportion.* Reading, MA: Addison-Wesley, 1980.

———, A. Zurek, and W. Zurek, eds. *Quantum Theory and Measurement.* Princeton, NJ: Princeton University Press, 1983.

White, J. *The Meeting of Science and Spirit.* New York: Paragon House, 1990.

Whitmont, E. C. *The Return of the Goddess.* New York: Crossland Press, 1982.

Wilbur, K. *No Boundaries.* Boston and London: New Science Library, 1985.

———. "Sex, Gender, and Transcendence." *The Quest,* Summer 1991.

Wilson, M. "Marital Conflict and Homicide in Evolutionary Perspective." In R. W. Bell and N. J. Bell, eds., *Sociobiology and the Social Sciences.* Lubbock, TX: Texas Tech University, 1980.

Wittelson, S. F. "Sex and the Single Hemisphere: Specialization of the Right Hemisphere for Spatial Processing." *Science* 193 (1976).

Wolf, F. A. *The Body Quantum: The New Physics of Body, Mind, and Health.* New York: Macmillan, 1986.

————. *Parallel Universe.* New York: Simon & Schuster, 1988.

Wolfram, S. "Cellular Automata." *Los Alamos Science* 2 (1983).

————. "Cellular Automata as Models of Complexity." *Nature* 311 (1984).

Wordsworth, W. *The Prelude.* Book II, 1805–6.

Zohar, D. *The Quantum Self: Human Nature and Consciousness Defined by the New Physics.* New York: William Morrow, 1990.

Zukav, G. *The Dancing Wu Li Masters: An Overview of New Physics.* New York: William Morrow, 1979.

Zullow, H. M. "The Interaction of Rumination and Explanatory Style in Depression." Master's thesis, University of Pennsylvania, 1984.

INDEX